Essential Series

Springer

London
Berlin
Heidelberg
New York
Barcelona
Hong Kong
Milan
Paris
Singapore
Tokyo

I

David Thew

Essential
Access 2000
fast

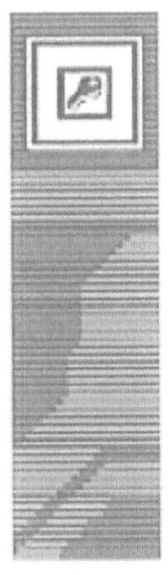

How to create databases
using Access 2000

 Springer

David Thew
Devizes, Wiltshire, UK

Series Editor
John Cowell, BSc (Hons), MPhil, PhD
Department of Computer and Information Sciences,
De Montfort University, Kents Hill Campus, Hammerwood Gate,
Kents Hill, Milton Keynes MK7 6HP, UK

ISBN-13: 978-1-85233-295-2   e-ISBN-13: 978-1-4471-0767-5
DOI: 10.1007/978-1-4471-0767-5
Springer-Verlag London Berlin Heidelberg

British Library Cataloguing in Publication Data
Thew, David
  Essential Access 2000 fast : how to create databases using
  Access 2000
  1.Microsoft Access 2000 (Computer file)
  I.Title II.Access 2000 fast
  005.7'565

Library of Congress Cataloging-in-Publication Data
Thew, David, 1958-
    Essential Access 2000 fast : how to create databases using Access 2000 / David Thew.
        p. cm. – (Essential series)
                    (alk. paper)
    1. Microsoft Access. 2. Database design. I. Title. II. Essential series (Springer-Verlag)

      QA76.9.D3 T4444 2000
  005.75'65—dc21
                                                00-033822

© Springer-Verlag London Limited 2000
Softcover reprint of the hardcover 1st edition 2000

Typesetting: PostScript file supplied by author

34/3830-543210 Printed on acid-free paper SPIN 10761967

Contents

1

Why Use Access 2000?

Introduction

In the mid - 1980's, Microsoft introduced the first version of a Windows GUI style database to complement their standard Office products. This product was to form a major part of what is now known as the Office product range.

Access is provided as part of the Microsoft Office product range but only in the Professional or Business editions. Access is a Relational Database Management System that integrates elements of Object Oriented Technology, enabling users to control how an object reacts by using a set of properties and methods built into the product. While spending a good deal of time working with various versions of Access, it occurred to me that what is often required is a quick and concise guide to using this software. People who are familiar with Office tools want to get on with using the product as quickly as possible; perhaps they only need to be shown around the user interface, while others do not have the time to wade through pages and pages of text in a guide book that often resembles a cross between an encyclopaedia and an experienced user's technical guide. This essential guide is aimed at those who want to get to grips with the basics quickly. I hope that I have been able to draw on my experiences of using Access professionally as a development tool to impart the basic concepts within the pages of this book.

What is Access 2000?

Access is a GUI desktop database designed to run under the Windows operating system; it is designed to allow you to create data lists of related information and to utilise that information by combining the following elements:

- Tables that contain list data.
- Queries to view selective lists or update table data.

- Forms to view the list data.
- Reports to print selective lists.
- Macros to provide automation of events.
- Modules to create Visual Basic programs.

Access will allow you to combine sets of records or data into common groups, produce selective lists based on your questions, count and summarise information onto your screen or within paper reports. All these things can be accomplished quickly with a few basic ground rules, which are covered within this book.

Is this book for you?

This book provides a complete overview of how to create and maintain data using Microsoft Access. It does not cover every aspect of Access; if it did it would be ten times the current size, but it does give you all the essential information you need to develop applications in Access *fast*.

It is assumed that you are familiar with Windows 95 or 98 operating systems and have a basic knowledge of PC applications such as word processors or even spreadsheets. Additional support information is available from Microsoft via its web-based information service and through its online guides. This book is designed to show you how to create, maintain and selectively view data within Access. The idea is to enable you to create a database in Access as quickly as possible. In addition, the book will provide you with an overview of database concepts.

What you need to run Access 2000

The Microsoft recommendation to run Office 2000 and Access is a Pentium 75Mhz-based computer with Windows 95 or later, 16Mb RAM for the operating system and an additional 4Mb of RAM for each application that is running (8Mb for Access or Outlook) and 217Mb of hard disk space for Word, Excel, Outlook, PowerPoint and Access. An additional 174Mb of hard disk is required for Publisher and Small Business Manager. In addition you will require a CD-ROM drive and VGA or SVGA card with monitor. The PC used to generate all the database examples in this book was a Pentium 350Mhz-based PC, with 64Mb of RAM and a 3Gb hard disk. This gave excellent performance.

How to use this book

To fully appreciate just how good Access is, you would need to understand all of the component parts as well as Object Oriented programming and ActiveX controls. This book describes the essentials to provide you with an overview of the product and allow you to create a database as quickly as possible.

You do not have to read this entire book to get started with Access; once you get the basic principle you may want to continue by experimenting on your own. The online help provided with Access is very comprehensive (once you know what to look for).

This book is not intended to be a definitive guide to Access and you may want to use it in conjunction with the documentation provided by Microsoft.

Conventions

There are a few conventions used in the book to make it easier to read:

- All menu names and options are in **bold**.
- All system-defined names are in **bold**.
- All user-defined names and variable names are in *italics*.

2
Starting with Access

Introduction

Before you can use Access you need to understand the component parts that make up the Access application. Access combines a number of elements within a single file - this is known as the database. Tables are used to hold the data while forms and reports are used to display the data in a more meaningful format; these database elements are introduced in this chapter.

In this chapter you will learn:

- How to use the Access interface.
- The difference between the individual Access components.
- How the individual components relate to each other.
- How to use the individual Access components to create a simple database.
- How to use some of the built-in functions within Access.
- Essential terminology.

The menu bar

The menu bar will be familiar to anyone who has used a Microsoft product before; the main changes are to be found in the way the menu items appear. The basic menu layout is shown in Figure 2.1.

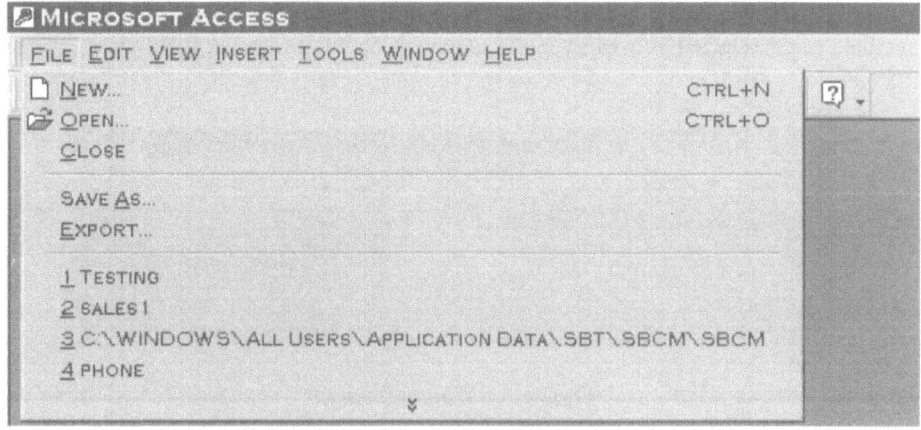

Figure 2.1 *Access menu example.*

Many of the menu options have additional items, these may only become available when you highlight the Extend Menu symbol as shown in Figure 2.2.

Figure *2.2 Extend Menu button.*

There are additional tool bars to facilitate features such as hyperlinks and HTML; the best way of finding out about these features is to use the **Help** menu. Look at the **Help** menu now to demonstrate how the extended menu features operate. Start Access from the Windows 95/98 menu bar, or use the shortcut icon if you have placed one on the desktop. When Access starts, select the **Cancel** option from the Access Create Database window as shown in Figure 2.3.

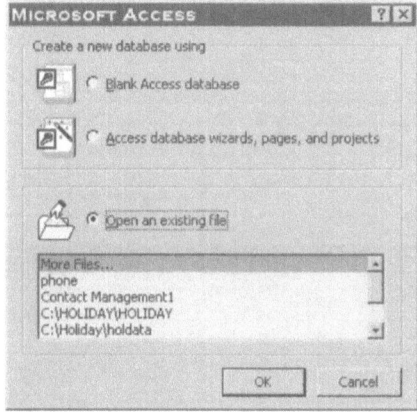

Figure 2.3 *Access Create Database window.*

Then place the mouse pointer over the **Window** menu to see the extended menu symbol; when selected you will see the extended menus as shown in Figures 2.4 and 2.5.

Figure 2.4 Window menu.

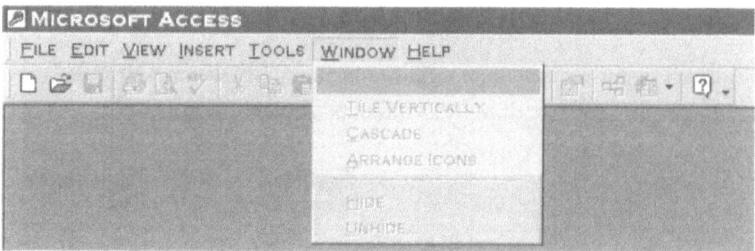

Figure 2.5 Extended Window menu.

By using the **Help** menu you can find out a bit more about the many features within Access 2000.

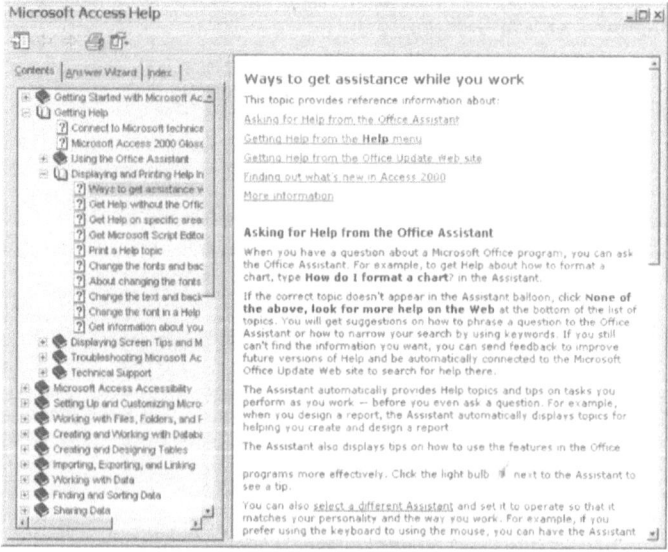

Figure 2.6 Help menu.

The **Help** menu is shown in Figure 2.6. Many of the help features work with Hyperlinks in the same way as Web Pages.

You can create a hyperlink in a table, a form, or a data access page to go to a variety of locations; for example, another Microsoft Access database, project, document or a Web page on the Internet. You can create a hyperlink from a command button, or a label or picture on a form or data access page. A hyperlink is normally seen as coloured and underlined text.

The options buttons are shown in Figure 2.7, these are:

- Hide (to show or hide the toolbar)
- Back (to move back to the previous topic)
- Forward (to move forward to the next topic)
- Print (to display the print dialogue)
- Options (to change the internet options and menu options)

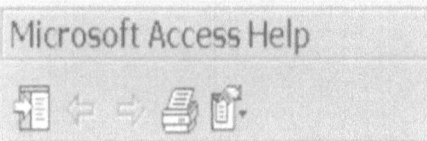

Figure 2.7 Help option buttons.

Now you have seen the menu structure it is time to start using it.

- Select File | New from the menu to create a new database.
- Select the **General** tab from the New window.

The other two tabs may vary in content depending on the options and templates you have installed.

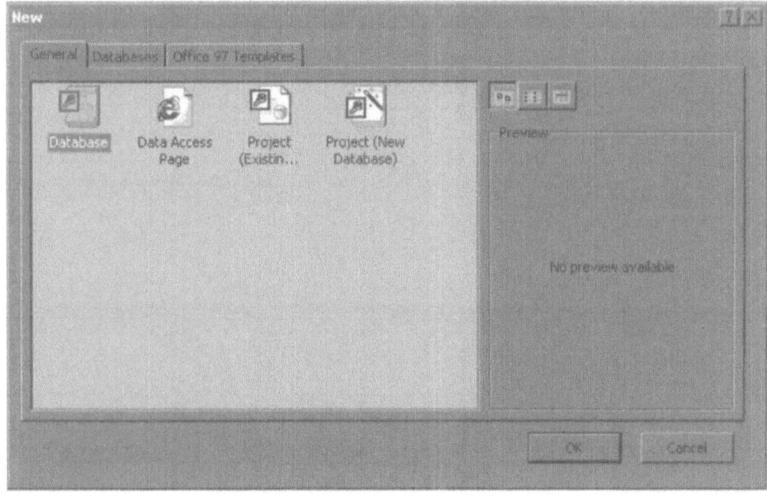

Figure 2.8 Selecting a template.

From the choices select **Database**; you do not want to create a **Data Access Page** or a **Project**. Having selected database as the option you need to supply a file location and a file name for your database. In this example *Testing* has been used as the database name. You can see the Access object tabs on the left hand side of the database window as shown in Figure 2.9.

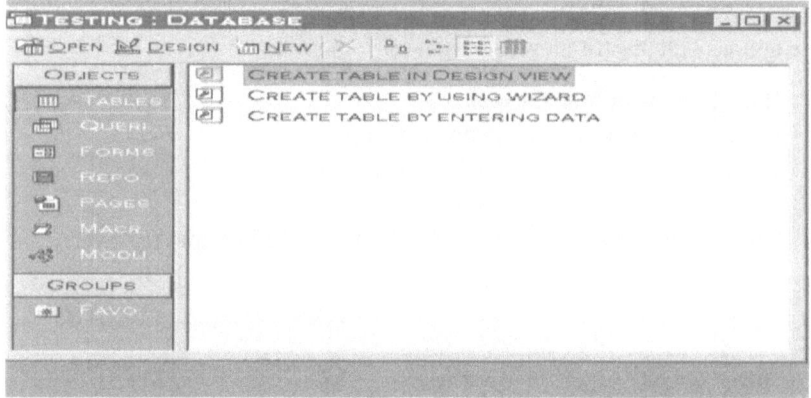

Figure 2.9 *Access object tabs.*

There are two main tabs:

- Objects
- Groups

These are used to open or close the list of items within each main tab; simply click onto each main tab with your mouse. Most of the time you will be using the **objects** tab, this is the area that you use to create each new item used within your database. The main database objects are:

- Tables
- Queries
- Forms
- Reports
- Data access pages
- Macros
- Modules

Tables

A table is used to collect your data about a specific subject; a separate table is used for each subject. Tables keep your data in columns (called fields) and rows (called records). You can add, edit, view, or delete the data in a table as well as filter out the records you do not want to use.

Forms

Forms allow you to visualise your data in a more familiar manner, they can be designed to look the same as the forms you use every day. You can control how the data appears on the form or even how much data appears on a form.

Queries

Queries allow you to phrase a specific question relating to your data. You can use queries over and over again to view, change or summarize your data. The most common form of query is used to select specific records based on criteria you specify; for example, selecting names and addresses of people from a personnel table.

Reports

Reports can be an effective way to present your printed data. Information in a report comes from a table or query; this is known as the report's data source. You can alter the appearance of everything on a report and control the information you want to see on it.

Data access pages

A data access page is a Web page designed to be viewed with intranet data that is stored in a Microsoft Access database or a Microsoft SQL server database. The data access page can include data from Microsoft Excel. The page is stored as a file outside the Access database, a shortcut to the file is added in the Database window.

Macros

A macro is used to hold a set of one or more commands; each can perform a particular task such as opening a form or printing a report. Macros are commonly used to automate common tasks.

Modules

A module is a collection of Visual Basic code contained within procedures; these can be used to control how Access or any Office application works. The latest version of VB is included with Access 2000, and contains similar features to Visual Basic. VB 6 provides Access 2000 with features such as support for additional ActiveX controls. In addition you can work with data and objects such as forms and reports using Microsoft Visual Basic. You can write procedures that create, delete, or modify data and objects. For example, you can write a procedure that performs a calculation on a form or that changes the colour of a field. You can refer to data and objects directly in your code.

3
Database Concepts

Introduction

Before continuing you will need to understand some of the essential features of database design. The principles of database design are relatively straightforward although the application can often become time-consuming and complicated. The basic elements are covered in the following chapter along with the terms you will become familiar with when working with your Access database.

Paper database

The paper file database is simple in design and favours the style of a card index system' similar to those you find on your desk with name and address details.

The design is straightforward to apply, as there are only a few ways to utilize the system. For example, to create a paper file database containing name and order information you could design a card index type system.

If you look at Table 3.1, the card shows six fields of information. Each relates to a customer. These are the *Customer Name, Company, Phone, Order No, Description* and *Qty*.

In a computerized database you need to identify the fields of information relating to each entry; this is part of the design stage. The card shown in Table 3.1 contains fields of information, each with its own heading or **field name** and each with its own column width or **field size**.

These are the three main design features of any database: **fields, field Names** and **field sizes**. There is a fourth element that will be discussed later, **field type**. This is used to define the type of information in the field.

Table 3.1 Example of a paper file system.

Name	Company	Phone	Order	Desc	Qty
Mr David Jones	The Black Pen Co	123-456789	1234	Black Ink	10
Mr David Jones	The Black Pen Co	123-456789	1234	Blue Ink	15
Mr David Jones	The Black Pen Co	123-456789	1234	Black Ink	10
Mrs Sally Smith	Mount Trading Stamps	333-123456	1235	Black Ink	12
Mrs Sally Smith	Mount Trading Stamps	333-123456	1236	Red Ink	10

Each row is called a record; all the items on one row are connected to each other in some way. In the next example each record relates to one person.

In the example shown in Table 3.1 there is a basic design fault: if this were to be used as it is there would be a lot of unnecessary typing. For example, what happens when a customer changes their phone number or the name of the contact changes? In other words there is a lot of redundant duplicated data; it would be better to eliminate this by splitting the **table** into two parts as shown in Tables 3.2 and 3.3.

Tables

Unlike other products Access holds all its component parts within one single file; this is known as the Database Container. This file has a normal extension of MDB (Microsoft Data Base). Having mentioned some of the Access component parts, you can now examine one of the key components, the table. Tables are designed by you to hold your information within your database; you design them by examining the items of information you want to store.

Perhaps you want to hold customer information in a **table** and relate this to a set of orders for goods placed by that customer; you might start with the customer information first and then move onto your customer's orders. You could design a simple *Customer* **table** as shown in Table 3.2. You may then go on to design a simple record of the orders as shown in Table 3.3.

Table 3.2 *Customer records.*

Customer Name		Company	Phone
Mr Jones	David	The Black Pen Co	123-456789
Mrs Smith	Sally	Mount Trading Stamps	333-123456

If you look at the two simple tables you may spot a problem: how do you know who the customer was on the list of orders in the *Orders* table?

Table 3.3 *Order records.*

Order No	Description	Qty	Cost	Date
1234	Black Ink	10	53.00	March 1st
1235	Black Ink	12	63.00	April 2nd
1236	Red Ink	10	53.00	March 1st
1234	Blue Ink	15	23.00	March 1st
1234	Black Ink	10	53.00	March 1st

What is required is some method of joining the two tables together. If you add the *Customer Name* to the *Orders* table then you will be able to relate them to each other; however, there could still be problems later on if you employ this method. What happens if you encounter more than one customer with the same *Customer Name*? What about using the *Company* name instead? There is still the possibility of a duplicated *Company* name occurring. This is a common problem when holding data in a paper database system or within another product such as an Excel spreadsheet; you are often faced with row upon row of duplicated data that is hard to relate. The answer would be to add a unique value to each customer in the *Customer* table; this is known as applying a **primary key**, a value that will not duplicate and is unique for each record. So if a **primary key** value was applied to the *Customer* table as shown in Table 3.4, you can identify each customer with ease.

Table 3.4 Customer records with a primary key.

ID	Customer Name		Company	Phone
1	Mr Jones	David	The Black Pen Co	123-456789
2	Mrs Smith	Sally	Mount Trading Stamps	333-123456

You can now use the **primary key** from the *Customer* table in the *Orders* table. However, there could be several orders relating to each customer. Microsoft Access will not allow any duplicate or blank values in a **primary key** field, so you can not use this on the **Orders** table. The answer is to apply a **foreign key**: a value that matches a **primary key** from another table that allows duplicate values. An example of a **foreign key** is shown in Table 3.5.

Table 3.5 Orders with foreign key in ID field.

ID	Order No	Description	Qty	Cost	Date
1	1234	Black Ink	10	53.00	March 1st
2	1235	Black Ink	12	63.00	April 2nd
2	1236	Red Ink	10	53.00	March 1st
1	1234	Blue Ink	15	23.00	March 1st
1	1234	Black Ink	10	53.00	March 1st

You could then use a query to join the two tables together using the *ID* values. This is known as building a relationship between tables.

Records

As mentioned earlier a collective set of data relating to one item is termed a **record**; these are stored in collective groups within your **table**. Before you can do this you have to create the **table**, so once you have decided what information you need to collect then you have to define the data type for the fields. If you look at the simple **table** layout in Figure 3.1 you can see that each row contains several fields of information. Each **field** is part of the individual record shown on a specific row, in this case contact names and addresses.

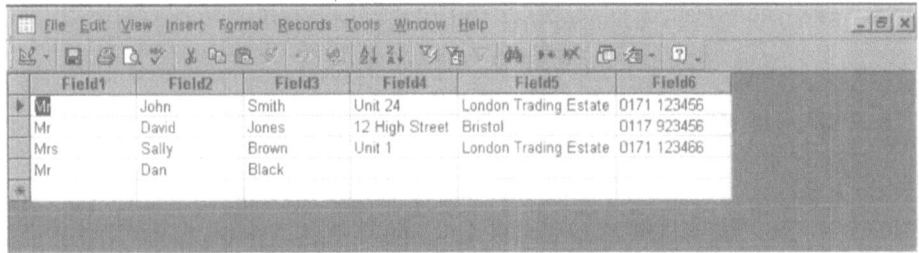

Figure 3.1 Example table layout.

Design ground rules

Deciding how to store your data can be difficult at first but if you remember a few simple rules, you will soon get to understand how to structure your tables in the optimum way. Remember that computerized databases can only find information based on the fields you use; it is no good trying to locate a record by using a surname if you did not store it in the table.

When using address data, try to break it down into its smallest component part. Split the address down into town, county and postcode; similarly, when using names, break them down into surname and first name. If you look at Figure 3.1 again you can see there are six specific fields of information, all of which contain text entries. The contact and address details have been broken down into the smallest component part of the information provided.

This allows you to use each **field** to search for specific **records** within the **table**; for example, you could search for a phone number or a surname or even a combination of fields. Computerized databases rely on pattern or character matching within fields to locate the data; this means you have to phrase your questions in a specific way. To locate a surname you have to specify the field that contains the surname and then the name of the person you are looking for. This might be expressed as: Field3 = "Brown". Notice that quotation marks are used to enclose the text of the surname you are searching for; this is a normally applied rule when using text data.

Design stages

Before you create your database there are a few questions you can ask yourself to help you avoid problems later on:

- What do you want to use your database for?
- What information do I need in my tables to achieve this?
- How is this information to be broken down into **fields** in the table?
- What type of **fields** should I use in the table?
- Do I need more than one table in order to avoid duplicating entries?

- How can I relate or join separate tables together to collect groups or data?

Normalizing data

There is a process called normalization that is used in the design of a database. This can be used to help organize your data and minimize duplication and often involves dividing the database up into several tables with a view to minimizing the amount of editing that takes place. The tables can then be related to each other and primary or foreign keys can be defined. There are several levels of normalization and a number of formal rules that are applied to this process.

The subject of Relational Database Management Systems, the formal rules that can be applied to their design, and the processes of normalization require more comprehensive coverage than can be given in this single volume. There are a number of excellent titles available on this subject and you will find some suggestions about further reading materials in Chapter 12.

Testing a design

Try to keep in mind the simplified guidelines listed under the earlier heading of Design stages. Keep the design as simple as possible, test your design with some sample data and examine what happens when you have to change a value in a **field**. Do you have to change another value somewhere else in the same or any other table? If the answer is yes then this indicates that there may be some redundancy in the tables. Taking the example in Table 3.1, there are several fields that contain duplicated or repeating data:

- Customer Name
- Company
- Phone
- Order No
- Description

If you were to change *Customer Name* from *Mr David Jones* to *Mr David Black* you would find that you need to enter this twice more as there are duplicated values for this customer. The same would apply to the *Order No* **field**; if this were to change from *1234* to, say, *1299* then you have to change all three entries, whereas the examples shown in Tables 3.4 and 3.5 correct some of the problems by splitting the table into two and applying keys to the tables. There is still, however, some duplication in the *Description* **field**: this could be overcome by introducing a third table for the order lines and a fourth table for the description of the goods as shown in Tables 3.6 to 3.9.

Table 3.6 *Customer records with a primary key in Cust ID.*

Cust ID	Customer Name		Company	Phone
1	Mr Jones	David	The Black Pen Co	123-456789
2	Mrs Smith	Sally	Mount Trading Stamps	333-123456

Table 3.7 *Orders with primary key in Order ID and a foreign key in Cust ID.*

Cust ID	Order No	Order ID	Date
1	1234	1	March 1st
2	1235	2	April 2nd
2	1236	3	March 1st

Table 3.8 *Order lines with foreign key in Order ID and Desc ID.*

Order ID	Desc ID	Qty	Cost
1	1	10	53.00
2	1	12	63.00
3	2	10	53.00
1	3	15	23.00
1	1	10	53.00

Table 3.9 *Product descriptions with primary key in Desc ID field.*

Desc ID	Description
1	Black Ink
2	Red Ink
3	Blue Ink

Therefore, you should be able to relate these tables to each other by using the primary and foreign keys. As you can see you only have to change the customer information, the order number or the description of the product once. You will find out more about using multiple tables in Chapter 9.

Field types

Before you start creating tables you need to look at the field types used with Access
tables; each is used for a specific data type.

Table 3.10 *Access field types.*

Data type	Use for	Size
Text	Combinations of text and numbers. Numbers that do not require calculations, such as phone numbers.	Up to 255 characters.
Memo	Lengthy notes or descriptions.	Up to 64,000 characters.
Number	Numeric data to be used for mathematical calculations.	1, 2, 4, or 8 bytes. 16 bytes for Replication ID.
Date/Time	Dates and times.	8 bytes.
Currency	Currency values. Accurate to 15 digits to the left of the decimal point and 4 digits to the right.	8 bytes.
AutoNumber	Unique sequential or random numbers automatically inserted.	4 bytes. 16 bytes for Replication ID.
Yes/No	Field that contains only Yes/No, True/False, On/Off.	1 bit.
OLE Object	Objects (such as Microsoft Word documents, pictures and sounds, created in other programs using the OLE protocol).	Up to 1 gigabyte (limited by disk space).
Hyperlink	A hyperlink can be a UNC path or a URL.	Up to 64,000 characters.
Lookup Wizard	A field that allows you to choose a value from another table or from a list.	The same size as the primary key field that is also the Lookup field; typically 4 bytes.

There are good reasons for using the correct field type for a specific piece of data. It will save space within the database and it will make the database more efficient as well as making it easier to locate data. Phone numbers are a good example; it is not sensible to add phone numbers together, even though they consist of a series of digits. There is usually no need to perform mathematical operations on phone numbers or people's names. So in general you may use text fields for descriptive data and numeric fields for mathematical data.

Fields have a direct effect on how the data can be used within the database. The field data types available in Microsoft Access are shown in Table 3.10.

If you look again at the **table** shown in Figure 3.1, the structure or design of the table shown would look like the one shown in Figure 3.2. You can clearly see the field names in the first column and the field types in the second column. The field names are simply shown as *Field1* to *Field6*, while each of the fields is designed to store Text only.

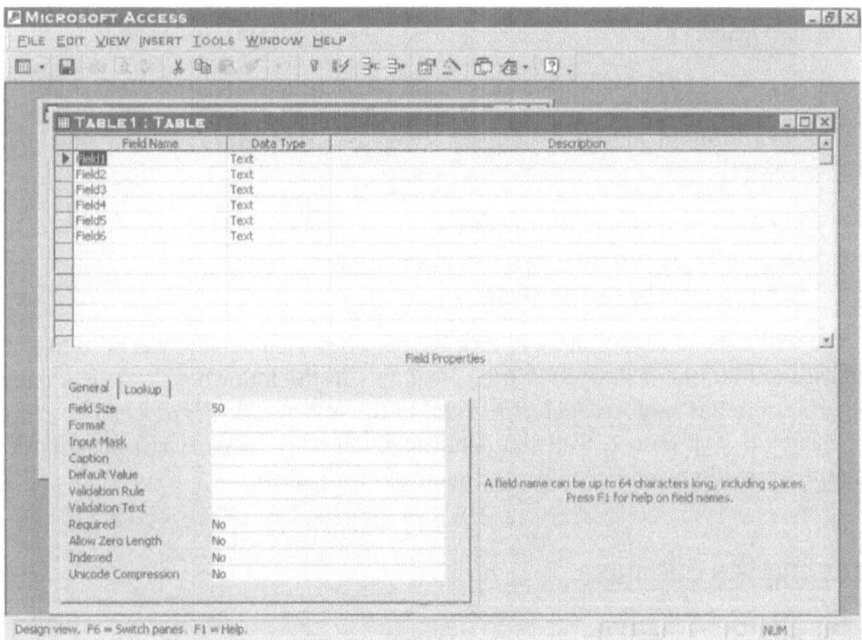

Figure 3.2 *Table structure.*

A text field may contain any number of characters from the keyboard; they are not normally used with mathematical calculations. So you could consider a telephone number, part number or account number to be suitable for a text type field, while a price or salary would be considered a genuine numeric field. That is to say the latter two types would be suitable for performing a mathematical operation.

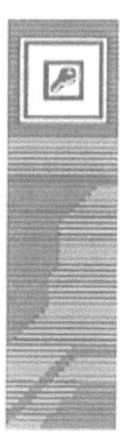

4

Creating a Table

Introduction

Now you have read about some of the basics it is time to look at the ways in which you can create a **table** in Access. There are three main methods of creating a table, these are:

- Use Design view to create a table
- Use the Table Wizard to create a table
- Create a table by entering data

You will look at each of these in turn but before you can do that you need to create a database to hold the tables you will be creating. In the following example a database called *Testing* has been created and stored in the folder called *Mydocuments*. It does not matter if you want to call the database by another name, you can still use the examples providing you remember the name of the database.

Creating the database

If you have not started Access then you will need to now. Start Access from the Windows 95/98 menu bar, or use the shortcut icon if you have placed one on the desktop. For the example, you are going to create a database using a Blank format rather than using an existing file or using the Wizard. Select the **Blank Access database** option and then click on the **OK** button.; see Figure 4.1.

Figure 4.1 *Creating a blank database.*

Creating the table with data entry

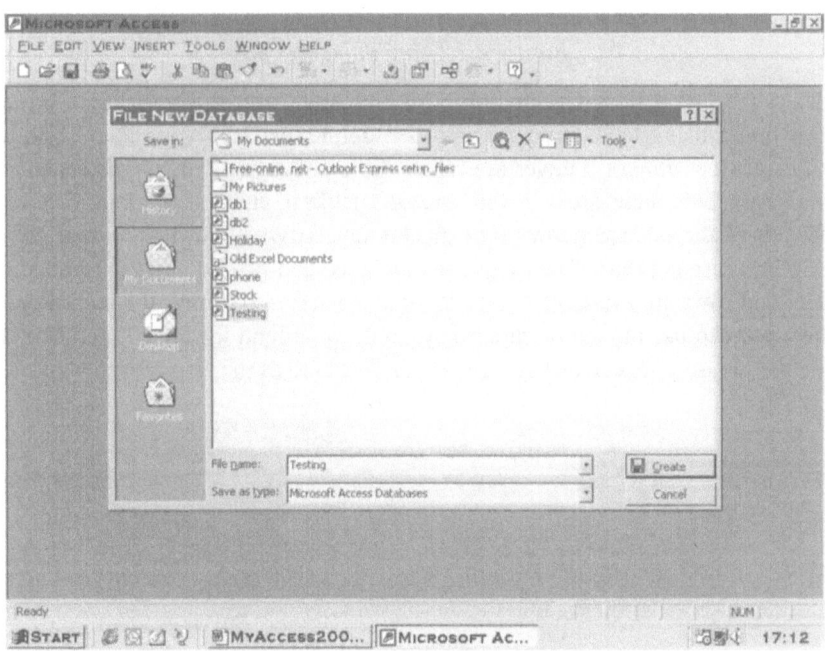

Figure 4.2 *Naming the new database.*

The next step is to name the database and specify the location or folder where it is to be stored, as shown in Figure 4.2. Once you have completed that and selected the **Create** button you will see the blank database with the **object** tabs on the left of the Database window. If you select the **tables** tab you will see the three main options mentioned before, as shown in Figure 4.3. Recreate the example table used earlier in Figure 3.1; this time you will modify the table structure to give each field a more meaningful name.

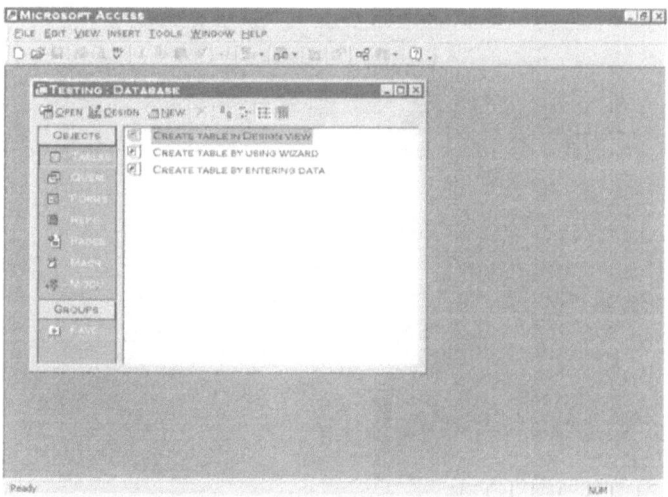

Figure 4.3 Using the tables tab.

Select the last option, **Create table by entering data**; this will allow you to type entries into a blank table structure and then define the field types later. You can see that the blank or unnamed tables are called *Table* and a suffix number is added to show how many tables there are. In this case the table is called *Table1* as shown in the upper left of the table window. The Access object type follows the name; the object type in this case is **table**. The fields are numbered and run from left to right across the screen, and rows are available to type the data entries into. Enter the records you used earlier; you can use the tab or cursor keys to move around the table if you do not want to use the mouse. The cursor keys are often referred to as the arrow keys.

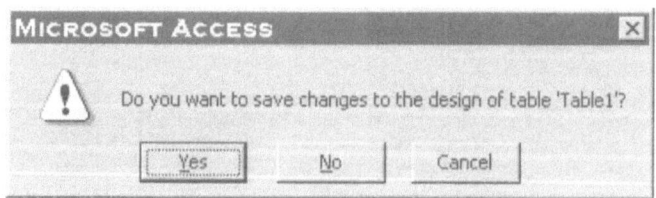

Figure 4.4 Save table prompt.

When you have finished, **close** the table and you will be prompted to save the table, see Figure 4.4, select **Yes** and then confirm the table name. In the example the table name is *Table1*.

You will then be warned that there is no primary key assigned and asked if you want to create one; do not worry about this for now, select the **No** button. When you have been returned to the database window you will see the new table in the list of table objects available. Primary keys are used in Access to help identify each record in a table by assigning a unique value to the record. For example, you would not want to have a part number that described a specific part held twice within your table. You could assign a unique value field for a part number and then use this as the primary key value. Access would not allow you to duplicate entries within this field. You will look at this in more detail later though, so for now you do not need to assign a primary key for this table.

Moving on, you can now examine how the table has been designed or structured. To view or change the structure of a table you need to highlight the table and then select the **Design** button on the toolbar; see Figure 4.5.

Figure 4.5 *Using the Design button on the toolbar.*

You can see how this particular table has been structured in Figure 4.6.

Field Name	Data Type	Description
Title	Text	
FirstName	Text	
SurName	Text	
Address1	Text	
Address2	Text	
PhoneNumber	Text	
LastOrderDate	Date/Time	

Field Properties

General | Lookup |

Format
Input Mask
Caption
Default Value
Validation Rule
Validation Text
Required   No

The field description is optional. It helps you desc and is also displayed in the status bar when you s on a form. Press F1 for help on descripti

Figure 4.6 *Modified table structure.*

Each of the fields has a name and a data type. To change the name of any field you only need to overtype it. To change the data type you need to select an option from the list. A little care must be taken when changing the data types of fields when data has already been entered-sometimes data already entered may be lost or even truncated. Access will issue a suitable warning before this occurs. One point to note: **AutoNumber** fields should only be changed to **Long Integer** data types. In the next example the field names have been changed and a new field added with a **Date/Time** data type. Use the example shown in Figure 4.6 and modify the design of *Table1* and then **close** the table and save the changes.

If you open the table from the database window by double clicking on the icon, you can view the changes you have made. Fill in the order dates as shown in Figure 4.7.

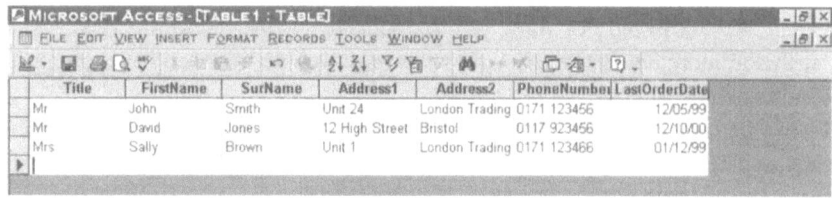

Figure 4.7 Modified records.

Creating a table using a wizard

The Table Wizard is designed to enable you to create a table based on a standard Access template. The principles are much the same, however the wizard guides you through the table design stage by stage.

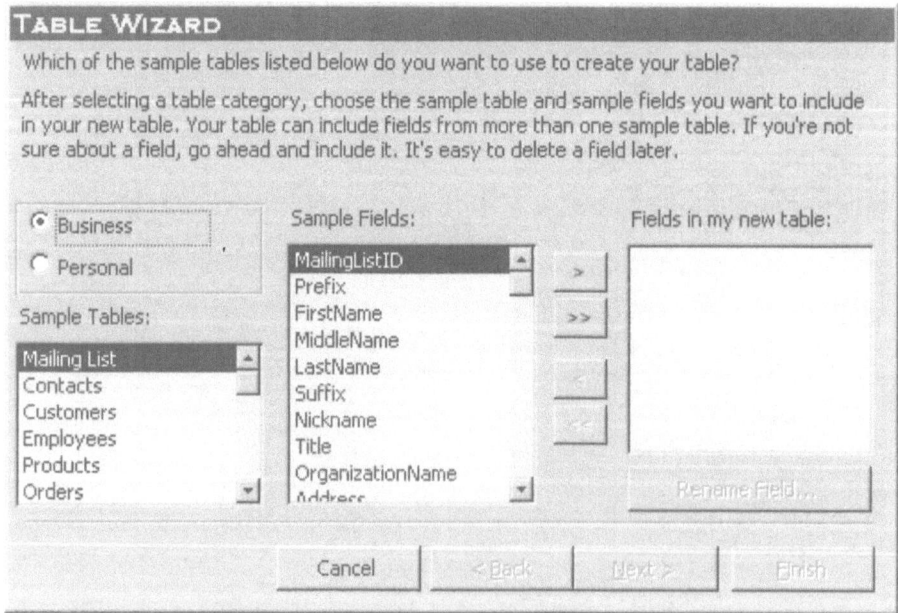

Figure 4.8 The Business or Personal templates.

To use the wizard you need to select the **table objects** and the use the **Create Table by Using Wizard** option. The Table Wizard allows you to select from one of two templates, either **Business** or **Personal**; a radio button is used to select the choice.

When you have chosen between these two options, the sample tables displayed will change to reflect this. The next step is to select the table that matches your requirement and then select from the list of supplied fields.

Fields are added to the **Fields in my new table** window by using one of two methods:

- Highlight one field at a time and add it to your table design by using the button, as shown in Figures 4.9 and 4.10.

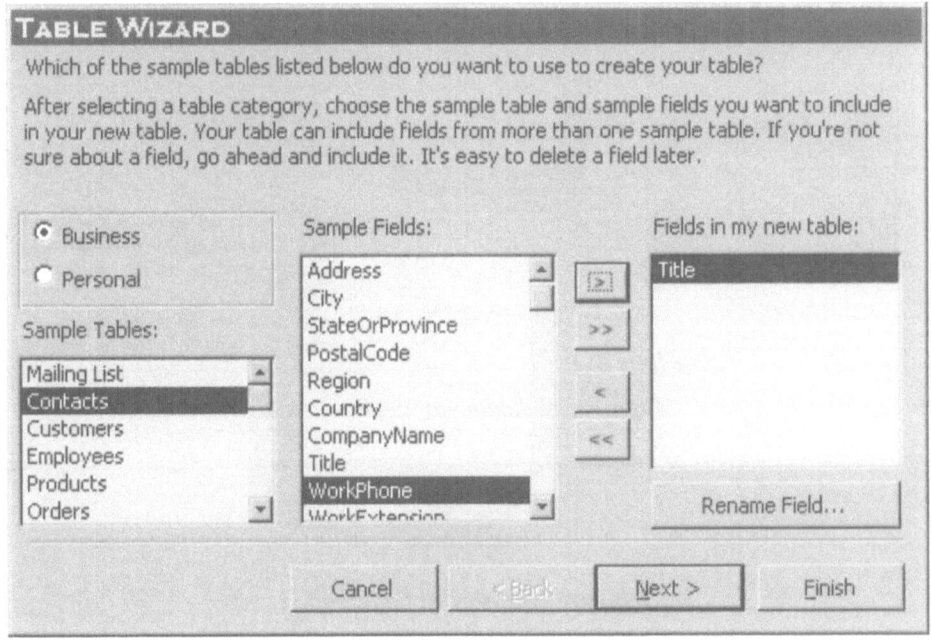

Figure 4.9 Adding single field to a table template.

Figure 4.10 Add a single field button.

- Select and add all the fields in one go to your table design by using the button, as shown in Figures 4.11 and 4.12.

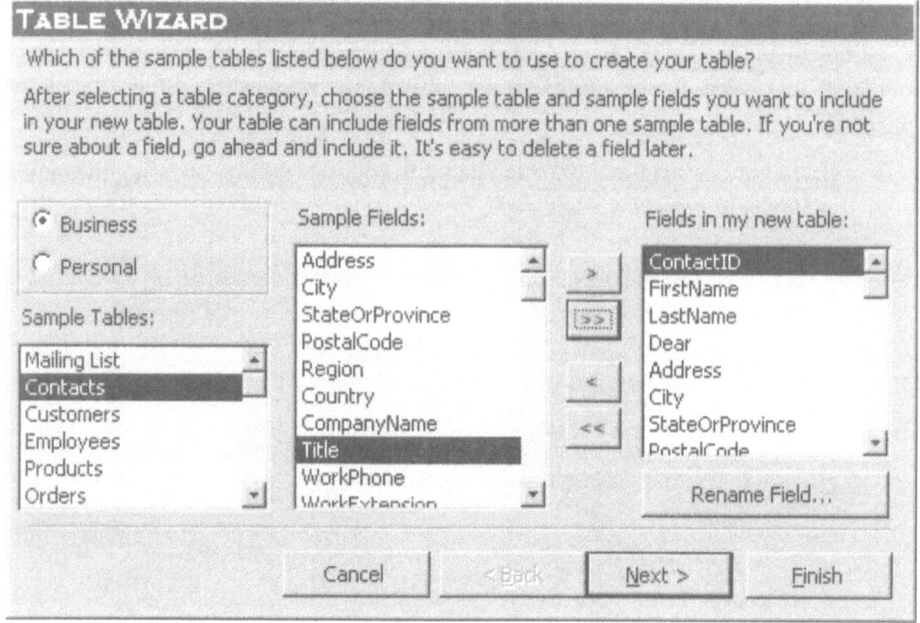

Figure 4.11 Adding all fields to a table.

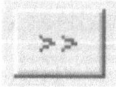

Figure 4.12 Add all fields button.

In the example shown in Figure 4.13, the **Business** templates radio button has been selected along with the **Contacts** table from the **Sample Tables**. The fields *Title, FirstName, LastName, CompanyName, Address, WorkPhone* and *LastMeetingDate* have been added one by one from the **Sample Fields** window. Fields may be renamed in the **Fields in my new table** window by using the **Rename Field ...** button.

When you have completed your field selection you move onto the next stage by using the **Next** button.

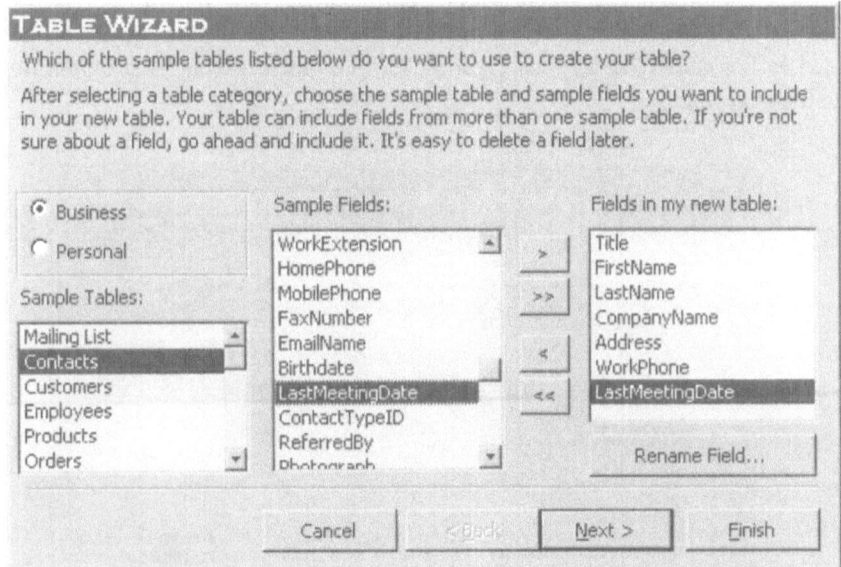

Figure 4.13 *Using the Table Wizard with a Business template.*

The next stage is to name the table and decide if you want Access is to assign a primary key field for you automatically. If so, each record will then be given a unique number; the default primary key is an **AutoNumber** field.

In Figure 4.14 the default file name is *Contacts* and Access has set the primary key for us.

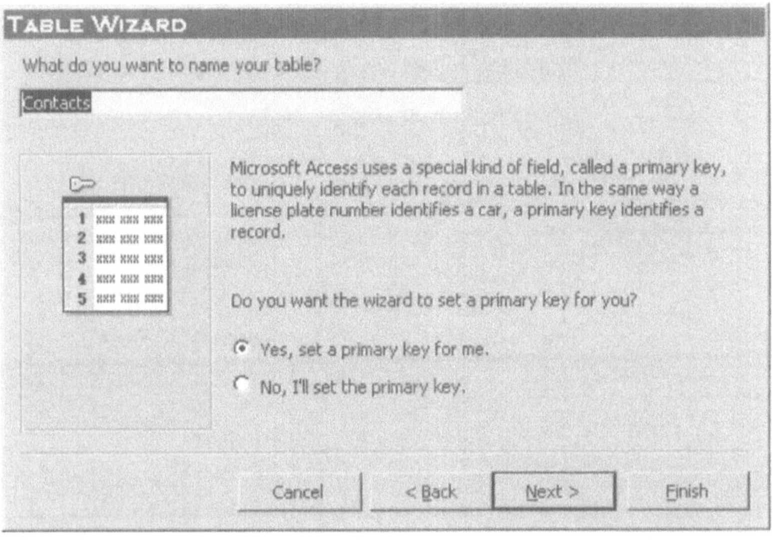

Figure 4.14 *Naming the table and assigning a primary key.*

If there is more than one table within your database, then you will be asked if they **relate** to each other in any way. In this case this new table is **not related** to the table created earlier called *Table1;* see Figure 4.15. You then use the **Next** button to move on to the next stage.

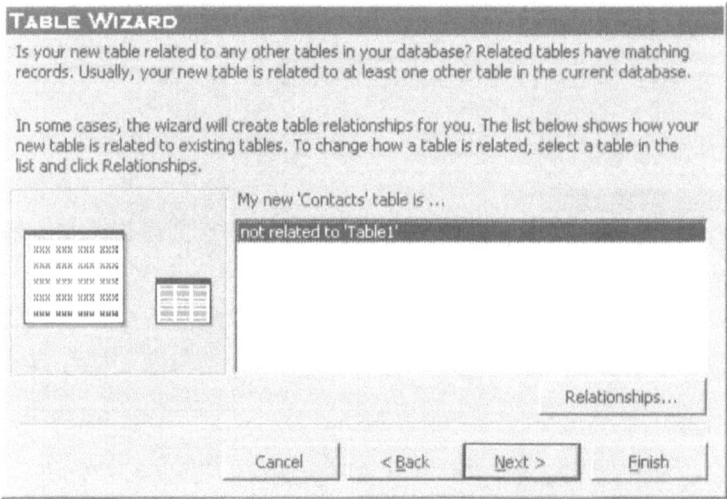

Figure 4.15 Setting relationships using the Table Wizard.

The final stage is to decide if you want to modify the table design, enter data directly onto the table or allow Access to create a form for data entry. If you choose the **Modify the table design** option, as shown in Figure 4.16 you can then see the tables structure.

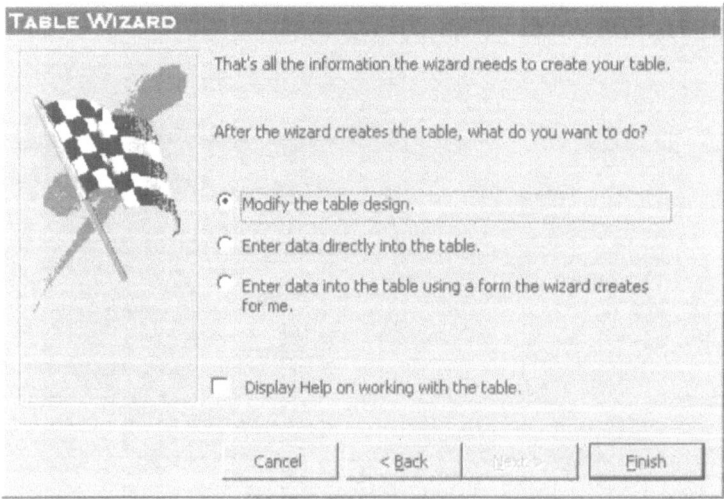

Figure 4.16 Defining the last option using the Table Wizard.

When you have finished looking at the new table structure, as shown in Figure 4.17, **close** it to return to the database window.

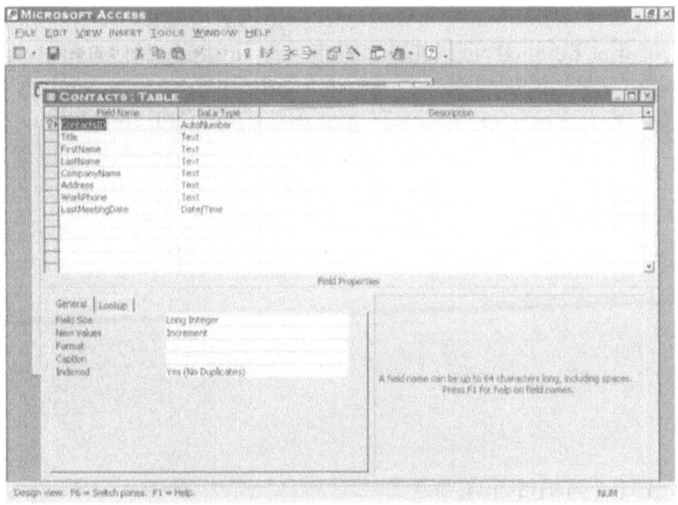

Figure 4.17 *The new table structure.*

Field properties

Now you have two **table objects** within your database and I hope some idea of how to create a table. If you decide to create a table using the **Design View** option, a blank table structure form is displayed as shown in Figure 4.18. This will allow you to type in your own field names and select your data types.

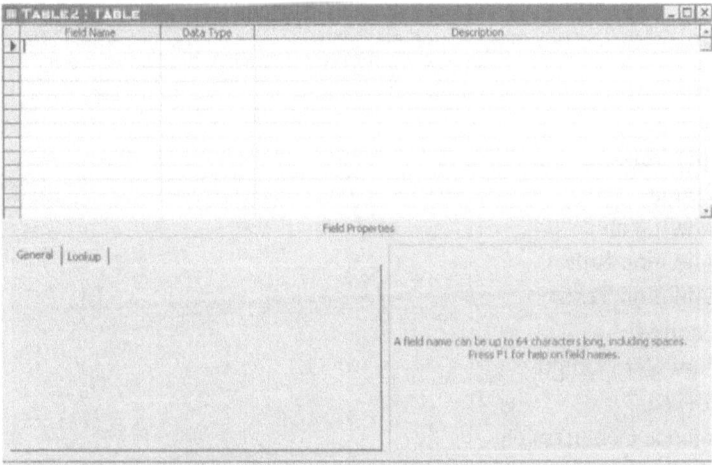

Figure 4.18 *A blank table structure in design mode.*

There are some additional features available to you when you create or change a table's structure. These are the fields' characteristics or **properties.**, If you **open** *Table1* in **Design** view, you can examine these properties in a little more detail.

By selecting any column within a single field row in the design you can view the **properties** for that field. If you look at the example in Figure 4.19, the *Title* field has been selected to view its properties. The properties will vary depending on the field's data type. This field has a text data type and so the properties reflect this.

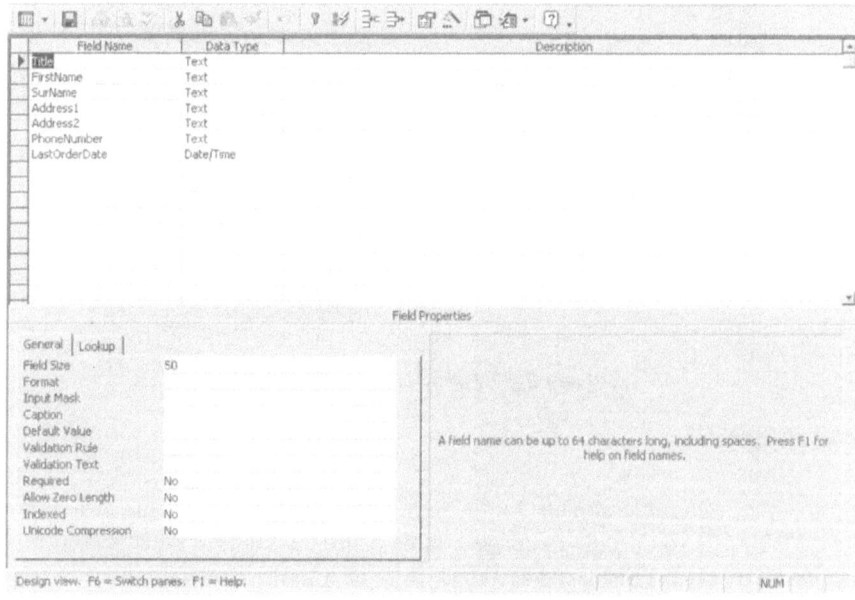

Figure 4.19 *Viewing the properties of the Title field.*

The General properties are:

- Field Size
- Format
- Input Mask
- Caption
- Default Value
- Validation Rule
- Validation Text
- Required
- Allow Zero Length
- Indexed
- Unicode Compression

The most common field properties can be seen in Figure 4.19. The field properties are used to give a specific field it's own unique characteristics: for example you could have two text fields that are identical in length but one could force all the entries into uppercase, while the other could leave the entries exactly as they were typed in. It is quite common for descriptive fields within a table to be converted to uppercase as this gives them all the same visual style and makes searching for entries a little easier later on.

Field Size

You can use the **field size** property to set the size for data stored in a field. With Text data types, enter a number from 0 to 255. The default setting is 50. You can specify the default field sizes for Text and Number fields. You should use the smallest possible **field size** property setting because smaller data sizes can be processed faster and require less memory

Format

You can use special symbols in the setting for the **Format** property to create custom formats for Text and Memo fields. You can create custom text and memo formats by using the following symbols; see Table 4.1.

Table 4.1 Formatting symbols.

Symbol	Description
@	Text character (either a character or a space) is required.
&	Text character is not required.
<	Force all characters to lowercase.
>	Force all characters to uppercase.

For example, a format symbol of > would convert "abcdef" to "ABCDEF" in the table. A format pattern of @ @ @ would allow for any three characters to be entered into the text field.

Input Mask

The **Input Mask** differs from a format in the following way:

- Input masks define how the data is to be stored and how much data can be entered; they can act to restrict the data to a specific number of characters.
- For example a format using the > symbol forces all the data entered to uppercase but does not restrict the number of characters (the field size dictates this). An input mask using the symbols: "LL99" specifies four characters maximum. The first two characters are required and must be an A - Z entry; the last two characters are also required but must be numeric.

An extract from the list of characters used with input masks is shown table 4.2.

Table 4.2 Input Mask symbols.

Character	Meaning
0	Used for 0 to 9 (entry required, plus [+] and minus [−] signs not allowed).
9	Used for digits or space (entry not required, plus and minus signs not allowed).
#	Used for digit or space (entry not required, plus and minus signs allowed).
L	Used for letter (A to Z, entry required).
?	Used for letter (A to Z, entry optional).
A	Used for letter or digit (entry required).
a	Letter or digit (entry optional).
&	Any character or a space (entry required).
C	Any character or a space (entry optional).

Caption

Field captions specify the text for labels attached as the column heading for the field in the table. These can be used to provide a more meaningful description of the field.

Default Value

You can use the **Default Value** property of a field to specify a value that is automatically entered into that field when you add a new record. For example, 100 could be used as a default numeric value.

Validation rule

A field validation rule is used to check the value entered into the field. It is validated after the user moves off the field. For example, you could define *">=10 And <=100"* as the validation rule for a Number field to allow only values from 10 to 100 to be entered. Some examples are shown in Table 4.3.

***Table 4.3** Validation operators.*

Operator	Description
<>0	Enter a value not equal to zero.
>100	Value must be over 100.
Like "AB???"	Value must be five characters beginning with AB.
<#1/1/99#	Enter a date before 1999.
>=#1/1/97# And <#1/1/98#	Date must be in 1997.

Try out the validation rule in the example shown in Figure 4.20. Notice that the field length has also been restricted to a maximum of four characters.

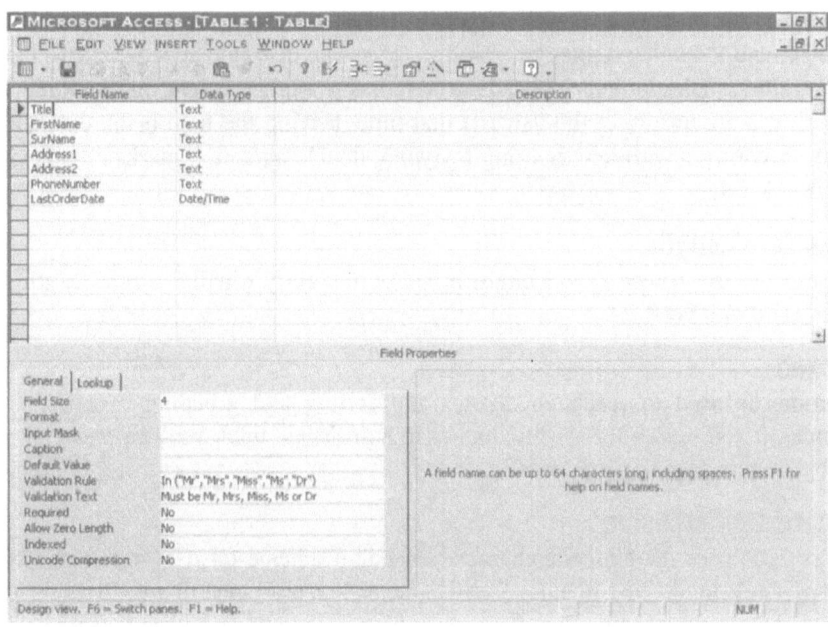

***Figure 4.20** Validation rule example.*

Validation text

Validation text is often used to replace the standard Access error message when data entry contradicts a validation rule. For example, if you had a **validation rule** of *>100* on a numeric field then you may have a validation text statement of "*Please Enter a Value of more than 100*". You can see a validation rule example in Figure 4.20. This has been used to check that the entries match one of those contained in the list. If an entry does not meet this requirement then the text entered as the **Validation Text** is displayed onto the screen. The word **In** relates to a specific function built into Access. Another example of its usage is shown next, along with the syntax or structure of the function. It is used to determine whether a value is equal to any value held in a specified list.

   [Not] In (value1, value2, . . .)

Value1, value2 etc are the expressions against which you want to evaluate an entry. If the entry is found in the list of values, the **In** operator returns **True**; otherwise, it returns **False**. You can use the **Not** operator to evaluate the opposite condition (that is, whether the value is **not** in the list of values). The following example checks to see if the value matches the words *London* or *New York*.

   In ('London','New York')

Required

You can use the **Required** property to specify whether a value is required in a field. If this property is set to **Yes**, when you enter data in a record you must enter a value in the field, and the value cannot be a **Null**. Access can distinguish between two kinds of blank values: **Blanks** and **Nulls.** If a table has a Numeric field and it is left blank because you are unsure of the value at that time, leaving the field blank enters a **Null** value. Entering a zero-length string by typing double quotation marks (" ") is classed as a **Blank** value.

Allow Zero Length

You can use the **Allow Zero Length** property to specify whether a zero-length string ("") is valid in a field.

Indexed

An **index** is used to speed up queries and sorting and grouping operations. For example, if you search for specific names in a *SurName* field, you can create an index for this field to speed up the search.

Unicode Compression

Access 2000 uses the **Unicode** character-encoding scheme for data in a **Text, Memo,** or **Hyperlink** field. In **Unicode**, each character is represented by two bytes instead of a single byte. Any scheme that stores each character in one byte limits you to a single **code page set** containing a maximum of 256 characters. **Unicode** can support a maximum of 65,536 characters, because it represents each character as two bytes. As a result, the data in a **Text, Memo,** or **Hyperlink** field requires more storage space.

Editing your data

Now you have covered some of the properties that can be applied to a **field** within a **table,** you can look at some of the features you can use to make life easier when entering or editing the data within your tables.

One of the first things to mention is the fact that, as with all Windows products, columns and rows can be selected and manipulated to alter their appearance. By way of example, open *Table1* as shown in Figure 4.21.

	Title	FirstName	SurName	Address1	Address2	PhoneNumber	LastOrderDate
▶	Mr	John	Smith	Unit 24	London Trading	0171 123456	12/05/99
	Mr	David	Jones	12 High Street	Bristol	0117 923456	12/10/00
	Mrs	Sally	Brown	Unit 1	London Trading	0171 123466	01/12/99
*							

Figure 4.21 Table1 example layout.

Click on the column heading for the *LastOrderDate* field to select the whole column of data. Now holding the mouse pointer on the field heading, drag the column to the left by one column and then release it. Your columns will now be arranged as shown in Figure 4.22.

	Title	FirstName	SurName	Address1	Address2	LastOrderDate	PhoneNumber
▶	Mr	John	Smith	Unit 24	London Trading	12/05/99	0171 123456
	Mr	David	Jones	12 High Street	Bristol	12/10/00	0117 923456
	Mrs	Sally	Brown	Unit 1	London Trading	01/12/99	0171 123466
*							

Figure 4.22 Rearranged Table1 layout.

To find data within the table, you use the **Find** button as shown in Figure 4.23, then you enter the text or value you are looking for. For example, say you want to **find** the surname *Brown*.

- Enter the word *Brown* in the **Find What** box.
- Change the **Look In** list to the name of the table e.g. *Table1*. Then use the **Find Next** button to locate the text within the table.

Figure 4.23 The Find button.

The cursor will be located over the first correct entry within the table as shown in Figure 4.24.

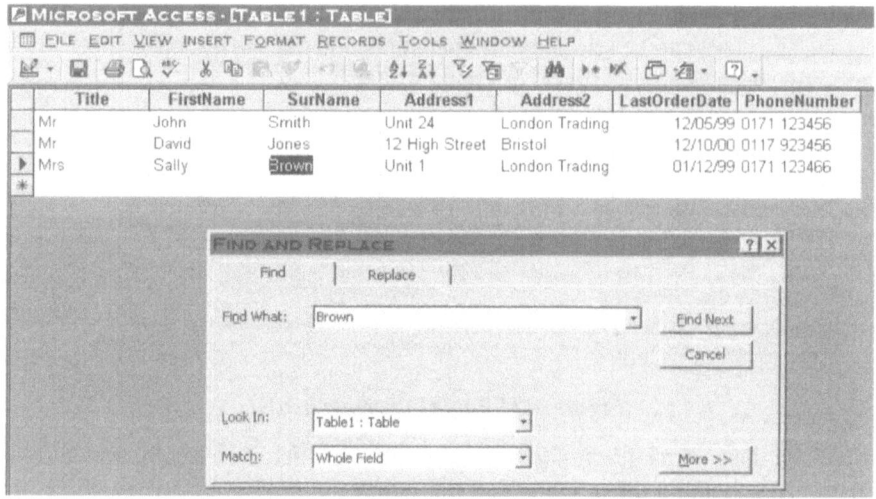

Figure 4.24 *Finding the first correct entry.*

Record navigation and editing

There are some basic features that can help when adding data to a table, as well as the standard cut and paste techniques. One useful feature is the **ditto** key combination that can be used when entering duplicated data in a table. Suppose you want to **add** a new record to the table and the *Address1* field is the same as the *Address1* field in record number three (the record navigation buttons are shown in Figure 4.25)

- Move to record number three and then onto the next record (new record).
- Place the cursor into the blank *Address1* field.
- Duplicate the entry above by using the following key combination: **CTRL** and ".

The entry above the current field will be duplicated as shown in Figure 4.26.

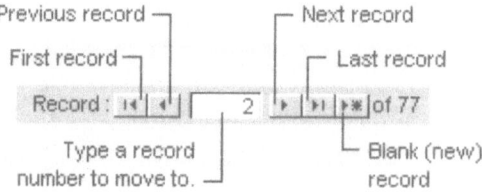

Figure 4.25 *Record navigation buttons.*

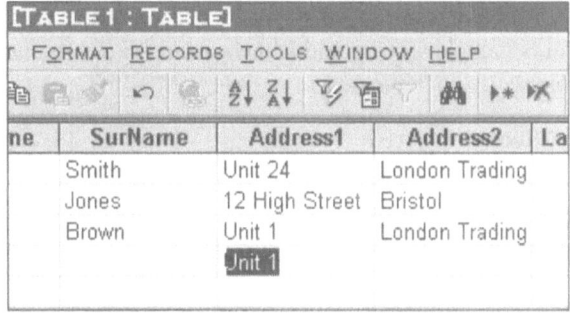

Figure 4.26 The duplicated field.

Deleting a record

To delete the new entry:

- Use the left hand side of the table to select the row that contains the record. It will be highlighted as shown in Figure 4.27.
- Use the **Delete** key to remove the entry and confirm that you do want the record removed by selecting **Yes** when the warning box is displayed, as shown in Figure 4.28.

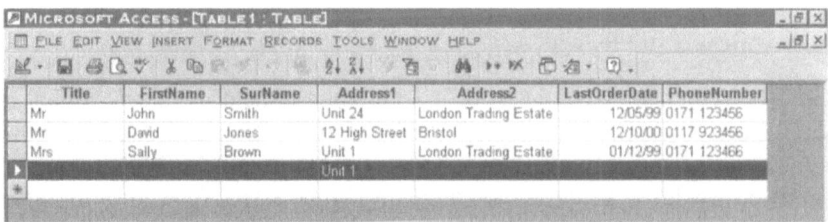

Figure 4.27 Highlighting a record.

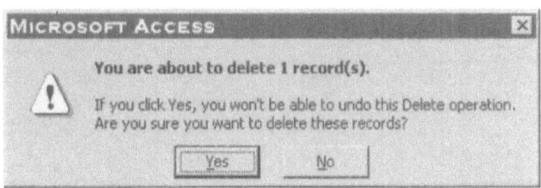

Figure 4.28 Confirming a record deletion.

Editing a record

To edit data in a table, place the mouse pointer onto the item and click on the entry to enable editing or use the **F2** function key.

Sorting data

Other useful features include **sorting** and **filtering** data. To sort a table by a particular column use the following quick method:

- Select the column.
- Select the **A-Z** sort button for ascending order or the **Z-A** button for descending order.

Most of the options you have just used can be selected from the **Records** or **Edit** menus.

Filtering data

Filtering can be very useful when you have a lot of data within a table and you only want to see a specific selection. The **filter** buttons shown in Figure 4.29 are listed below, in order from left to right:

- Filter By Selection.
- Filter By Form.
- Apply/Remove Filter.

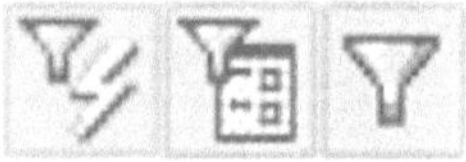

Figure 4.29 *Filter (By Selection, By Form, Apply/Remove) buttons.*

Filter by selection works by selecting the current field's contents to act as the criteria for the filter. If the cursor was positioned on the *SurName Smith*, as shown in Figure 4.30, and the **Apply Filter** button selected, for example, only records matching this surname would be displayed, as shown in Figure 4.31. To remove the filter use the **Apply Filter button** again.

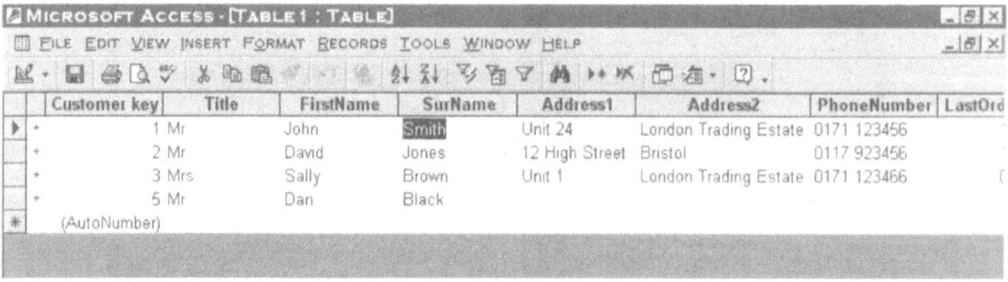

Microsoft Access - [Table1 : Table]
File Edit View Insert Format Records Tools Window Help
Customer key | Title | FirstName | SurName | Address1 | Address2 | PhoneNumber | LastOrd
1 Mr John Smith Unit 24 London Trading Estate 0171 123456
2 Mr David Jones 12 High Street Bristol 0117 923456
3 Mrs Sally Brown Unit 1 London Trading Estate 0171 123466
5 Mr Dan Black
(AutoNumber)

Figure 4.30 *Selecting a surname before applying a filter.*

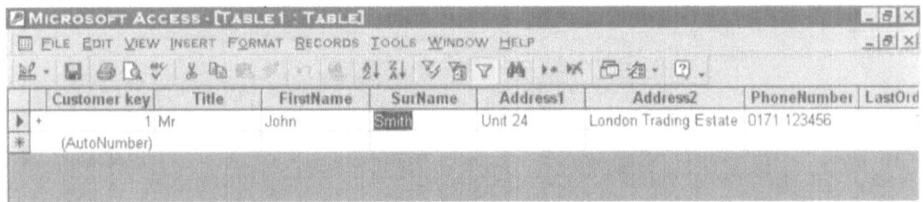

***Figure 4.31** The results of filtering by selection.*

The **filter by form** option works by displaying a **list box** above any field selected and allowing you to pick any entry from within the table, as shown in Figure 4.32. In this way you could be more selective: you could select all the records whose *Title* is equal to *Mr* and all the records whose *SurName* is equal to *Smith*.

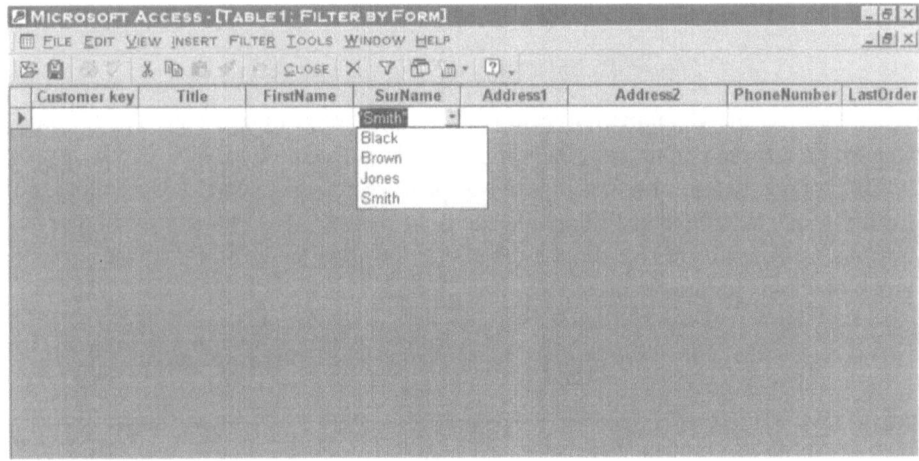

***Figure 4.32** Filtering by form.*

Printing and deleting tables

When you have finished experimenting with the features you have looked at so far you may be wondering how to print a copy of a tables' structure.
To achieve this:

- Close your table and return to the database window
- Select **Analyze** from the **Tools** menu.
- Then select **Documenter** from the submenu as shown in Figure 4.33.

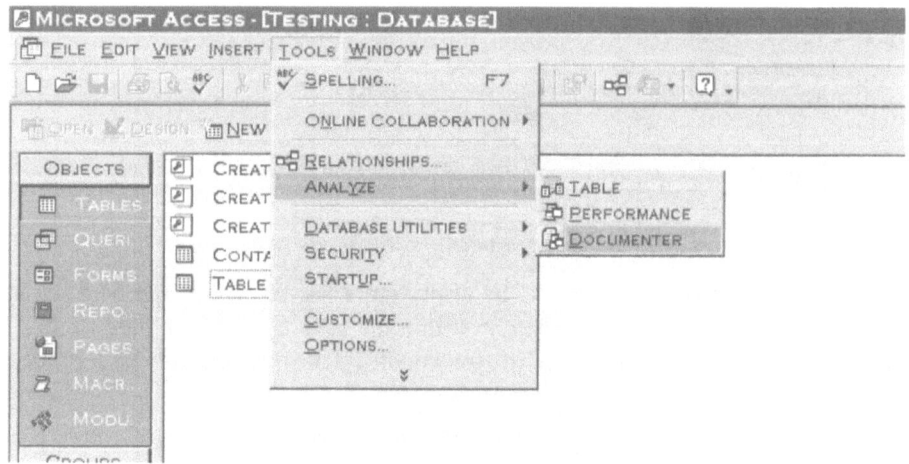

Figure 4.33 *Selecting the Documenter feature.*

When you use the **Documenter** feature you are expected to select the Access **object** you want **analyzed** and then set the **options** for the printout.

The options define how much detail to produce for the report; for a simple table listing it may be sufficient to list only the **field names**. The example in Figure 4.34 uses the table you created earlier as the selected **object**; notice that you can select any group of objects for analyzing.

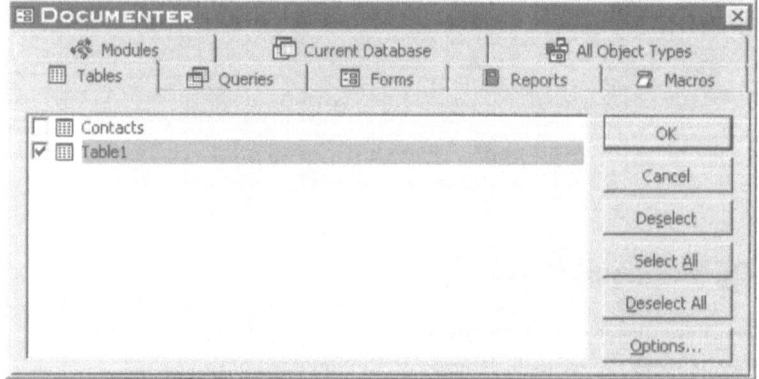

Figure 4.34 *Selecting a table object to document.*

In Figure 4.35 the **properties** for the table along with the **Names**; **Data Types** and **Sizes** of the fields have been selected for printing.

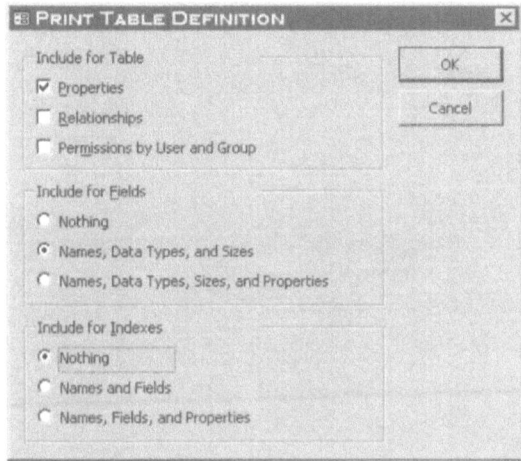

Figure 4.35 *Setting the Print Table Definition.*

The resulting printout is shown in Figure 4.36.

				12 October 1999
Table: Table1				Page: 1

Properties

Date Created:	11/10/99 16:43:43	Filter:	((Table1.Title="Mrs"))
GUID:	Long binary data	Last Updated:	12/10/99 00:07:12
NameMap:	Long binary data	OrderBy:	Table1.Title
OrderByOn:	True	Orientation:	0
RecordCount:	3	Updatable:	True

Columns

Name	Type	Size
Title	Text	4
FirstName	Text	50
SurName	Text	50
Address1	Text	50
Address2	Text	50
PhoneNumber	Text	50
LastOrderDate	Date/Time	8

Figure 4.36 *Example output from Documenter feature.*

Deleting an object from the database

To remove an **object** from your database you will need to:

- Select the **object group** from the **tabs** on the left of the **database window**.
- Select the **object** and use the **delete** key.

For example, to remove the table you created earlier using the table wizard.

Highlight the *Contacts* table and then press the **delete** key. When the warning message appears, confirm that you want to delete the object; see Figure 4.37.

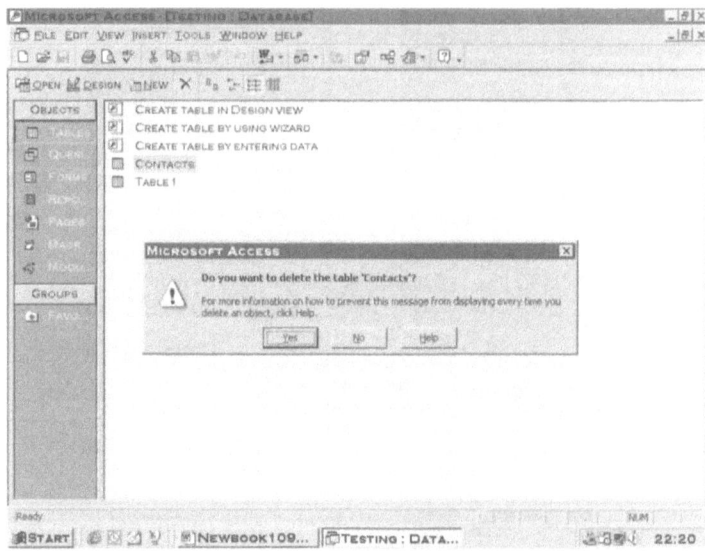

Figure 4.37 *Confirming deletion of an object.*

In the next chapter you will be looking at using forms to organize the way you view or edit the data from a table.

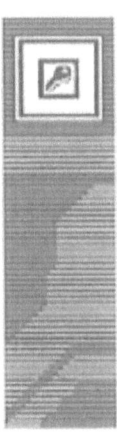

5
Creating a Form

Introduction

Forms are one of the most efficient ways of displaying your data from a table. You can decide how you want to display the data, which fields should be displayed and even which ones can be edited.

The principles are simple: you specify the table you want to base the form design on, place the fields onto the form and then arrange them to suit your needs. You can then set the properties for the objects on the form and even set the properties for the form itself.

In this chapter you will examine how forms can be created, what the difference is between the form types and how to set properties for form objects.

Using the Form Wizard

As with tables the quickest way to design a form is to use the Form Wizard; this will guide you through the creation process and cut out much of the manual input.

To create a simple form based on the *Table1* table use the following steps.

- Select the **Forms** object tab from the database window.
- Choose the Create Form By Using Wizard option.
- Select *Table1* as the table to base the form upon.
- Then select all the fields from the field list; see Figure 5.1.

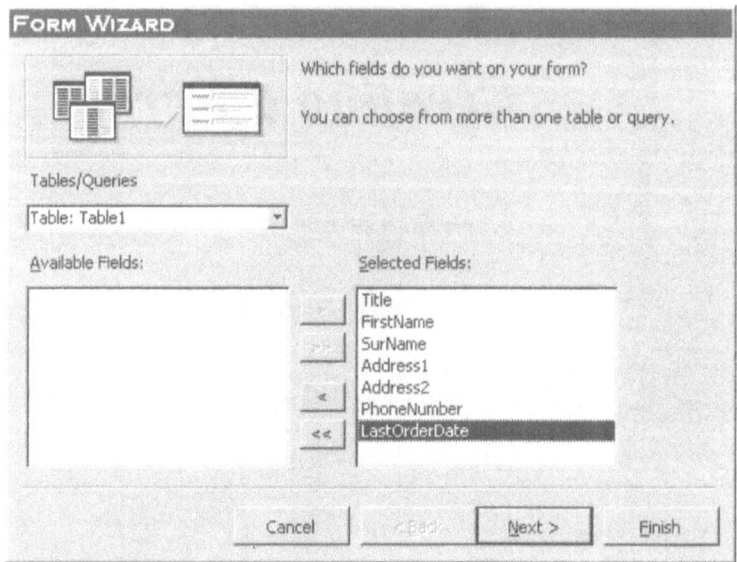

Figure 5.1 *Selecting a table and all available fields using the table wizard.*

- Select the **Next** button to move on and define the **form type**.
- Select a columnar layout.
- Then select the **Next** button to choose the **form style** as shown in Figure 5.2.

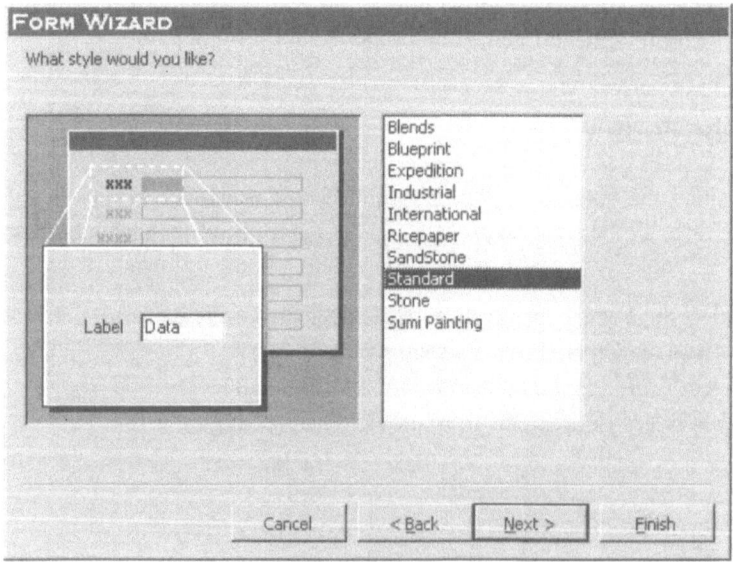

Figure 5.2 *Selecting a form style.*

- Select a **standard layout**.
- When you have selected your layout use the **Next** button to move on.
- Fill in a **title** for the form.
- Select the **Open the form to view or enter information** option and then select the **Finish** button to generate the form, as shown in Figure 5.3.

The completed form is shown in Figure 5.4.

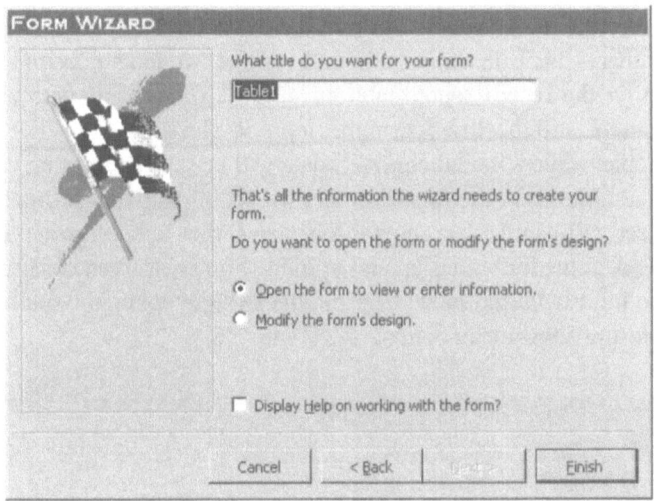

Figure 5.3 *Selecting form title and the open option.*

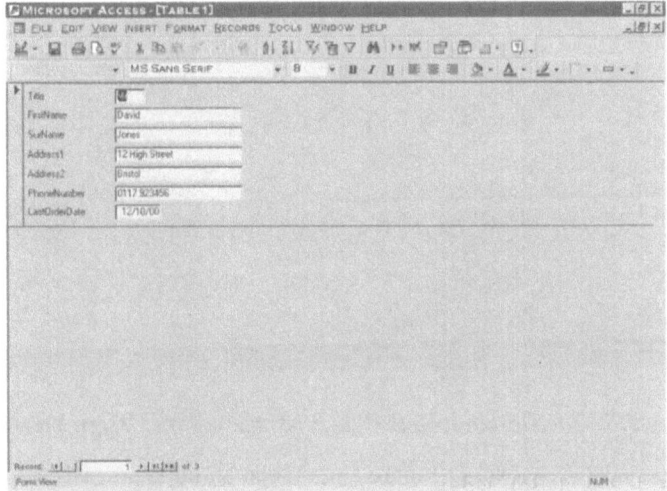

Figure 5.4 *A completed form design (in column format).*

The form **objects** consist of the **fields** from the underlying **table**. Each **object** has two parts: a **text box** and a **label**. The **text boxes** are **bound** to the underlying tables fields, while the **label** normally appears on the left of this. Labels are displayed on the form to indicate what the **text box** is used to store, and the **text box** itself is used to display the data from the field it is bound to in the table; it can be used to store the data back into the **table** when it is changed in the **text box** on the form. Text boxes normally have the same name as the underlying field it is **bound** to. A control or field that is used to enter or display information is normally tied to an underlying table or query known as the record source. In turn the control can be tied to a specific field on the table or query, this is known as **a bound control**, while an unbound control has no related field on the record source table or query. This means data entered into an unbound **control** will be lost when the form is closed as it is not saved on the underlying table, while a **bound control's** data will be saved when the form is closed.

Each of the **objects** on the **form** has its own set of **properties**; this helps to define how the object will handle data, how it looks and what happens when data is entered into it. To look at the form's design and examine how it has been constructed,

Open the form in design mode by using the **Design** tool on the **toolbar** or by using the **View | Design View** menu option; see Figure 5.5.

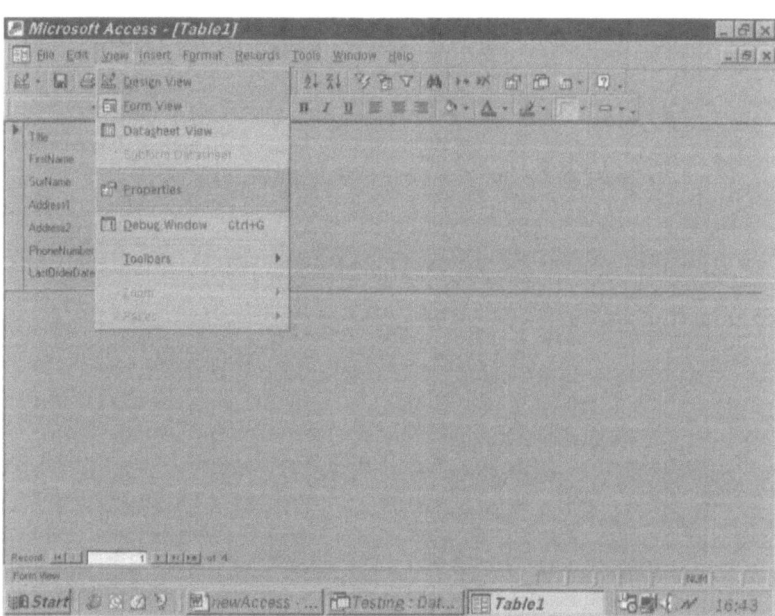

Figure 5.5. The Design icon and the View menu with Design View option.

The form design is shown in Figure 5.6. When an **object** is selected a set of small black squares will appear around the selected **object**. These allow you to resize the **object**, while the large black square in the upper left of the selected **object** is used to move the **object** around the **form**.

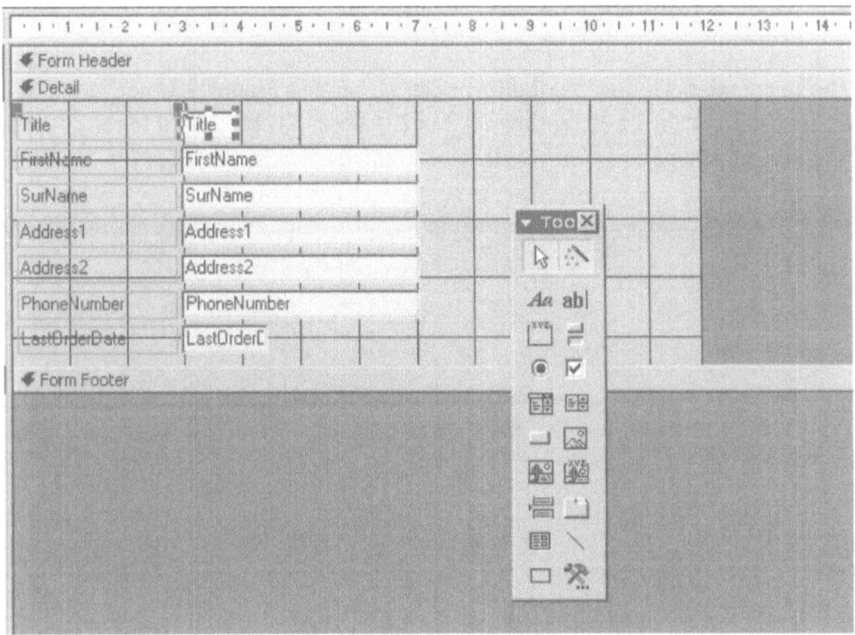

Figure 5.6. *A form in Design View mode.*

As you move the mouse you will notice that the mouse pointer will change its shape depending upon its intended action and position over the **object**.

Manually designing a form

To create your own form from scratch you will need firstly to close the current form.

- Return to the **Database window**.
- Select the **Forms object** tab.
- Then select **Create form in Design view**.

Setting the record source

This will place you in the design window on a blank layout. The first thing to do is decide which **table** your **form** is to display the data from. You will need to identify the **source** of the data for the **form**; this is known as the **record source**. To set the form's **record source** you will need to view the form properties; these are the characteristics of your form.

To view a form's property you will need to either:

- Select the **View | Properties** menu options.

- Right-click the mouse on the **form** to view the **shortcut** menu and select **Properties**.

The **properties** window for the **form** can be seen in Figure 5.7; notice that a pull-down **list**, (often called a **drop-down list** or **list box**), has been used to select the **table** for the **record source** row. The **table** used in this case was called *Table1*.

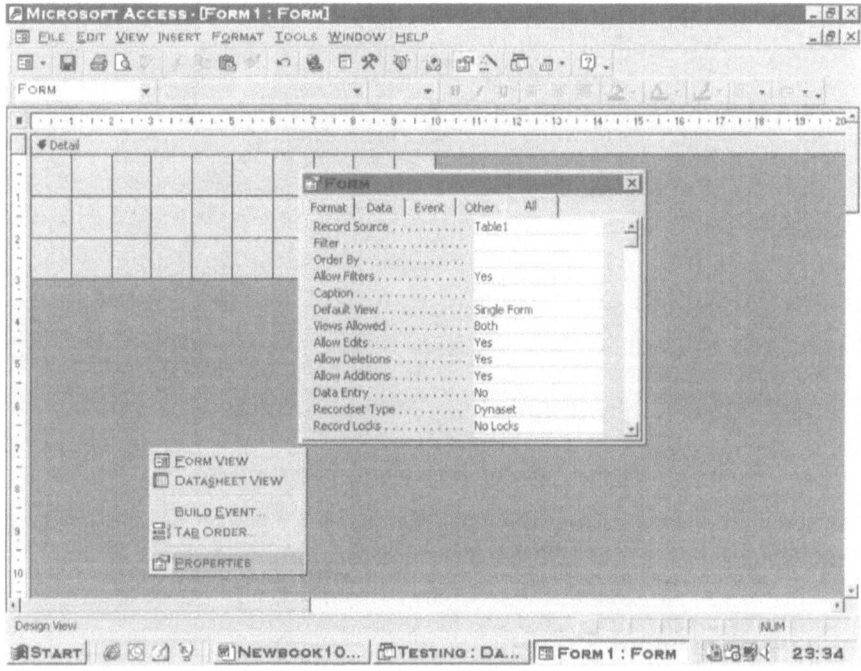

Figure 5.7 *Using the shortcut menu to select a form's property.*

Form properties

The **properties** box is divided by **tabs** to help locate the options from the full lists that appear in the **All** tab group. The tabs are:

- **All**, containing all the form's properties combined into one list.
- **Other**, containing properties relating to how the form is displayed and which menus are active.
- **Event**, containing properties relating to events that occur on the form.
- **Data**, containing properties relating to the source of the data.
- **Format**, containing properties that relate to the font and style of the form.

See Figures 5.8 to 5.11.

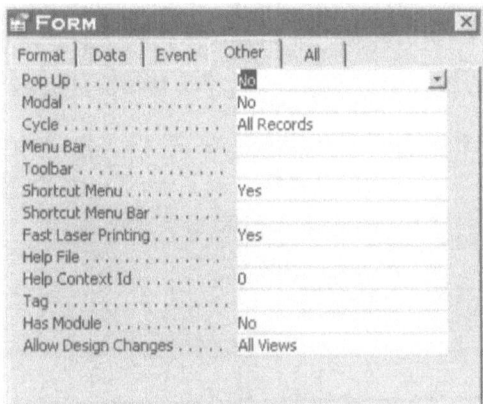

Figure 5.8 *The Other properties tab.*

Figure 5.9 *The Event properties tab.*

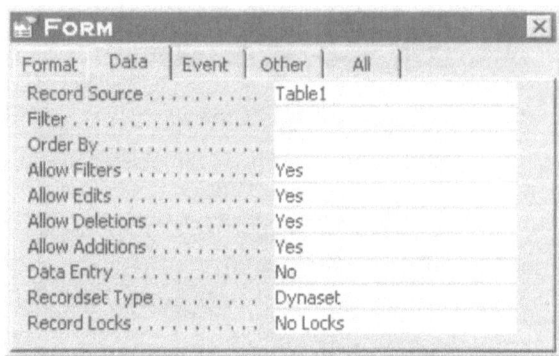

Figure 5.10 *The Data properties tab.*

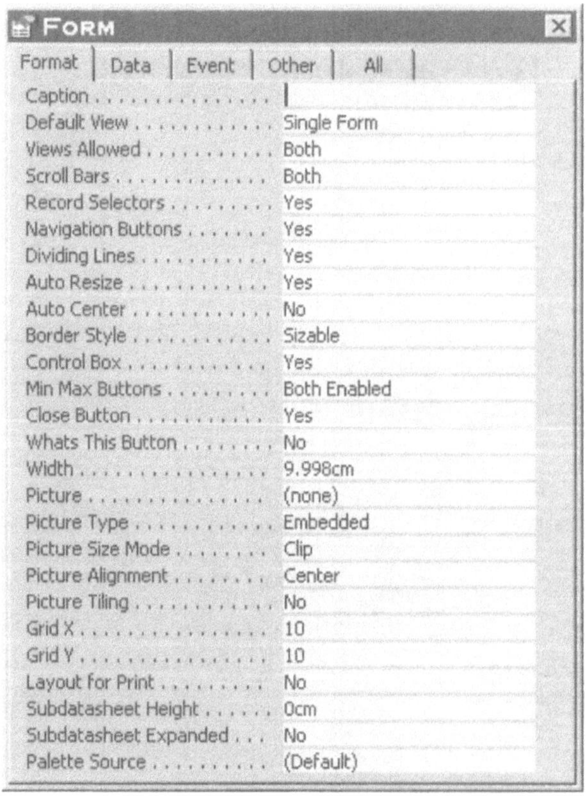

Figure 5.11 *The Format properties tab.*

There are two **properties** you should always set when using a form with underlying **tables** and these are:

- The record source

- The default view

The **record source,** as you have already seen, is the source of the **data** for the form.

The **default view** will affect how the records are shown on your **form**; in the example the **default view** is set to **single form**. This means that only one **record** at a time is displayed on the form. The other two **default view** options are **Continuous Forms** and **Datasheet**. The **Continuous Forms view** will display several **records** on a **form** at the same time, while **Datasheet view** will make the **form records** appear as if they were in a **table**.

To continue with the design of the form:

- Set the default view to Continuous Forms.
- Place the fields from your table onto the form in the position you require.
- To place fields onto a form you will need to open the field list window. Remember that each field comprises of two parts, the label and the text box containing the data.
- Use the Field List button on the tool bar or use the **View | Field List** menu option; see Figures 5.12 and 5.13.

Figure 5.12 *The field list icon on the toolbar.*

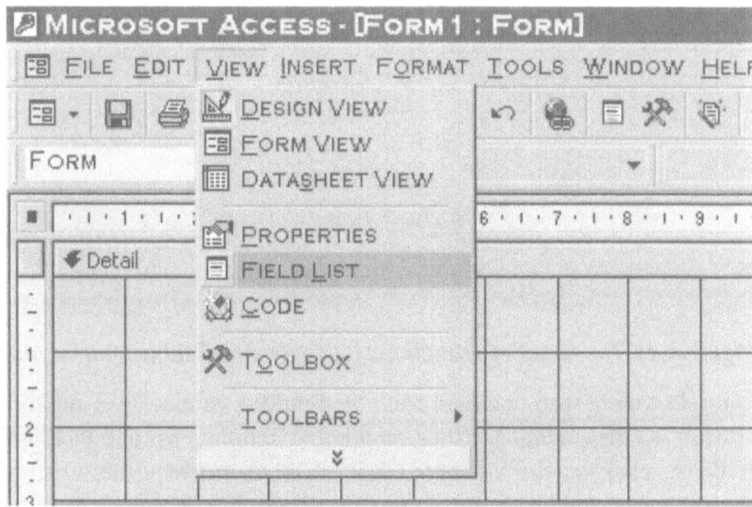

Figure 5.13 *The field list option on the View menu.*

When you have opened the **field list** window you need to drag the **fields** from the **field list** onto the **form**, placing them inside the **detail** area of the **form**, as shown in

Figure 5.14. Figure 5.15 shows the result of dragging the *Title* **field** onto the **detail** area of the **form**.

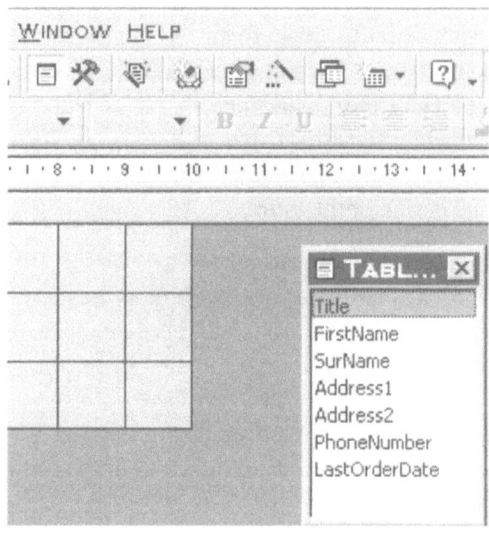

Figure 5.14 *The field list window.*

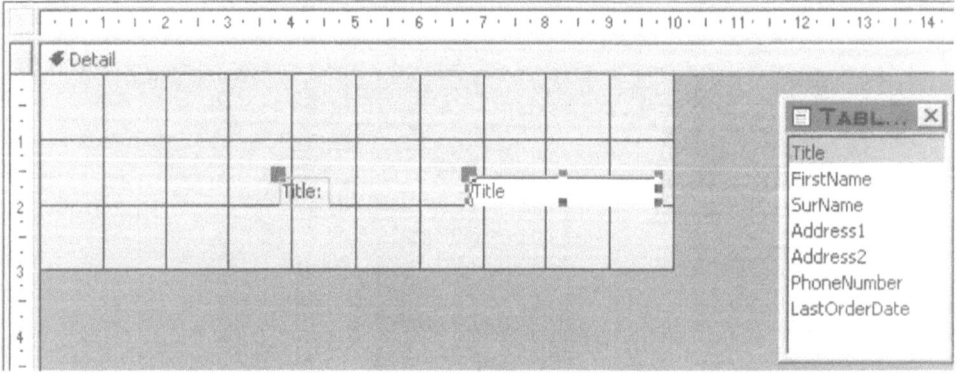

Figure 5.15 *The result of dragging a field from the field list onto a form.*

You can select more than one **field** from the **field list** window by using the standard Windows **Shift + Click** method. Click on the first item in a list and then, holding the **shift** key down, click on the last item. All the items between these two points are highlighted; they can now be dragged onto the form. For example, if you click onto the *FirstName* **field** and use **Shift + Click** on the *LastOrderDate* **field**, they will all be highlighted; you can then drag them onto your form as shown in Figure 5.16.

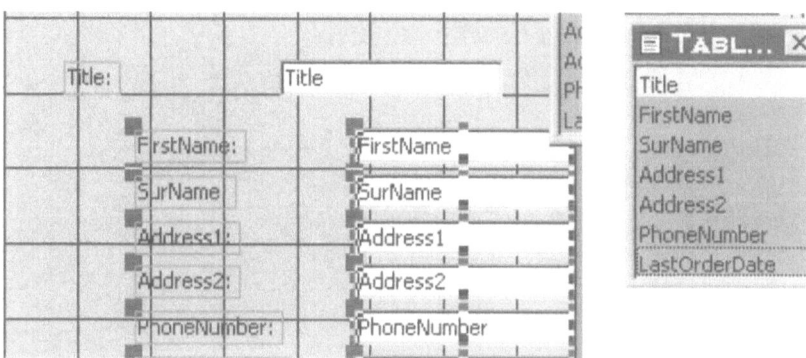

Figure 5.16 Selecting fields using Shift + Click and dragging onto the form.

You may want to do some tidying up of the items placed on the **form**, to do this you can use the **Format I Align** menu to **align** a group of items. In the example shown in Figure 5.17 the *Title* **field** is shown slightly to the left of the other items; you can **align** all the items to the leftmost item in a selection. You will need to select the items in the group to do this:

- Place the mouse pointer above and to the left of the first item in the group.
- Hold down the left mouse button and drag the mouse over the remaining labels in the group; an outline will appear as you drag the mouse.

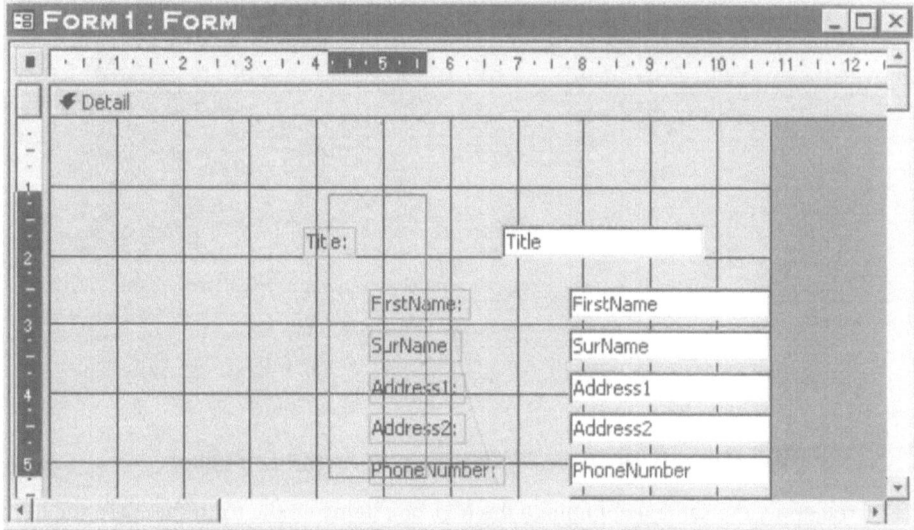

Figure 5.17 Dragging the mouse over a group of label objects.

- Either select **Format I Align** from the menu bar or use the right button on the mouse to obtain the shortcut menu and select **align** from this.
- Then select **Left** from the submenu, this will **align** the **labels** to the left.

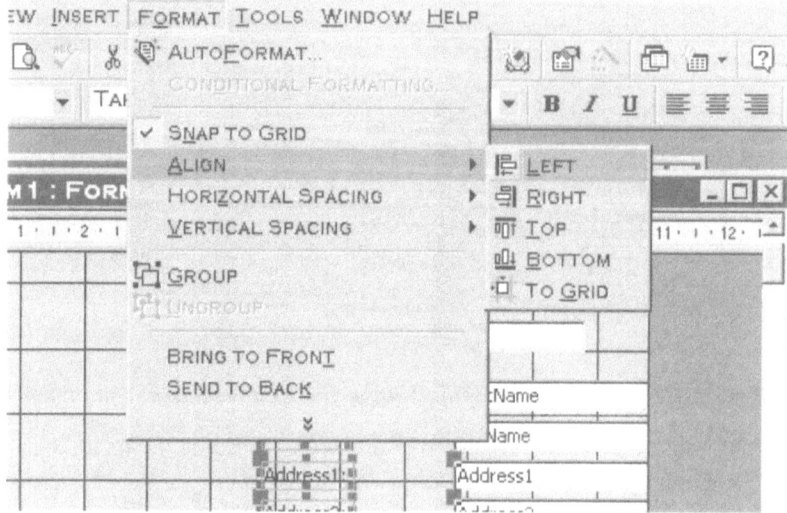

Figure 5.18 *Using the Format | Align | Left option.*

The **Format** menu is shown in Figure 5.18 while the results are shown in Figure 5.19.

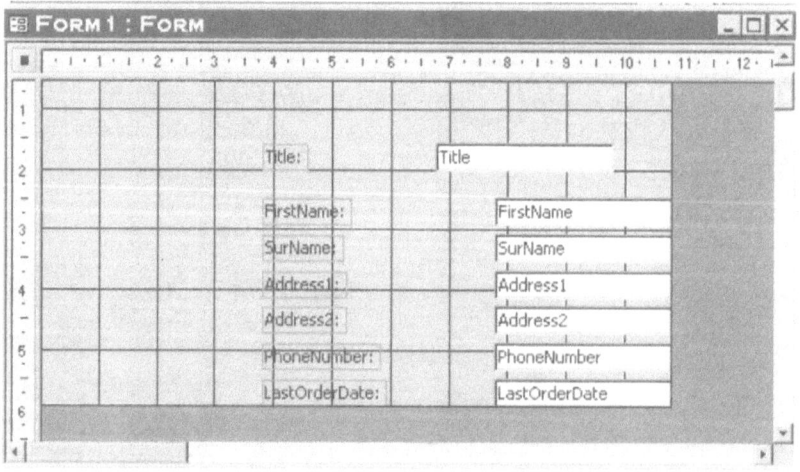

Figure 5.19 *The results of using the Align | Left option.*

If you apply the same technique to the **text box** items on the form these are the items to the right of the **labels** the results will be similar to those of the **labels**. In the example shown in Figure 5.20, the **field** items have been selected as a group and the **Format | Vertical Spacing** menu has been used to set the **vertical spacing** to **Make Equal**. This makes the space between the **fields** equal.

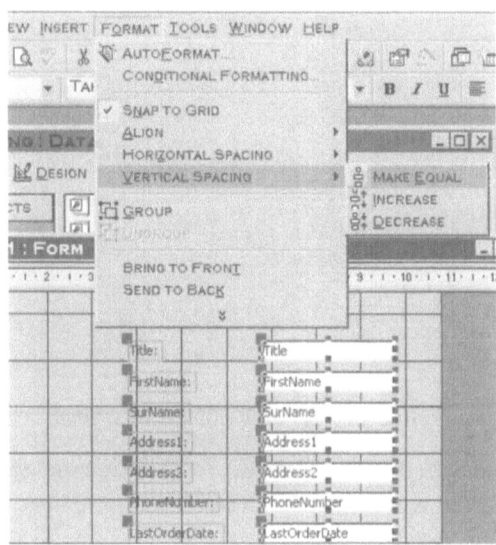

Figure 5.20 *Setting the vertical spacing of objects on a form.*

Now you have done some basic tidying up you can now look at moving the **objects** around. You can move **objects** around a **form** by selecting the large box in the top left of a selected item and dragging the item.

When you click on an **object** on a form, Access displays a group of boxes around the object; these are referred to as the move and sizing handles. The largest of these boxes in the upper left is the move handle; all the others are sizing handles. There is another method you can use if you wish to move both the label and the field at the same time; place the mouse pointer into the centre of an **object** and then drag it holding the mouse button down. Both the **label** and the **text box** will be moved until you release the mouse button. Try moving the **objects** as shown in Figure 5.21. If you need to deselect an item click the mouse onto any blank area of the **form**, this will cancel the selection. Remember, if you get it wrong you can always use the **Edit | Undo** menu.

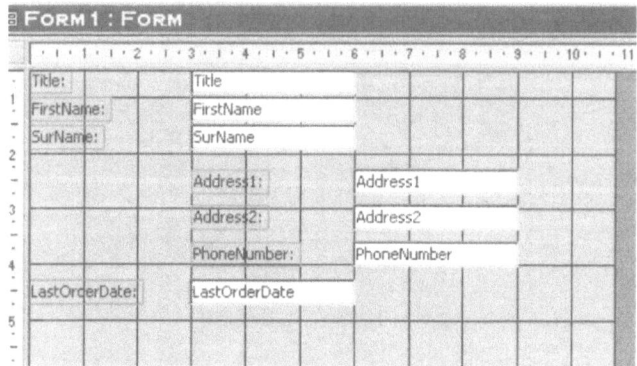

Figure 5.21 *Moving objects on a form.*

Leaving the form design as it is, **Close** the **form** design and **save** it; in the example the **form** has been closed and the default form name *Form1* has been used. Now you can look at the **Toolbox controls**.

Using the Toolbox

To add features such as **lines, boxes** and **buttons** to your **form** you use the **Toolbox**. As you move the mouse over the icons on the **Toolbox**, text is displayed to show you what each icon is for. This text is known as a **ToolTip**. You can also use the **What's this?** feature from the **Help** menu. These tools place **objects** on the **form**; these are often referred to as **controls**. The Toolbox icons are shown in Figure 5.22.

You can use an **option button** to display a **Yes/No** value from an underlying **record** source. For example, if the **option button** is selected, the value is **Yes**; if not, the value is **no**. An **option button** example is shown in Figure 5.25

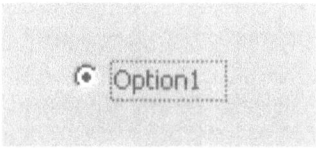

Figure 5.25 A completed option button.

Drop-down lists and combo boxes

It is easier to select a value from a list than to remember a value to type. With a drop-down **list box**, you can select from a list. A drop-down **list box** shows only one line until you click to expand the contents. You cannot type new values in a drop-down list box; however, a **combo box** allows you to make new entries if required. Figure 5.26 shows a completed **combo box**.

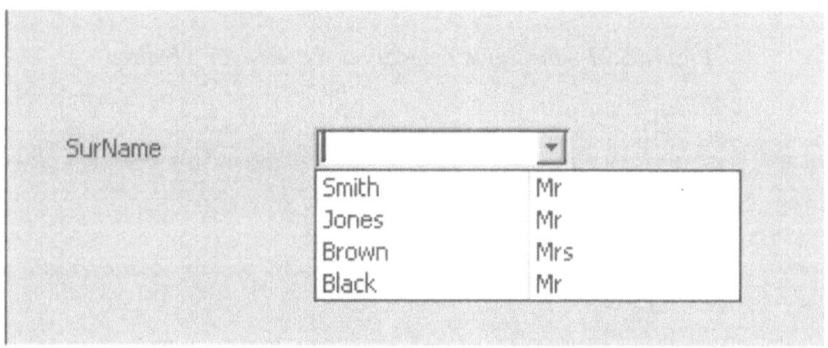

Figure 5.26 A completed Combo box.

Command button

The **command button** does just that: it places a button on the **form** to run a specific command. If you use the **Toolbox Control Wizard** you will be guided to select the type of command you need. You can create over 30 different command buttons with the **Button Wizard**; Access creates the **button** and the **event procedure** for you.

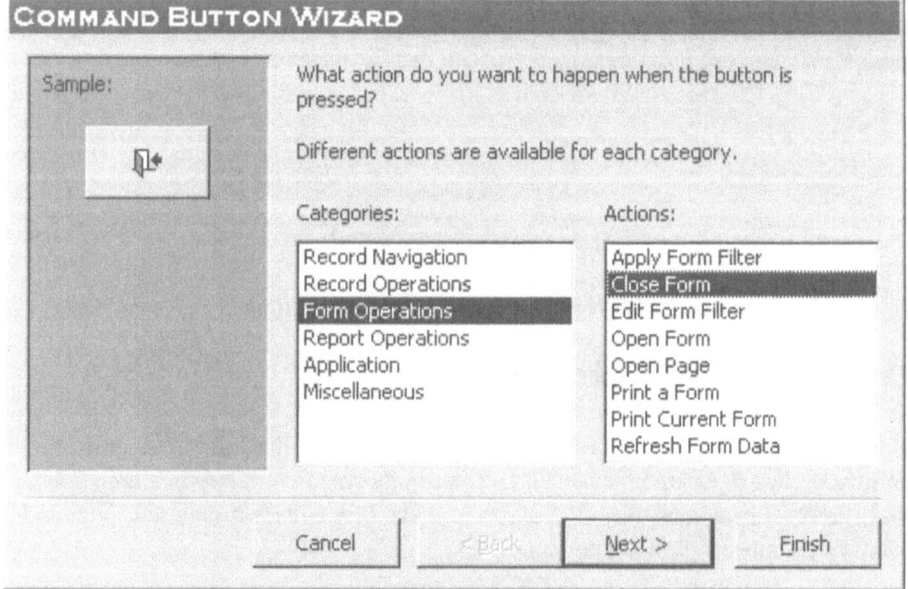

***Figure* 5.27** *Selecting a category and action for a button.*

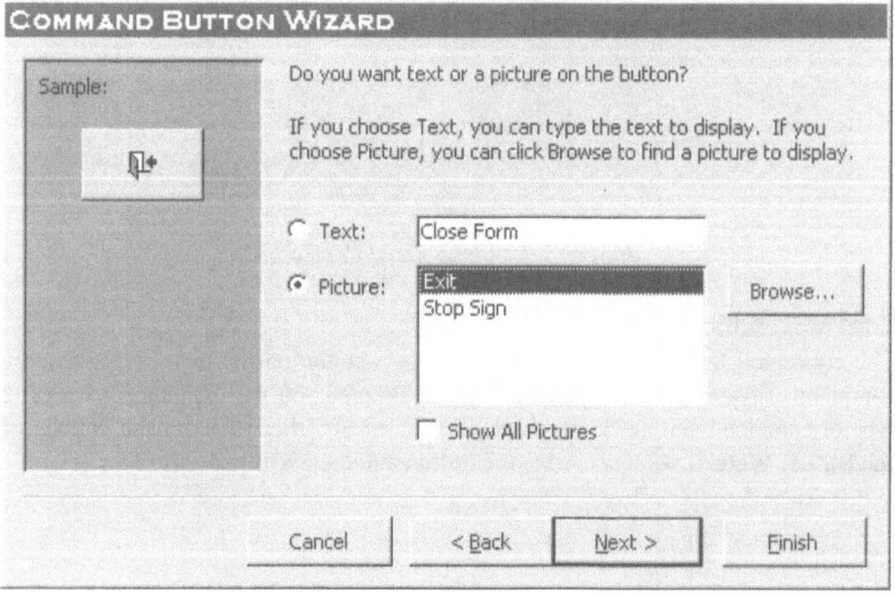

***Figure* 5.28** *Selecting text or picture for a button.*

Figure 5.29 *A completed command button.*

Unbound/bound object frame and image control

If you want to add a background picture, you use the **Picture property** of the form. If you want to add a picture that appears in a **control**, use an **image control** or an **unbound object frame**.

If you do not need to update the picture, add the picture using **image control**. If you need to update the picture, add the picture as an **unbound object frame**. You can insert pictures or you can link to them. When you insert a picture, Access stores the picture in your database. If you modify the picture, it is changed in your database.

When you link to a picture, you can make changes to it, but the changes are stored in the original object file, not in your database file.

Page break

A page break marks where the form will scroll to when **Page Up** or **Page Down** is pressed.

Subform

A **subform** is a **form** within a **form**.

Customer key:		Address1:	Unit 24		Close Form	
Title:	Mr	Address2:	London Trading Estate			
FirstName:	John	PhoneNumber:	0171 123456	Text13:		
SurName:	Smith	LastOrderDate:	12/05/99			

					Calculate Total	
CustomerKey:	Order Number:	date:	qty:	cost each:	Total value:	
1	12345GG	12/10/00	100	£11.00	£100.00	
1	12333GK	01/10/99	0	£6.00	£1.00	
0			0	£0.00	£0.00	

Record: 1 of 2

Record: 1 of 4

Figure 5.30 *A main form/subform example.*

The primary **form** is called the **main form**, and the **form** within the **form** is called the **sub form**. A main form/subform combination is often referred to as a **parent/child form**. **Subforms** are effective when you want to show data from **tables** or **queries** with a **relationship** to another **table**. For example, you could create a **form** with customers and a **subform** to show data from an orders **table**. The data in the customers **table** is the **one** side of the **relationship**. The data in the orders table is the **many** side of the **relationship**. This gives you a **one-to-many relationship** between the **tables**. An example of a main form and subform is shown in Figure 5.30.

Text box

You use **text boxes** to display data from a table. This type of **text box** is called a **bound text box** because it is **bound** to data in a **table**. **Text boxes** can also be **unbound**. For example, you can create an **unbound text box** to display the results of a calculation on the **form**.

Rectangle

Click anywhere on the **form**, report, or data access page to create a default-sized rectangle, or drag to create a **rectangle** that's the size you want.

Tab control

You can use a **tab control** to present several pages of information as a single set. For example, you might use a **tab control** on a contacts **form** to separate general and personal information. A **tab control** is shown in Figure 5.31.

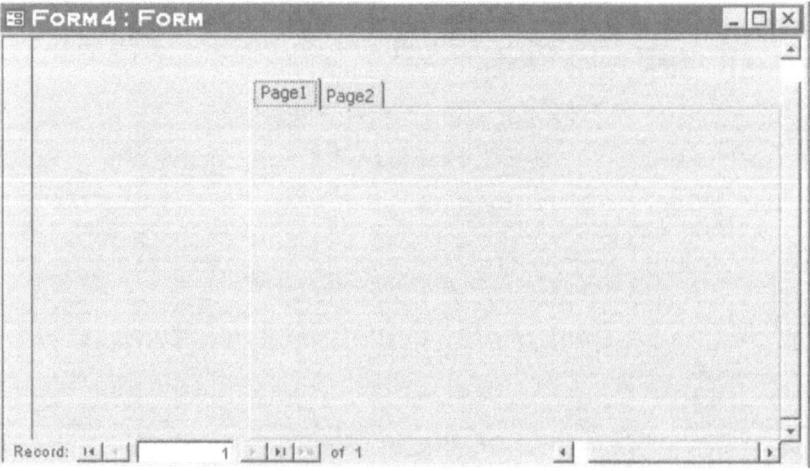

Figure 5.31 An example of a tab control.

Toggle button

You can use a **toggle button** on a **form** as a stand-alone **control** to set a **Yes/No** value. For example, the **toggle button** data type is **Yes/No**. When the button is pressed in, the value is **Yes**. When the button isn't pressed in, the value is **No**.

Check box

You can use a **check box control** to display a **Yes/No** value, in a similar fashion to the **toggle button** or **option button**.

Line

To draw horizontal or vertical lines on a **form** or **report**, click the **Line** tool and then drag it to create the line. To make small adjustments to the length or angle of a line in **forms** and **reports**, select the line, hold down the **Shift**, and press one of the **Cursor** keys on the keyboard. To make small adjustments in the placement of a line, hold down the **Ctrl** key and press one of the **Cursor** keys.

Rectangle

To place a **rectangle** around information on the form, select the **rectangle** icon from the **toolbox**. Then place the mouse pointer in a position above or below the group of **objects** you want to place the rectangle around. Drag the mouse to stretch the outline around the **objects** and release the mouse button when complete. See the example in Figure 5.32.

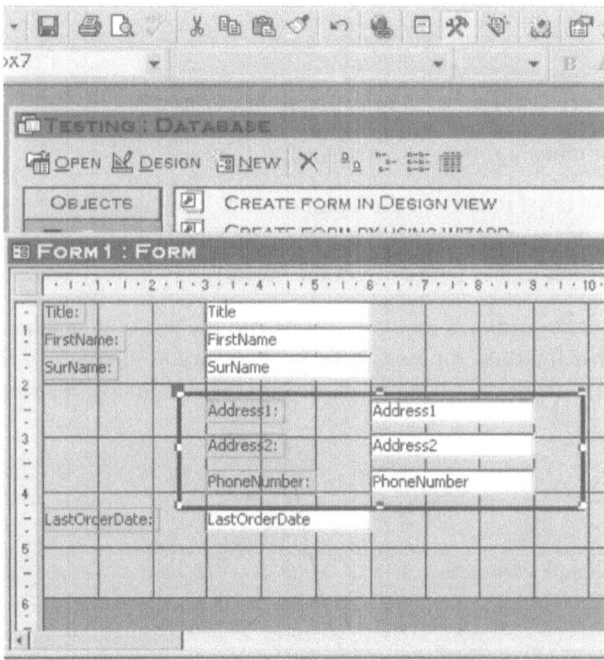

***Figure 5.32** A rectangle placed around text boxes on a form.*

In the earlier example a **rectangle** was added. Changing the **Width property** of the **object** has increased the border width. You can use the **properties** button or right-click onto the selected **object** and show the **properties** from the **shortcut menu**. See Figure 5.33 for the **rectangle object properties**.

RECTANGLE: Box7   [X]

| Format | Data | Event | Other | All |

Name Box7
Visible . . . .   Yes
Display When . . . .   Always
Left 2.499cm
Top 2.199cm
Width 7.399cm
Height 2.099cm
Back Style . . . .   Transparent
Back Color   16777215
Special Effect . . . .   Flat
Border Style . . . .   Solid
Border Color   0
Border Width . . . .   2 pt
Tag . . . .
On Click . . . .
On Dbl Click . . . .
On Mouse Down . . . .
On Mouse Move . . . .
On Mouse Up . . . .

***Figure 5.33** Rectangle object properties.*

To place a **label** on a **form,** perhaps as a heading:

- Select the **label** icon from the **Toolbox**.
- Position the mouse on the **form** at the point you want to place your text.
- Click the left mouse button to fix the position and start typing your text.

The text entry box will expand as you start typing. You can change the text size for the selected **label** by using the **Font Size list** box on the **toolbar**. If the text is larger than the text box, double click on one of the corner selection boxes; see Figure 5.34.

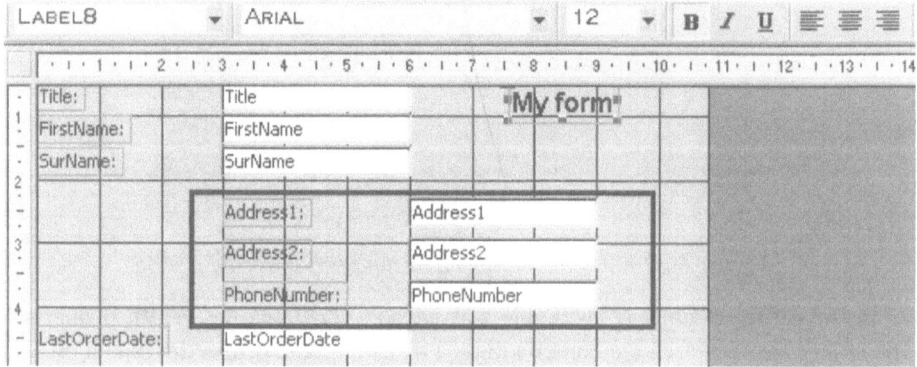

***Figure 5.34** Placing a label on a form.*

Placing a command button on a form

- Using the **Toolbox** select the **Command Button icon** and then place the mouse pointer onto the **form**.
- Click the left mouse button to drop the **command button** at this position making sure the **Toolbar Control Wizard** is turned on.

Figure 5.35 shows the **Command Button** icon on the left of the **Toolbox** and the **Control Wizard** on the right.

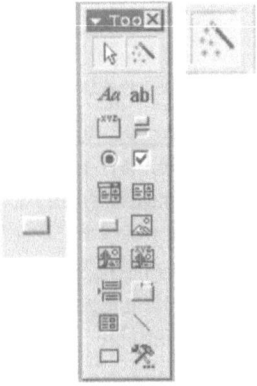

Figure 5.35 *The Command Button icon and the Control Wizard button.*

- With the **Toolbar Control Wizard** turned on, select a **category** and then the **action.**
- In this case the **Form category** and the **Close Form** action have been selected; this action will close the form.
- Select the **Next** option and fill in your choice of either text or an **Icon** for the button, then select **Next** again and confirm the button name.
- Click **Finish** to place the button on the **form;** see Figures 5.36 and 5.37.

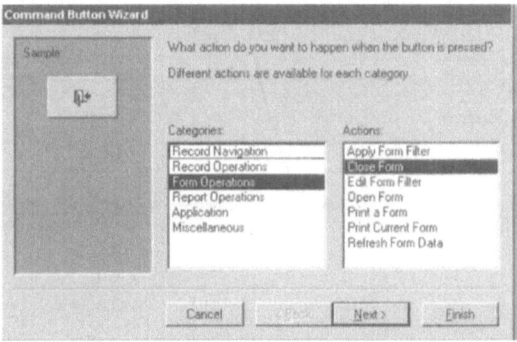

Figure 5.36 *Selecting a category and action for a command button.*

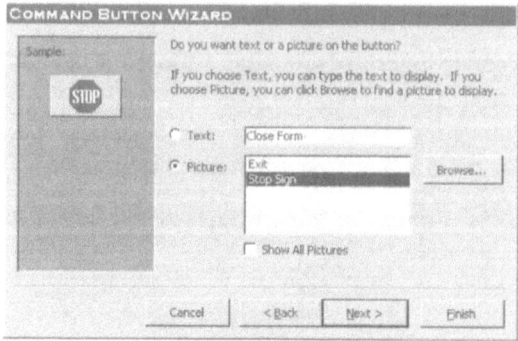

Figure 5.37 Selecting an icon for the command button.

If you have placed text on the button you may edit this by displaying the **properties** and changing the **button text**. To delete an **object** from a **form**, select the **object** and then use the **Delete** key on the keyboard to remove it. Alternatively, use the **Edit |** **Delete** menu to delete the item. Try some of the **Toolbox** features such as a **command** **button** to close a **form** or perhaps a **rectangle** or **check box**. Add them to the form you used earlier called *Form1*, and then **open** the **form** to see what it looks like. Figure 5.38 shows the **View** options available.

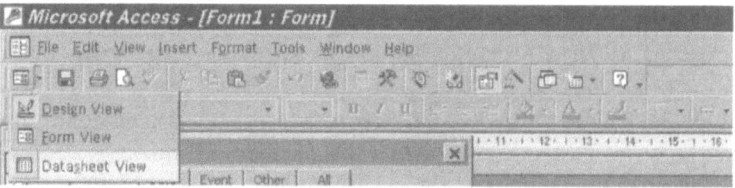

Figure 5.38 The View options.

Form types

So far you have looked at some of the **properties** for **controls** or **objects** on **forms**; the **Default view** was only mentioned earlier. There are three options for the **Default view** **property** of a form; (shown in Figure 5.39); these are:

- Single Form
- Continuous Forms
- Datasheet

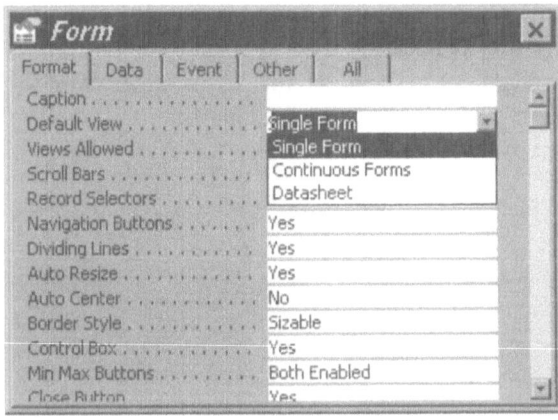

Figure 5.39 The view options available for a form

Single Form

Single form view is normally used to show one record per page. If you use the **form** designed earlier and then set the **forms properties** for **Default view** to **Single form,** then the result will be similar to that shown in Figure 5.40, depending upon the layout changes you made.

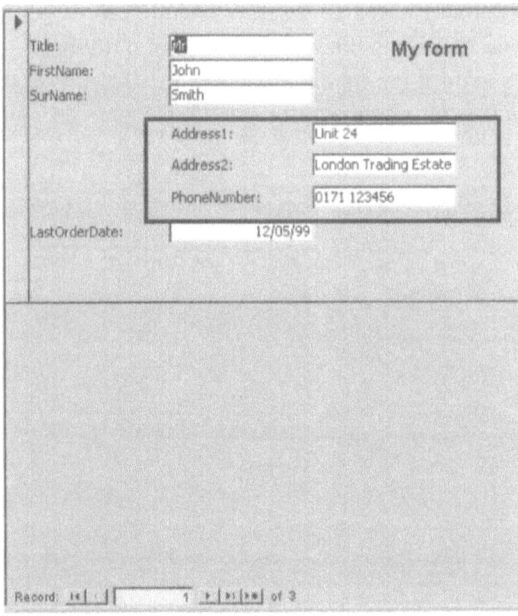

Figure 5.40 An example of a single form view.

Continuous forms

Continuous forms view is normally used to display several records per page. If you use the **form** designed earlier and set the **forms properties** for **Default view** to **Continuous forms** then the result will be similar to that shown in Figure 5.41, again depending upon the layout changes you made.

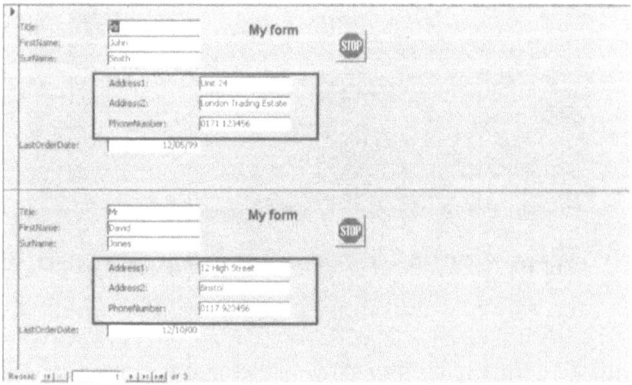

Figure 5.41 *An example of a continuous form view.*

Datasheet

Datasheet view is normally used to display several records per page but similar in layout to a **table;** you lose all the **headings, buttons** and **labels.** If you use the **form** you designed earlier and set the **forms** properties for **Default view** to **Datasheet** then the result will be similar to that shown in Figure 5.42, again depending upon the layout changes you made.

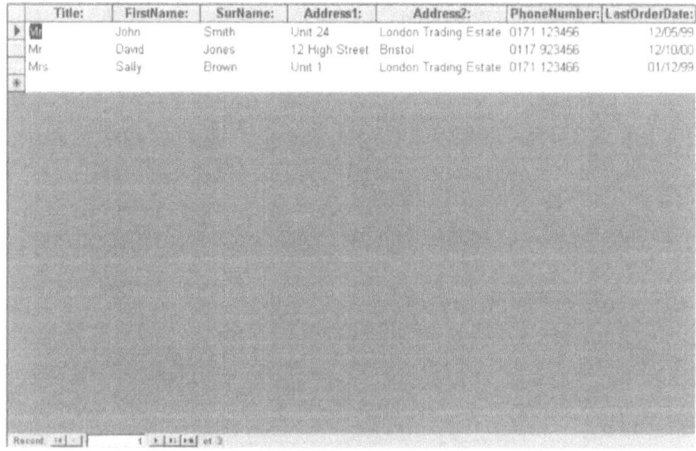

Figure 5.42 *An example of a Datasheet view.*

Form properties

Look again at the **form** you designed called *Form1* and add a **header** to the **form**; before you do this, set the **forms default view property** to **single form**.

Using the **View** menu (you may have to expand the menu options), select **Form Header/Footer**.

You will see two extra sections at the top and bottom of the form. These areas can be altered in terms of the amount of vertical size they occupy by placing the mouse onto the top of the vertical bar for the **Detail** or **Footer** and then dragging the bar up or down the screen.

In the example, the **command button** and the **label** have been dragged onto the **header** area of the form. If you view the **form** it will be similar to that shown in Figure 5.43.

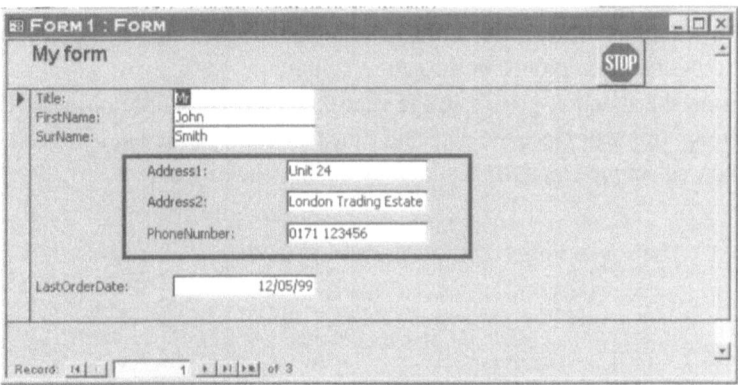

Figure 5.43 *Using a form header.*

Now you will examine how to create a field on the **form** that does not exist on the **table**, a calculated field. These are referred to as **unbound text boxes**; they are not **bound** to any **field** in an underlying **table**. Say, for example, that you want to show a box on the **form** to calculate how many days have elapsed between today and the date of the last order shown in the **table**. There are three steps involved in this process:

- Add the unbound text box to the form.
- Alter the labels text.
- Enter into the **text box Control Source** property the required calculation expression.

To add an unbound text box to the form:

- Select the text box control from the toolbox and click onto the form in the area you want to place the textbox.
- Two items are placed on the form: the **label text** on the left and the **unbound text box** on the right.

- To alter the **text** within the **label** on the left, select the item and view the **properties**, then type in the new **caption text**.
- You may have to widen the text **label** on the **form**; to do this double-click or drag a sizing box with the mouse. In the example the **caption** has been set to *Days From last Order*.

Now you need to alter the **Control Source property** for the **unbound text box**. This will be set to the calculation that works out how long it has been since the date of the last order. To do this you will need to **build** a calculation; Access has a number of built-in **functions** to help out. To help you do this you will use the **Expression Builder** tool.

- View the unbound text box properties, then select the Control Source row.
- Select the Expression builder button as shown in Figure 5.44.
- From the list of Access objects in the left hand column double-click on the Functions object.
- Now double-click on the Built-In Functions object; this will place the built-in Access function groups in the centre column.
- From the function groups in the centre column click once onto the **Date/Time** group; this will place the date and time **functions** in the left hand column.
- Now select the **DateDiff** function by double-clicking onto it.

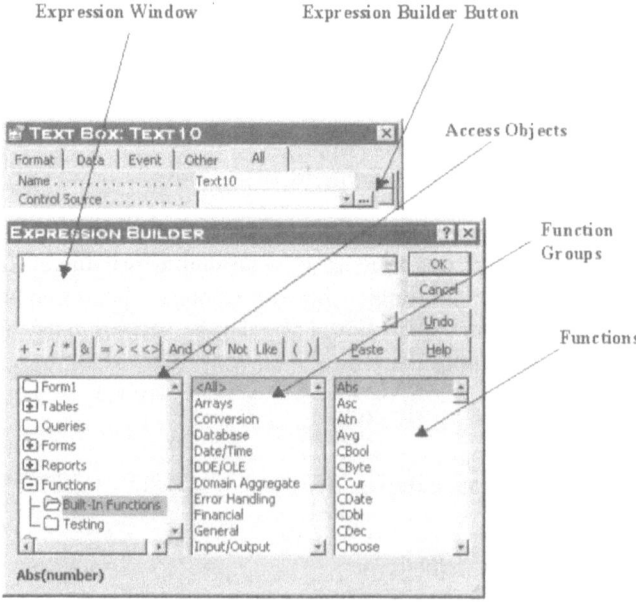

Figure 5.44 *Using the expression builder.*

The expression is placed in the **expression builder** window but it is not completed; you will have to supply the variable information required. The unfinished expression looks something like this:

= *DateDiff («interval», «date1», «date2», «firstweekday», «firstweek»)*

You do not need to use all of the options but you do need the following three:

• Interval
• Date1
• Date2

The **DateDiff** function provides the difference between two **date objects** in Access; in this case the difference between the last order date and today's date. The variables *date1* and *date2* used in this **function** will be the *LastOrderDate* on the **form** and **today's** date supplied from the PC. The interval determines how the result is to be calculated: in days, weeks or months. The interval is specified as a **character** or **string**; for example *d* is used for days, *m* is used for months and *y* is used for years.

The first date is the **bound object field** on the **form**. This **field** is called *LastOrderDate*. The second date is the date supplied from the PC; this can be obtained by using another **function, Now,** from within the Access **Date/Time functions**.

When you refer to a field's name it is usual to enclose the **field name** in square brackets *[ ]*. There are exceptions to this rule; for example, when a **field name** does not contain a space. For example, a field called *ADD LINE 1* will require the use of brackets while a field called *ADDLINE1* would not. You may also use an underscore instead of brackets when a field name contains a space; for example *ADD_LINE_1* would be acceptable.

So the final **expression** will look like the one shown in Figure 5.45. When the expression is built in the **expression builder** window, click on the **OK** button. The expression is then returned into the **Control Source property** of the **unbound text box**.

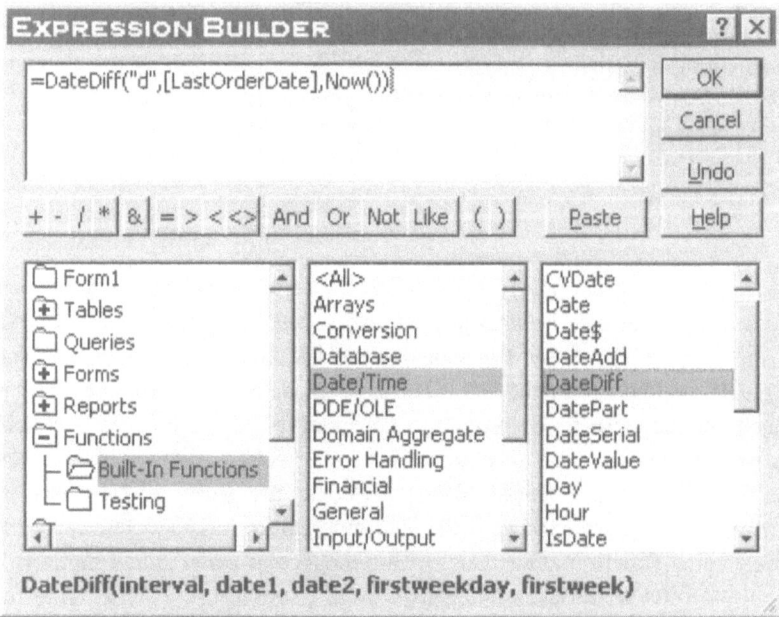

Figure *5.45 The completed expression.*

If you view the **form** now you will see the resulting calculation displayed in the **unbound text box** you created. Do not forget that as the field is **unbound** it means the data will not be stored on the underlying **table**. Figure 5.46 shows the view of the **form**.

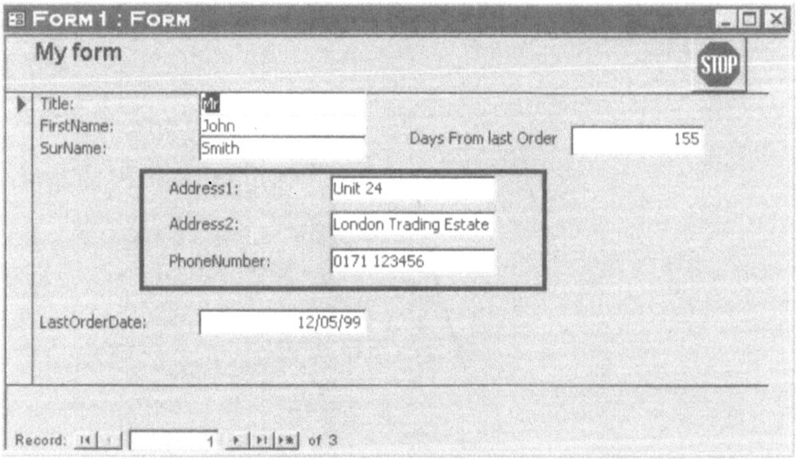

Figure *5.46 A complete unbound text box with calculation.*

To complete this chapter you need to look at the **properties** for the **command button** you placed onto the form earlier. Open the form you have been using in the previous examples, this time use **design view**. Then examine the **properties** for the **Close** button you placed onto the **form;** see Figure 5.47.

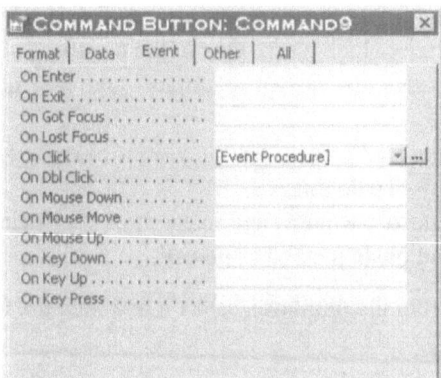

Figure 5.47 *Command button properties.*

If you select the **event tab** you will see that there is an **Event Procedure** shown within the **On Click** row. This means that there is an underlying **event** that takes place when this **button** is clicked; this is usually a **Visual Basic procedure**. To look at the **procedure** click onto the **Expression Builder button** for this **event**. The code can be seen in Figure 5.48.

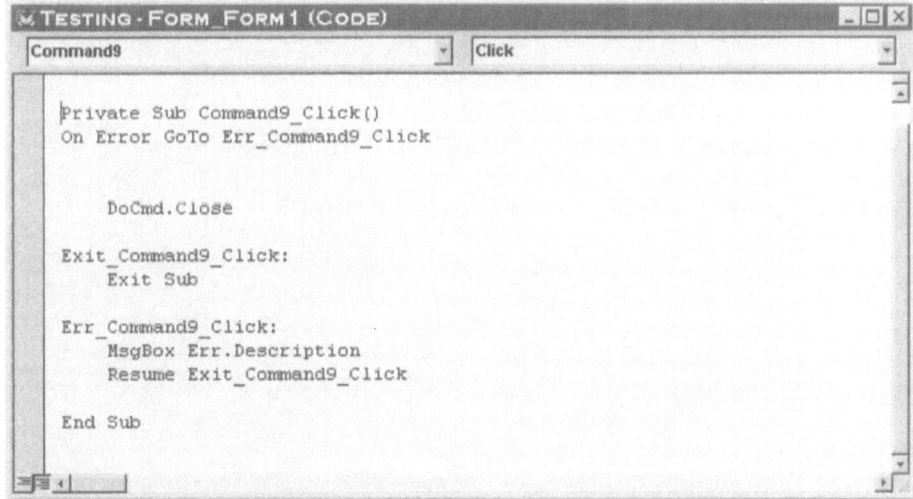

Figure 5.48 *An example of a command button's On Click event.*

The **Command Button Wizard** will build **Visual Basic** statements into the **event** on a button for you. The actual statement to close the **form** is:

DoCmd.Close

So **command buttons** placed onto a **form** can have **events** as well as **properties** that control the appearance or contents of a **field object**. There are so many **properties**, options, **functions** and combinations that it would be almost impossible to cover them all in a small volume such as this. It does however give you a taste of what's on offer and where to look for it. One of the most important things to remember is that all items on a **form** are classed as **objects** and each **object** will have a set of **properties**.

When you have completed a **form** you may want to reuse it by making a copy and then modifying the copy. To do this:

• Return to the database window and select the form by clicking onto it once.

• Use the **copy** and **paste** method as normal.

To remove a **form** from the **database**, select it and then use the **delete** key.

6
Queries

Introduction

You have already looked at using the **find** function when viewing data from a **table**, but that does not always provide you with enough flexibility to find what you want. **Queries** provide you with selective views of your data or allow you to update a selection of records. In this chapter you will look at the simplest form of query, the **select query**. This allows you to choose how you want to see your data when selecting a specific set of records, by setting search criteria.

Building a simple query

The first thing to get to grips with is the design of a simple **select query**. To design a **new query** use the following steps.

- Select the queries object tab from the database window.
- Click on the create query In Design view option.
- Select the table that will supply the data for your query.

In the **query design window** the **Show Table window** is displayed; here you can specify the source of the data for a **query**. This can be **Tables, Queries** or **Both**. The standard or default query type is a **select query**.

In the example shown in Figure 6.1 the only table available to use is *Table1*. Highlight this **table** and use the **Add button** to add the **table** to the design grid. Then use the **Close button** to close the **Show Table window**. Your selected table is shown in the upper left of the **query design grid.**

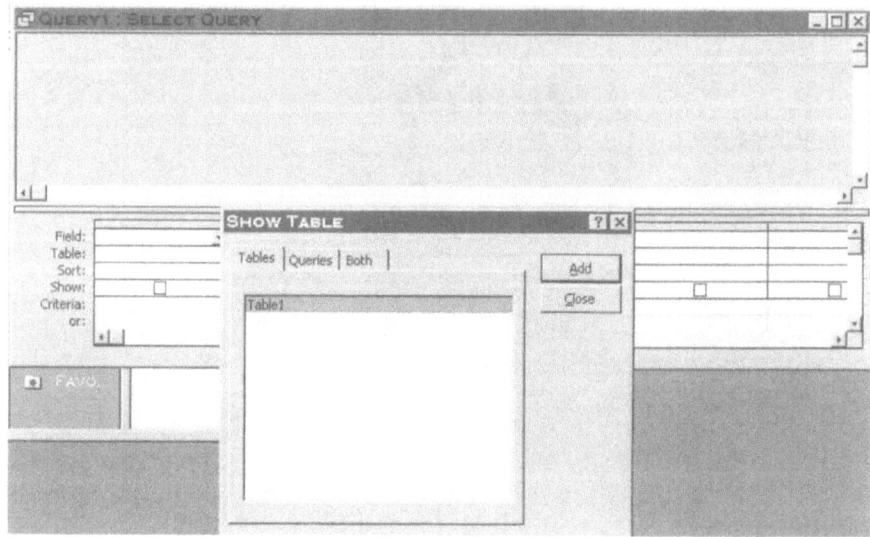

Figure 6.1 *Adding a table to the query design grid.*

The **table** or **tables** are shown in the upper left of the **query design window**; the lower part of the window is the **design grid**. To this grid you add the fields you want to display using the field row. The **design grid** consists of blank columns and rows; each column is used to identify a **field** from your **table**. The rows are provided so you can specify how to **sort, select** or **update** the records. Figure 6.2 shows the blank **design grid** with a **table** in the top left of the window.

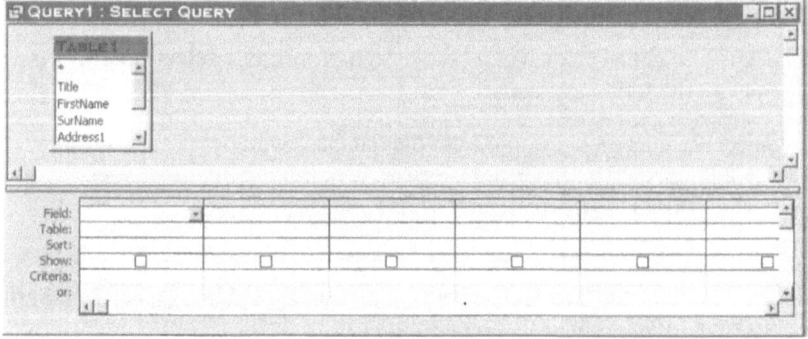

Figure 6.2 *A blank design grid with an added table.*

Selecting fields

There are several ways to add fields from your **table** into the **design grid**:

- Drag the **field** from the **table** onto a column within the **Field row** using the mouse.
- Drag multiple selected fields from the table onto the design grid.
- Double-click on a field within the table to add to the next available column.
- Use the **list box** at the top of each column within the **Field row**.

To select a block of fields:

Select the first **field**, hold down the **Shift** key, and click onto the last **field**.

For a non-contiguous selection of fields, hold down **Ctrl** key as you select each of the **fields**.

To select all the fields from a **table,** double-click on the **title bar** of the **table** window or the **asterisk**.

In the example shown in Figure 6.3, three **fields** have been added to the **design grid**; *Title*, *SurName* and *LastOrderDate*. Only these three **fields** will be displayed when you view the results by running the **query**.

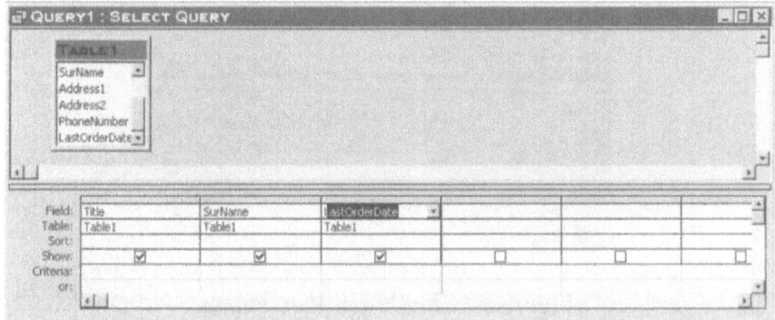

Figure 6.3 *A selection of fields added to the design grid of a select query.*

The **query** results can be viewed by using the **Query | Run** menu or by using the **Run button,** as shown in Figure 6.4.

The Run Button

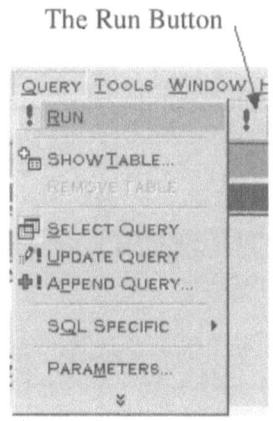

Figure 6.4 *Using the Run button or the **Query | Run** menu.*

The results are shown in Figure 6.5. In a standard Access **table** view, you may **edit** or **delete** the **records** shown in this view.

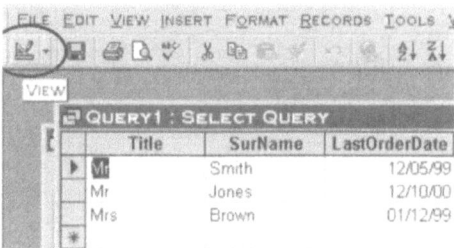

Figure 6.5 The results of a select query.

To return to your **design,** use the **Design View button** as shown in Figure 6.6, or use the **View | Design View** menu.

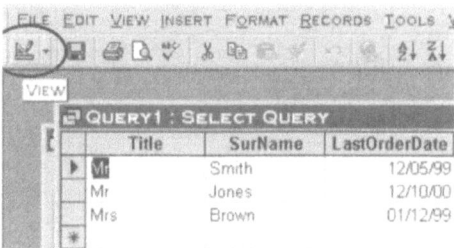

Figure 6.6 The Design View button.

Sorting records

The **records** are shown in **data entry order;** to **sort** them into a different order you need to apply a **sort** on the selected **field**. Using the **design grid** again you can specify if a field is to be sorted into **descending** or **ascending** order. The example in Figure 6.7 shows how this is applied to the *LastOrderDate* field.

In this case the **records** will be **sorted** by the *LastOrderDate* with the latest order date first. You can use fields for **sorting, grouping** and selection, even when they are not going to be displayed.

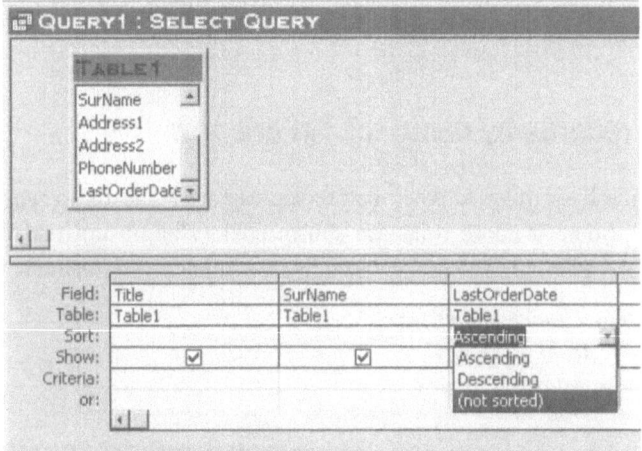

Figure 6.7 Applying a sort to the LastOrderDate field.

Showing and hiding fields

The **Show check box** is used to indicate if a **field** will be shown or not. In the next example the *LastOrderDate* column has been dragged to the left of the **design grid** and the **Show check box** has been turned off, as shown in Figure 6.8.

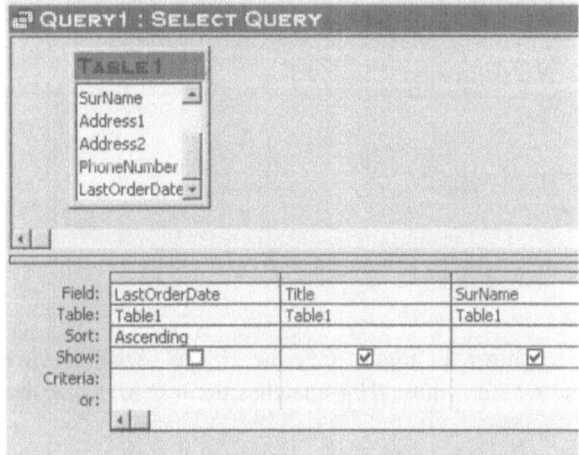

Figure 6.8 Controlling the visibility of fields.

This means you have the ability to **sort** or select by several **fields** even if they are not being shown in the results. In the next section you will look at how can you select **records** for your **query**. The **criteria row** is provided for you to specify how you want your **records** to be selected.   You can select by simple character matching or by buiding complex **expressions** using the Access **functions**.

Selecting records by using the Criteria row

There are some basic rules to cover before you can start selecting **records** by defining the **criteria**. Some of these rules are shown next. When using **text fields**; type the words under the selected field and enclose them in quotes. For example:

Field row = PhoneNumber
Criteria = "0171 123456"
Field row = Address1
Criteria = "Unit 24"

When using **date fields**, it is best to enclose them using the hash symbol, *#*. For example:

Field row = LastOrderDate
Criteria = #01/12/99#

When using **numbers**, type in the number without quotes. For example, if you were using a **numeric** salary **field** called *Salary:*

Field row = Salary
Criteria = 18000

When using **logical field** types in a **query** use **Yes/No, True/False, 1/0** (zero = **false**) to select them. For example, if you had a **logical field** called *NewCustomer:*

Field row = NewCustomer
Criteria = Yes
Or
Field row = NewCustomer
Criteria = True
Or
Field row = NewCustomer
Criteria = 1

In the example shown in Figure 6.9, the selected set of **records** is specified by asking for all the records whose *Title* matches the text *Mr* note; that the search word *Mr* is enclosed in quotes.

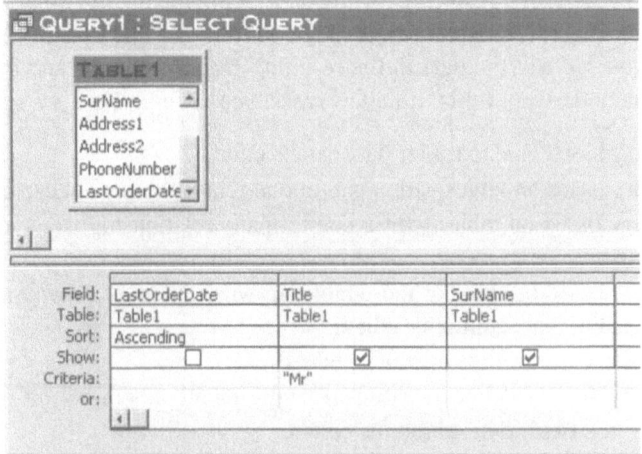

Figure 6.9 *Selecting the criteria for a text field.*

You can see the results of the **query** in Figure 6.10.

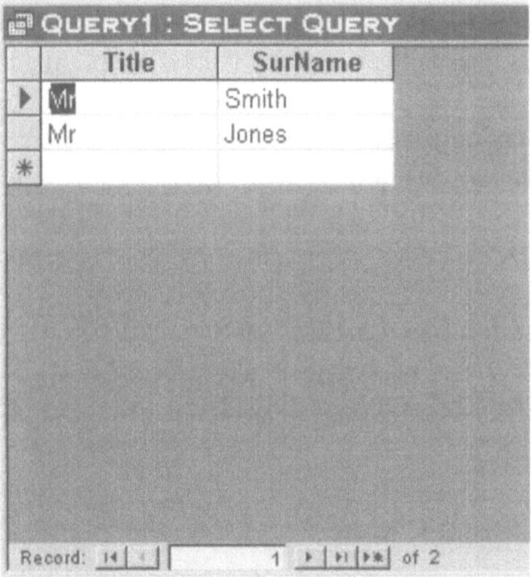

Figure 6.10 *The results of selecting all the Title fields that are equal to Mr.*

You can see that although there are three **records** in the **table** you created, only the two that match your criteria are shown.

The data displayed as a result of most **select queries** is known as a **dynaset**. You can normally **edit** the results of a **query** if there is a single **table** in use or when there are several **tables** and they have a **one-to-one relationship**. For **query** results that contain several **tables** with a **one-to-many relationship**, you cannot edit the data from the join field on the one side of the **relationship** unless you have enabled the **cascade update** option when the **relationship** was defined between the tables. However, some types of **query** display results in the form of a **snapshot**, this also means that no **records** can be edited. A **Crosstab query** produces results that cannot be updated. In most cases, you can edit the data in the resulting **Datasheet view** and this will change the data in the underlying **table**. In a few cases, you cannot. Here are some examples.

- A query based on one **table:** data can be edited.
- A query based on tables with a one-to-one relationship: data can be edited.
- A query based on tables with a one-to-many relationship: some of the data can be edited.
- A query based on three or more tables in which there is a many-to-one-to-many relationship: data cannot be edited.
- A Crosstab query: data cannot be edited.
- A query that calculates a **sum, average, count** or other type of **total** on the values in a **field:** data cannot be edited.

You can obtain a full list of these rules by looking up the **Recordset** keyword from the Access **Help** menu.

Using expressions and functions in criteria statements

There are times when you will need more than a simple match to select records. To help with this there are a number of **functions** you can use; in this section you will examine the most commonly used.

Two of the more common **functions** are:

- **Like**
- **Between**

You may also use the **like operator** to search for words that may be contained within the **field**. The use of **wildcards** is also acceptable with the **like operator**. For example, to find all the *Address1* records that start with the word *Unit*:

Field Row = Address1

Criteria = Like "Unit"*

The above **criteria** will find two **records** in the sample table with the following *address1* **field** contents; *Unit 24* and *Unit 1*.

The * is used to replace the remainder of the word with any number of characters. The **? Wildcard** character is used in a similar way, except that each question mark symbol is used to represent a single character. So if you used the following **criteria**:

Field Row = Address1

Criteria = Like "Unit??"

You would end up finding only one **record**, with an address containing *Unit1*. This is because the **wildcard** is only searching for a maximum of six characters, of which the first four must match the word *Unit*.

For example, say you wanted to find all the **records** whose *LastOrderDate* field contained dates **between** the *1st May 1999* and the *30th December 1999*. You could use the **Between operator**.

Field Row = LastOrderDate

Criteria = Between #01/05/1999# AND #30/12/1999#

This would return two **records** with *LastOrderDate* containing dates *12/5/99* and *01/12/99*.

Date functions

There are a number of **date functions** available with Access to help you handle **date** information. The **DatePart function** is used to supply a part of any **date;** the **month, day, year** or perhaps the **quarter**. The **syntax** for this function is:

DatePart(part, date)

The **part** argument is an abbreviation of the **part** of the date you want returned. For example using *YYYY* will return the **year** part of the date as a four-digit **year** while *Q* will return the calendar **quarter**.

The **date** argument is either a **field** name that holds **Date/Time** data or a literal **date** such as *7-Dec-99*.

The following are examples of **expressions** that apply the **DatePart function** to the *LastOrderDate* **field** from the example **table**.

DatePart("m",[LastOrderDate]) = 6

Only records with a month of 6 (June) will be selected.

DatePart("yyyy",[LastOrderDate])=1999

Only records with a year of 1999 will be selected.

The **Now() function** is used to show today's date as set by your PC. For example, say that today's **date** is *12/12/1999* and you want to select all the *LastOrderDate* **fields** that are less than this **date** i.e. before this date. The **criteria** would be:

Field Row = LastOrderDate
Criteria <Now( )

This will select all the records with a **date** prior to today's date.

Generating temporary fields in a query

You can create temporary **fields** within your **query** to show the result of a calculation. Perhaps you need to see how many **days** have expired between today's **date** and the *LastOrderDate*, while showing today's **date** as well.

To create a **calculated field** you need to enter your expression in a spare column within the **field row**. If you look at the example in Figure 6.11, you can see the two **expressions** used, *Now()-[LastOrderdate]* and **Now()**. Once the **expression** is entered and you move to another column or press enter, the **expression** is given a default heading by Access.

The first **expression** is headed *Expr1*, while the second **expression** has the heading *Expr2*. So the first **expression** has a default heading of *Expr1*, the second *Expr2*, the third *Expr3* and so on.

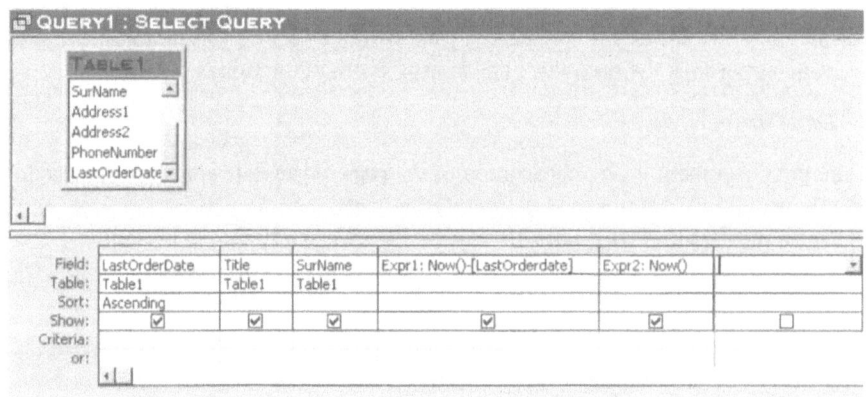

Figure 6.11 *Using a date expression with a default heading.*

Other calculations can be used whether they are mathematical in nature or not: many of the built-in **functions** you see when using the **expression builder** can be used within a **query**.

For example, say that you wanted to calculate the effect of a 10% increase on a cost field in a **table**. If the field holding the cost was called *Cost* then the calculation might look something like this:

*[Cost]+([Cost]/100*10) or ([Cost]*1.10)*

If you return to the **Design view** of your **query** for a moment you can change the temporary column headings. To **rename** a column place a colon, : , between the field **expression** (calculation) and the field **heading**, which you supply, see Figure 6.12. The text *Days since last Order* and *Today's date* have been used as the column headings.

You can also rename a field heading within a query. If you wanted to change the column heading for the *Title* field in the **query** to *Salutation*, then the **field row** would contain the following statement:

Salutation : Title

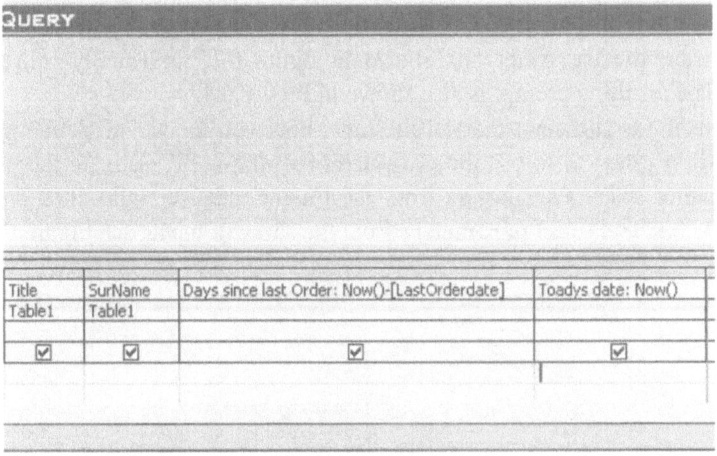

Figure 6.12 *Changing a column heading in a query.*

Using parameters in a query

A parameter is the name given to any piece of information supplied to a **function** or task by the user, before that task in performed. In the **query** examples used so far a **constant** value has been used, that is to say a value that does not change. Sometimes you do not know what the value is going to be. Taking the example shown in Figure 6.9 a **constant** value of *Mr* was used to select the records in the *Title* field.

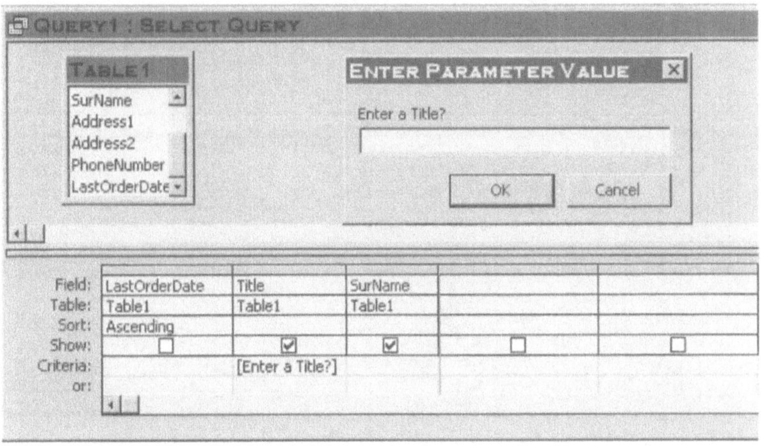

Figure 6.13 *Using a variable value with a parameter query.*

In Figure 6.13 the query has been modified and the **constant** value has been replaced with a **variable parameter**. The **parameter** value has been enclosed in square brackets [ ] to define it as a **parameter**; rather than give the **parameter** a name, a meaningful phrase has been used. This will appear on the screen when the **query** is run; the parameter box shown in figure 6.13 is actually called *[Enter a Title?]*. The resulting prompt is also shown in Figure 6.13.

This method is sufficient most of the time; however, the way to define **parameters** used within a **query** is to use the **parameters window**. To activate the **parameters window** either select **Parameters** from the **Query** menu or right-click on the query design **title bar** and select **parameters** from the shortcut menu; see Figure 6.14.

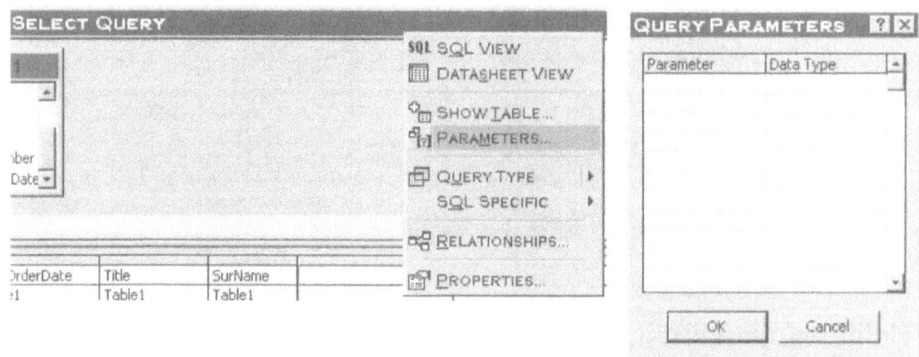

Figure 6.14 Selecting the parameters window.

You are required to supply the **parameter** name or phrase and define its **type** by using the drop-down list on the right. Make sure that you place your **parameter** name in square brackets when using it within your query.

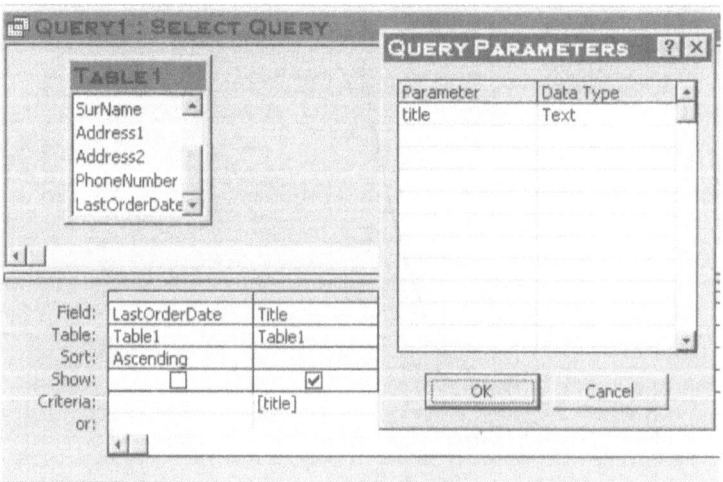

Figure 6.15 Matching the parameter name in the query to the parameter window.

In the example shown in Figure 6.15 the **parameter** name matches the one used within the **criteria row**, with the exception of the brackets.

You can use the **Shift** and **F2** function keys to zoom into a field on the **query design grid**. Remember to match the **parameter type** to the **field type** you are using.

Using a query to update information

One of the most useful types of **query** after the **Select** query is the **Update** query; this allows you to select a set of records and then specify how to **update** or change them.

For example, say you wanted to set all the *LastOrderDate* **fields** to the date, *12th May 1999*. To change an existing query to an update query you would need to change the **query type** to an **Update query** using the **Query** menu, or by using the right-click short-cut menu. An extra row is added to the **query design grid;** this is the **Update To row** and here you specify what the **field** will be **updated** to. See Figure 6.16.

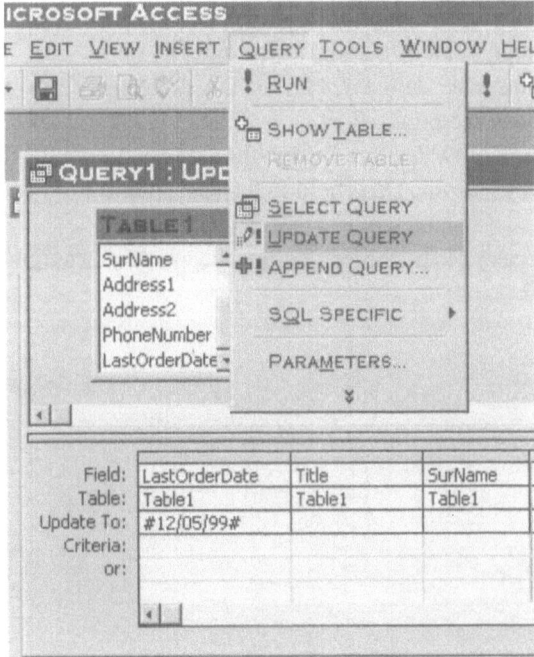

Figure 6.16 *Updating a query.*

Once the **query** has been run, all the *LastOrderDate* records will have been **updated** to the *12th May 1999*. To be more specific in an update you need only to specify your **criteria**.

Creating a crosstab query

A crosstab query is ideal for producing summary **totals** and **averages** by **groups** of records. For example, you might like to view the **count** of the number of customers within *Table1* by *LastOrderDate* and *Customer key* as shown in Figure 6.17.

LastOrderDate	1	2	3	5
				1
12/05/99	1			
01/12/99			1	
12/10/00		1		

Figure 6.17 Example of a crosstab query.

To recreate the example above you will need to:

- Return to the **database window** and select the **query object tab**.
- Select the new query button from the toolbar.
- Choose Design View as shown in Figure 6.18.
- Now add the table called *Table1* to the design grid and then close the Add Table window; see Figure 6.19.
- Now add the *LastOrderDate* field to the first column of the design grid.
- Then add the *CustomerKey* field to the second and third columns of the design grid.
- Using the query menu change the **query type** to a **crosstab query** as shown in Figure 6.20.

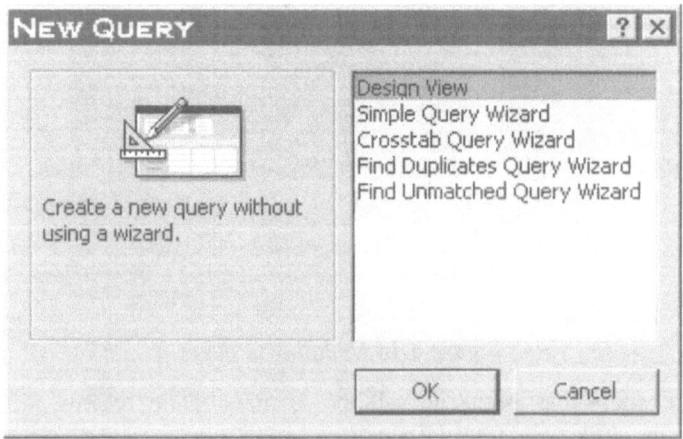

Figure 6.18 Using Design View to create a new query.

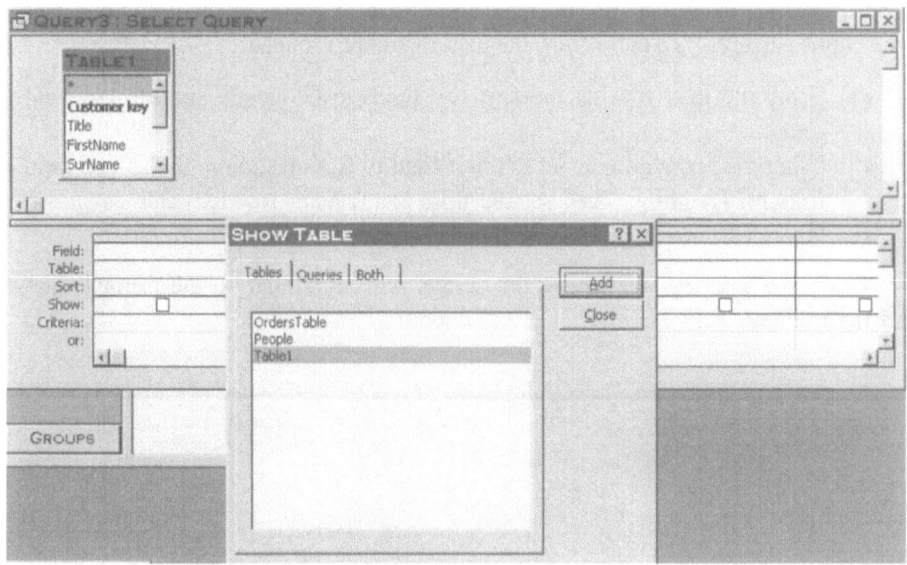

Figure 6.19 *Adding the table to the design grid.*

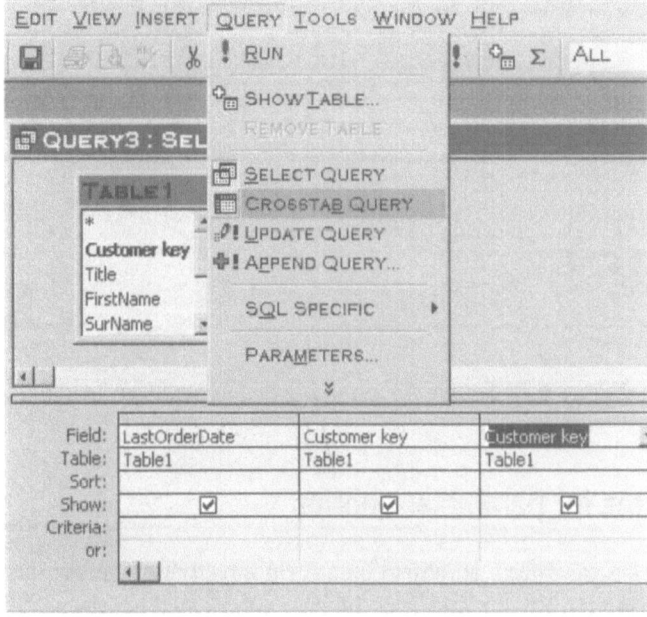

Figure 6.20 *Converting the query from select to crosstab type.*

The next stage is to define the **fields** to be used as **column or row headings** and then set the **field** to be used as a **count variable**. In the example shown,

LastOrderDate is used as the **row heading**, *Customer key* as the **column heading** and the **count variable**. To define how the data should be grouped:

- Using the total row set the first two fields to Group By and the last field to Count.
- Using the **crosstab row** set the first **field** to **Row Heading**, the second **field to Column Heading**, Then set the third field's total row to Value as shown in Figure 6.21.

When you **preview** the **query** the results will be similar to the example shown earlier in Figure 6.17.

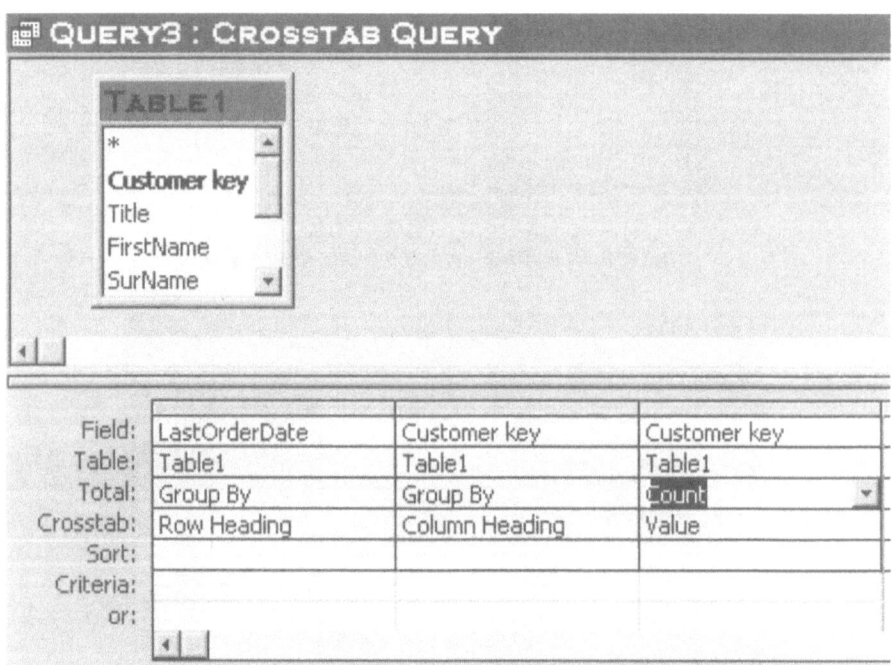

Figure 6.21 Setting the grouping and column/row headings.

Using forms for parameter queries

You can pass a value from an **object** on a **form** directly to a **query**; this can be useful if you are using **parameter queries**. Suppose you wanted to select a customer from a pick list (**combo box**) on a **form** and then run a **query** to show all the details for that customer. You would need a **form** with a **combo box object** and a **select query** for your customer's table that uses the **combo box object** on the **form** as the **criteria**. This is shown in the next example.

The first thing to do is set up your form with its combo box, this will allow you to specify the criteria for your query.

- Select the **forms object tab** from the **database window** and then click on the **New** button on the toolbar to create a new form in design view. DO NOT enter a table for the **data source**, leave this blank.
- In the form design window open the toolbox and ensure the toolbox wizard is turned on.
- Select the combo box tool and drag it onto the detail section of the form. The Combo Box Wizard will ask you to identify how the values are to be selected for the combo box.
- Select 'I want the combo box to look up the values in a table or query' option; see Figure 6.22.
- Select the Next button to move on and choose the table that contains the values you require for the combo box; in this case use Table1 as shown in Figure 6.23.
- Select the Next button again to move on and choose the fields to be used in the list, use the *Customer key* and *SurName* fields as shown in Figure 6.24.

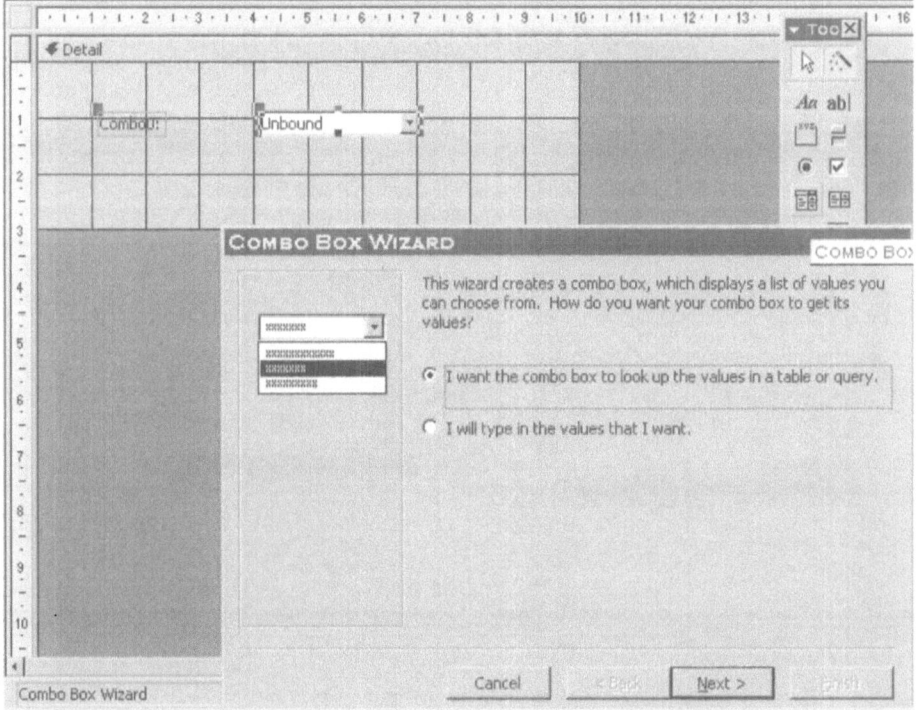

Figure 6.22 *Using a combo box with the toolbox wizard.*

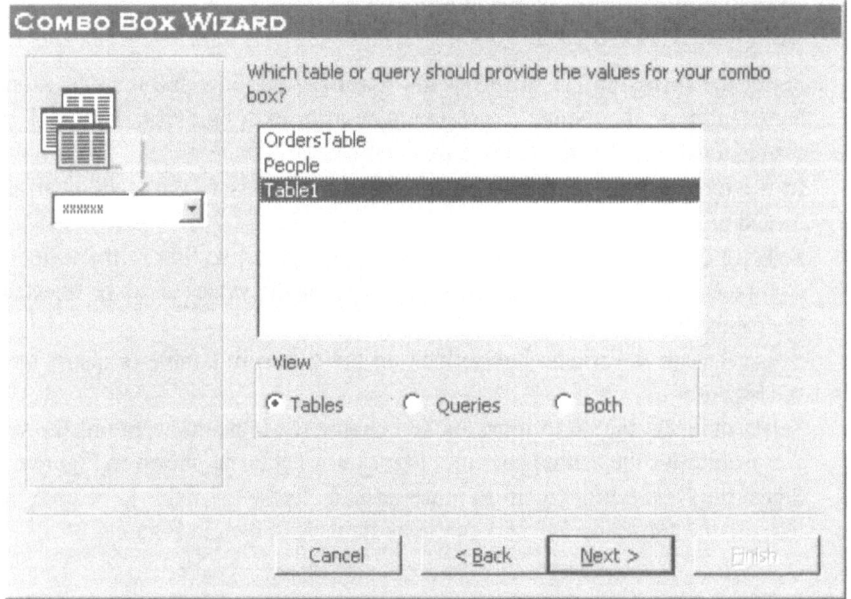

Figure 6.23 *Selecting a table for a combo box.*

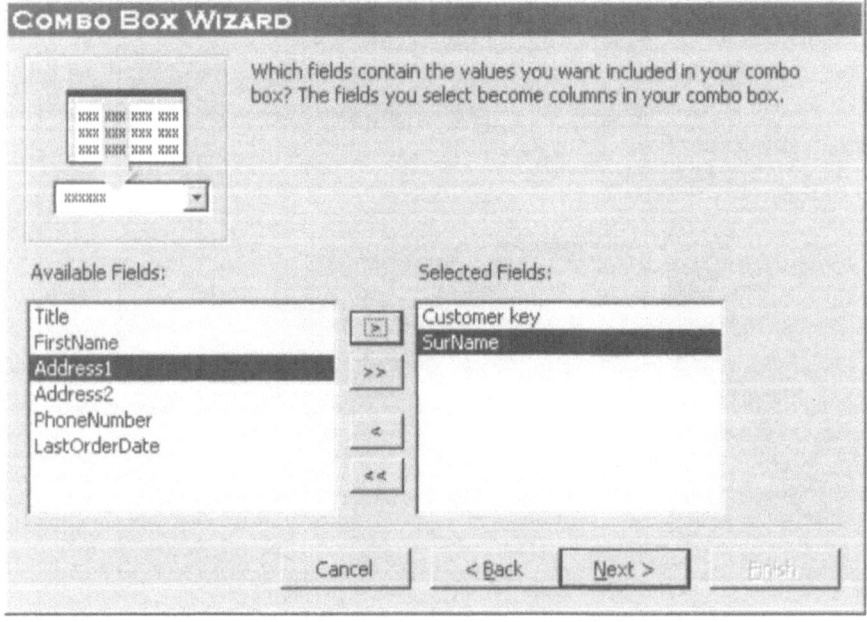

Figure 6.24 *Selecting the fields for a combo box.*

- Move on using the **Next** button enabling you to adjust the width of the columns if required.
- Use the mouse pointer and drag the left hand edge of the visible column to the width you require.
- Turn off the check box option to hide the key column, as you would like to see this value displayed; see Figure 6.25

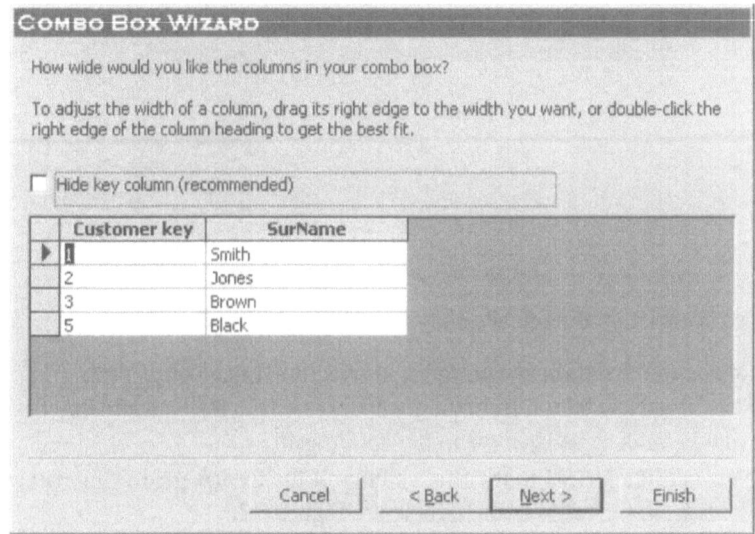

Figure 6.25 *Adjusting the width of a column.*

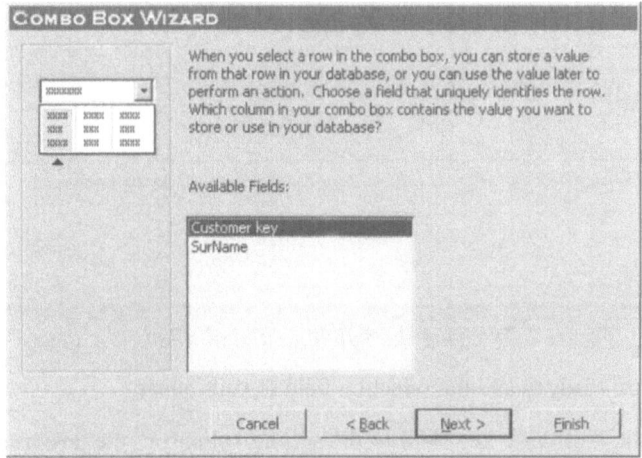

Figure 6.26 *Setting the field value for a combo box.*

- Select **Next** to move on again to set the **field** that will contain the value you want to hold in the **combo box**; set this as the *Customer key* **field** as shown in Figure 6.26.
- Select **Next** to move on and then confirm the name for the **combo box** by selecting **Finish**, in this case the combo box is called *Combo0*.
- When you have returned to the **form design close,** and **save** the **form** calling it *PickCustomer*, as shown in Figure 6.27.

Figure 6.27 *Saving the form.*

Now you can set up the **select query** for the **form**. To do this:

- Return to the **database window** and select the **query object tab**.
- Select the New button from the toolbar to create a new query using design view.
- Add the table called *Table1* to the design grid.
- Now add the *** field** to the first column of the **design grid.** This will add all the **fields** from the **table** to the **query**; see Figure 6.28.

Figure 6.28 *Using the * field to add all fields to a query.*

Now you are ready to add the selection field to your query.

- Add the Customer key **field** to the second column of the **design grid** as shown in Figure 6.29.
- Turn the Show **check box** Off for this **field**; you do not want it to be shown a second time.

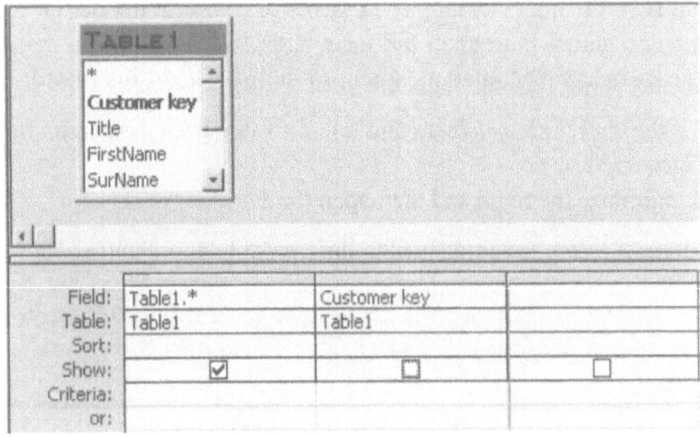

Figure 6.29 *Add the Customer key field.*

Now you can add the following statement to the **criteria** row of the *Customer key* column:

Forms![PickCustomer]![Combo0]

This will set the **criteria** for the *Customer key* **field**; the value will be passed to the **query** from the **form** called *PickCustomer* and the **object** on the **form** is called *Combo0*. The **query** will now look similar to the example shown in Figure 6.30.

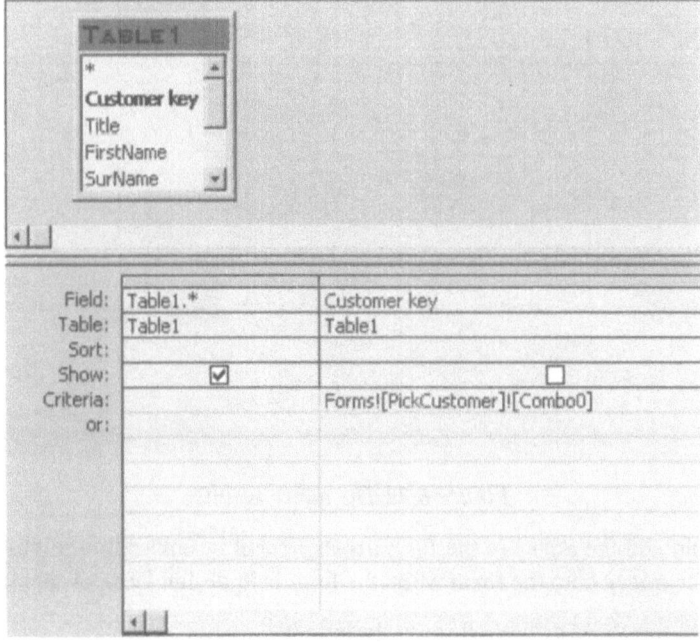

Figure 6.30 *The query with criteria selected from a forms combo box.*

Close and **save** the **query** calling it *PickCust* to complete the design of the query. Now all that is required is to **open** the **form** and **pick** a value from the **combo box**, **minimize** the **form** and then **open** the **query** to show the matching records.

- **Open** the *PickCustomer* **form** and select a value from the **combo box** as shown in Figure 6.31.
- Now minimize the **form** and then **open** the *PickCust* **query.**

The results will match the value held in the **combo box** for the *Customer key* **field**.

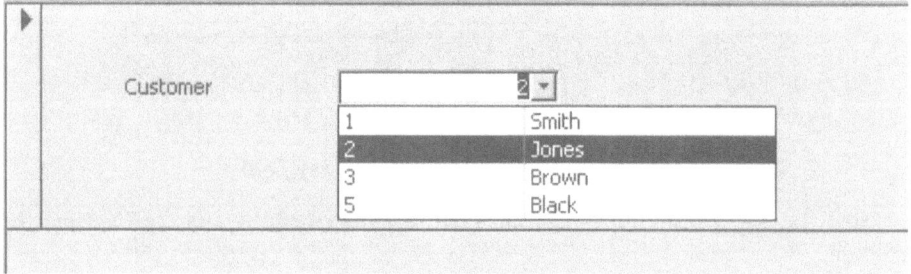

Figure 6.31 Picking a value from the combo box.

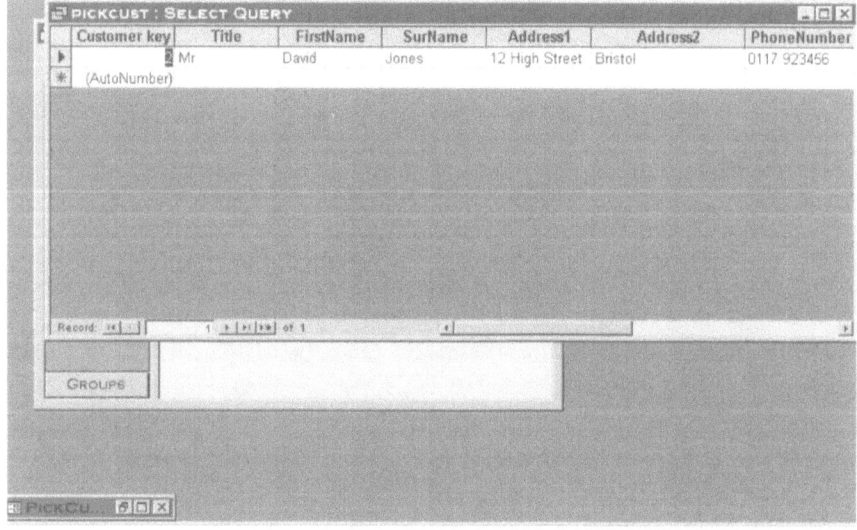

Figure 6.32 The query results.

You could add the **query** to the *Pickcustomer* **form** by embedding it into to **form** by dragging the **query** onto the **form** while the form is in design view. To do this:

- Open the *PickCustomer* form in **design** view.

- Use the **Window | Tile Vertically** menu option to display the database window alongside the form design window as shown in Figure 6.33.

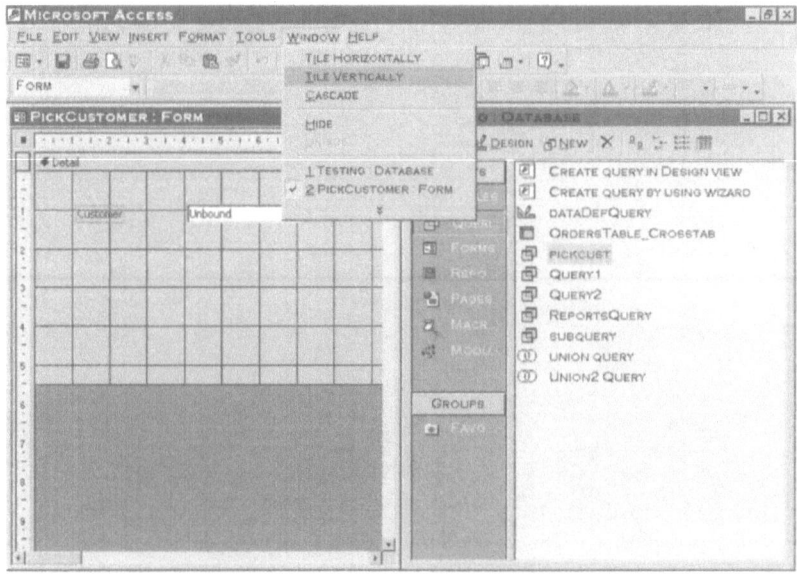

Figure 6.33 *Displaying two windows vertically.*

- Select the **query** tab from the **database window** and then drag the *PickCust* **query** onto the **form** design. Just below your **combo box** the **subform wizard** will appear and ask you to name the **subform** as shown in Figure 6.34.
- Confirm that you want to use the default name by selecting the **Finish** button.

Open the *PickCustomer* form to display the **subform** containing the *PickCust* **query** as shown in Figure 6.35. In this example the column widths in the **subform** have been adjusted to show more of the data.

There is one small problem: when you pick another customer from the **combo box** the data in the **subform** is not refreshed. This is because the query has already been run once when the *PickCustomer* form was opened; it will need to be rerun to **requery** the data in the **subform** each time the **combo box** contents is changed. To correct this problem you need to re query the **sub form** each time the **combo box** is updated by using the **After Update event property** for the **combo box**.

Open the *PickCustomer* **form** in **design view** and select the **combo box After Update event property** row as shown in Figure 6.36.

Use the **expression builder** button on the right of the row to open the **Choose Builder window**, then select the **Code Builder** option and click on the **OK** button as shown in Figure 6.37.

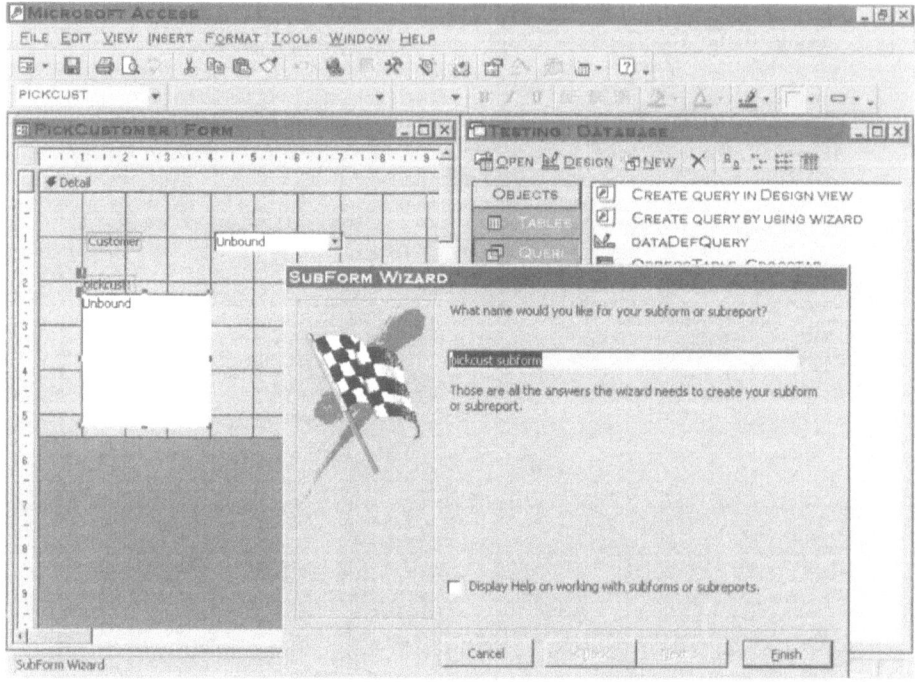

Figure 6.34 *Dragging a query onto the form design and the subform wizard.*

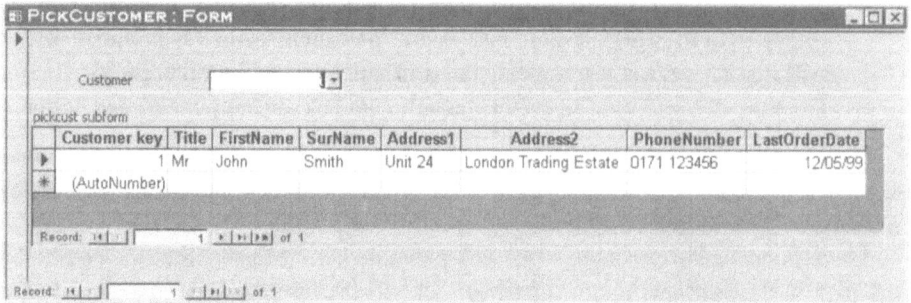

Figure 6.35 *The PickCust query shown in the open form.*

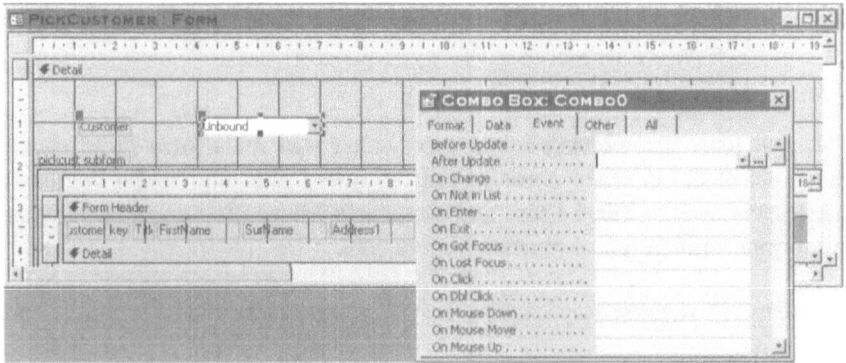

Figure 6.36 *Selecting the event properties for the combo box.*

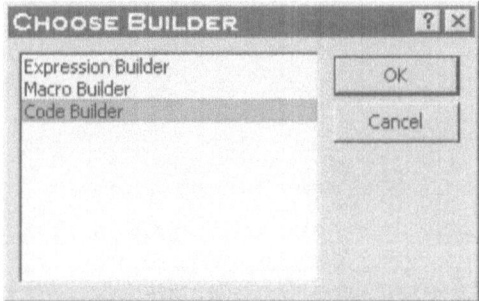

Figure 6.37 *Selecting Code Builder after using the expression builder button.*

Now you can enter the code for the **After Update event** of the **combo box** as shown in Figure 6.38.

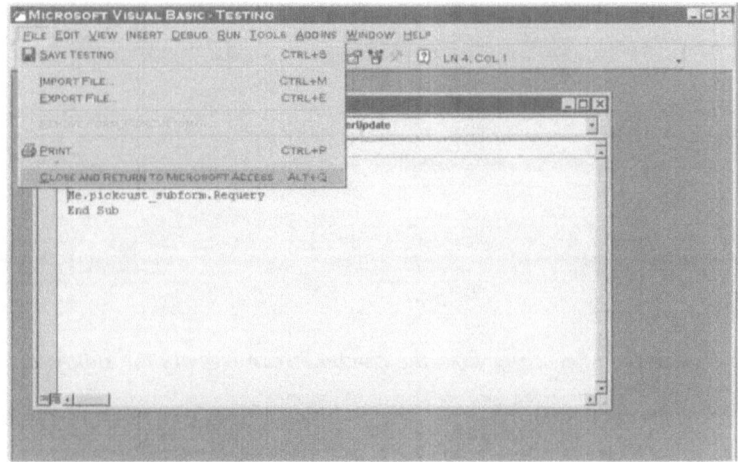

Figure 6.38 *Closing the code window to return to the form design.*

Enter the following line of code between the *Private Sub Combo0_AfterUpdate( )* and *End Sub* lines:

Me.PickCust_subform.Requery

This will force the **subform** called *Pickcust* on your main **form** *PickCustomer* to **requery** the data. In other words re run the **query** after the **combo box** has been updated. Now use the **File | Close and Return to Microsoft Access** menu option to return to your form design as shown in Figure 6.39.

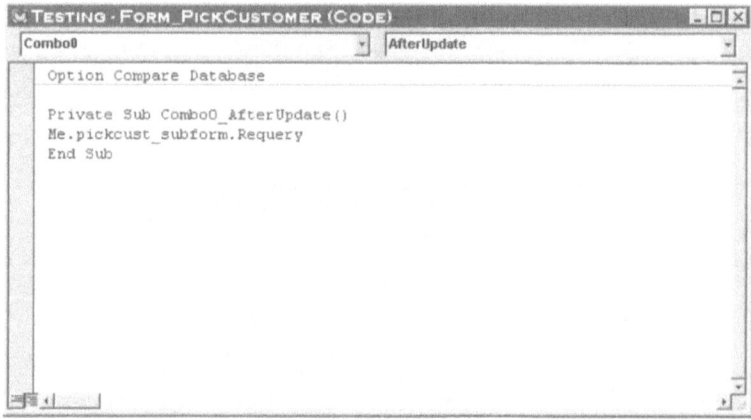

Figure 6.39 *Entering the code for the combo box after Update event.*

Open the form in form view and then select another customer from the combo box as shown in Figure 6.40.

The data in the subform will change to match the value in the combo box.

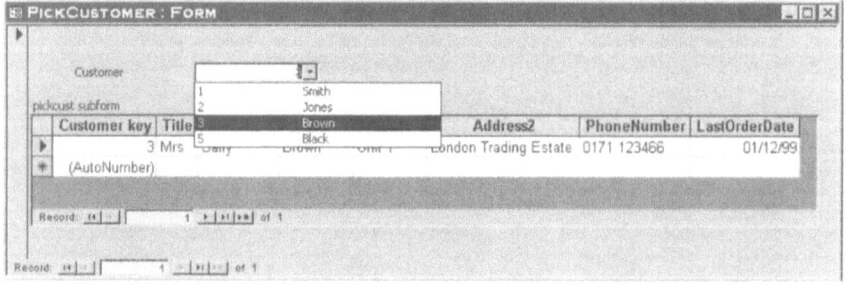

Figure 6.40 *Selecting from the combo box to requery the subform.*

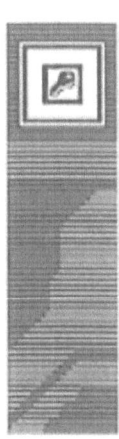

7
Basic Reports

Introduction

A **report** is a way to present your data in a printed format; you can control the size and appearance of everything on a **report**. The data is displayed in the way you want to see it. Information in a **report** comes from an underlying **table**, **query**, or **SQL** statement. Other information in the **report** can be created in the **report's design**.

Types of report

There are three main types of **report**; **tabular, single column, label format**. While variations are possible these cover the types most people use. When you create a new **report** you can see the options available, see Figure 7.1.

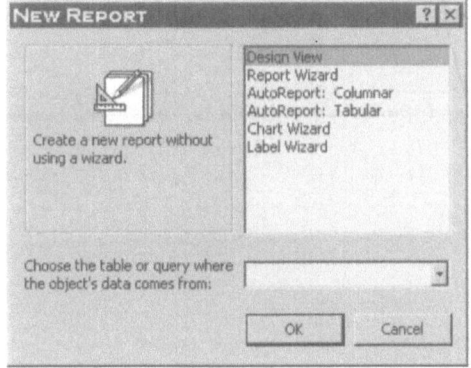

Figure 7.1 *Selecting the type of report to create.*

Tabular report

In a **tabular report** the data runs across the page from left to right; the example shown in Figure 7.2 shows seven **fields** of data running across the page. The data is held within the **detail** area of the report, while the column headings are positioned within the **page** or **report heading** area.

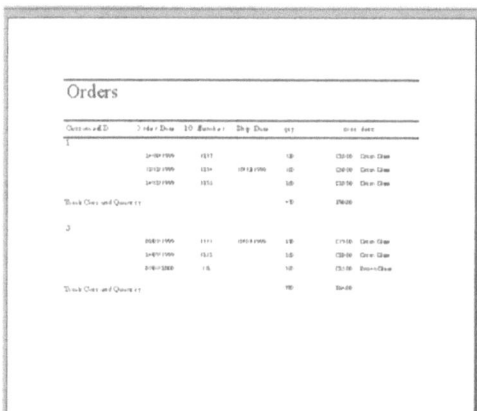

Figure 7.2 *A tabular report example.*

Column report

In a **column report** the data runs down the page in a single column; again the data is held within the **detail area** of the report. An example is shown in Figure 7.3.

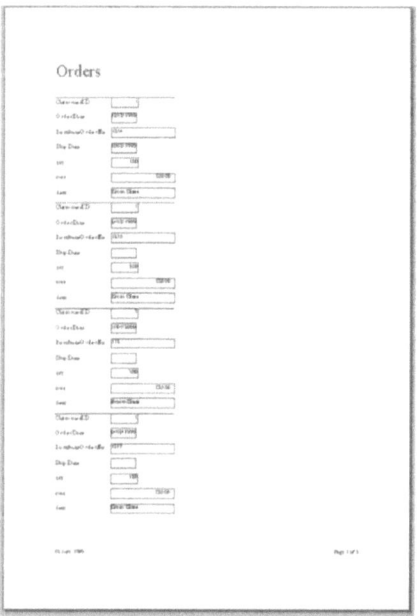

Figure 7.3 *A column report example.*

Label report

A **label report** is normally set up to produce a layout for printing on labels, data normally runs from left to right, with one complete **record** on each label. An example is shown in Figure 7.4.

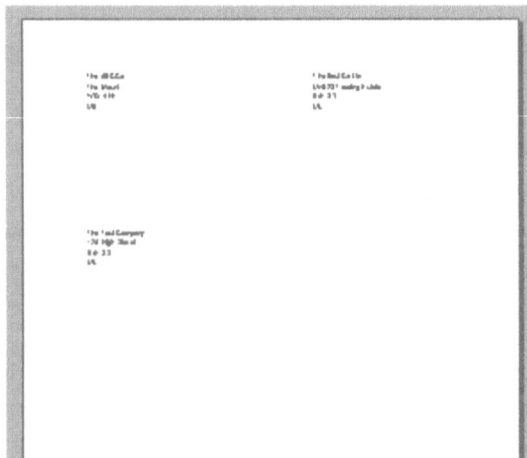

Figure 7.4 *An example of a label report.*

Creating a new report using the AutoReport feature

To produce an example, generate a quick **report** to show your customer contacts as shown in Figure 7.6.

To create a new **report** using the **Auto Report** feature:

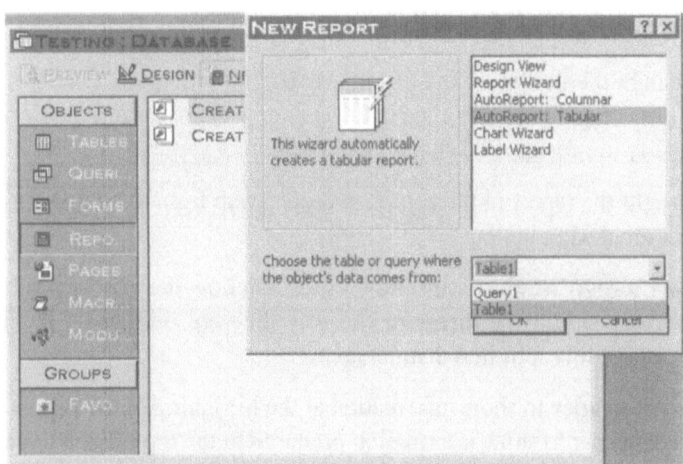

Figure 7.5 *Using the AutoReport feature.*

- Select the report objects group from the database window.
- Select the **new** button from the toolbar.
- Select the AutoReport: Tabular option.
- Select the customer table, *Table1*. Select the OK button to continue, as shown in Figure 7.5.
- The **AutoReport** Wizard will complete the layout and the results will be shown on the screen as seen in Figure 7.6. In the example the report has been **saved** and named *Table1*.

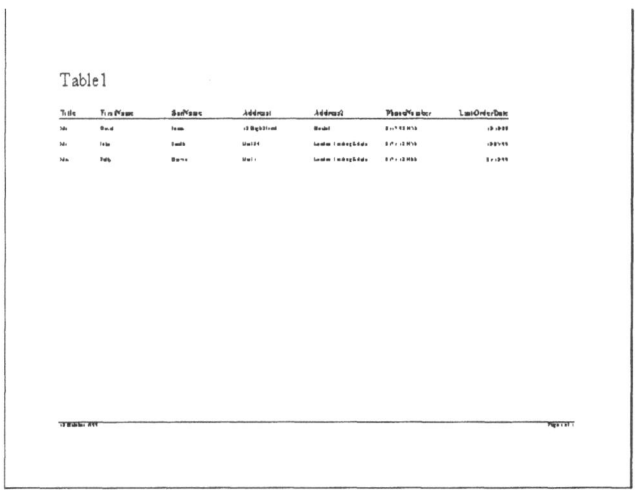

Figure 7.6 An example of a tabular AutoReport.

Changing the design of a report

You may change the design of any existing **report** at any time. One of the best ways of learning how **reports** are designed is to generate a **report** using the **Report Wizard** and then modify the design. To change the **design** of a **report:**

- Highlight the report in the **report objects** group from the **database** window.
- Select the **design** button.

The **report design window** will allow you to see how the **report** has been created. **Reports** are very similar to **forms** in the way they are designed. If you look at a **report** you can see it is split into distinct areas.

- A report **header** to show information at the beginning of the **report**.
- A page header to show information produced at the top of each page.
- A detail block to show the actual detail of each chosen record.
- A page footer to show information at the base of each page.
- A **report footer** to show details at the end of the **report**.

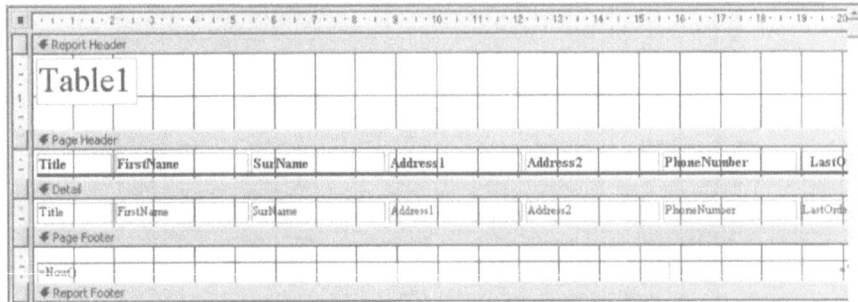

Figure 7.7 *A report design example.*

In the example shown in Figure 7.7, the **labels** are shown in the **page header**, while the **bound text fields** are shown in the **detail block**. **Unbound text boxes** containing information such as page numbers are shown in the **page footer**. The **report header** also contains the **report title** within an **unbound text box**.

You can view the **properties** for an **object** on the **report** by using the **View | Properties** menu or by using the mouse right-click method to open the shortcut menu.

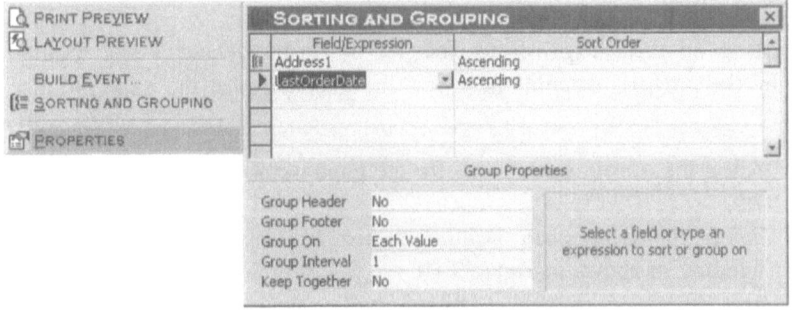

Figure 7.8 *Setting grouping options.*

One of the other options available on the shortcut menu or the **View** menu is the **Sorting** and **Grouping** option. Grouping allows you to **group** the records together and to display a **header** and **footer** for each **group.** For example you may want to **group** records by the company address to **count** how many orders there are by each company. **Sorting** just lists the records in a particular order. In the example shown in Figure 7.8 the grouping option has been set for the *Address 1* **field**.

If you look at the **page footer** area of the report a page-numbering **object** is shown. The **page** numbers are placed within an **unbound text box** with the actual **text** to be displayed at this position on the **page**. The **control source** is an **expression**. The **expression** consists of the word *Page* then a text box with a control source of *[Page]* next to this, then the word *of* and finally *[pages]* next to it. Translated this means show the **text** *Page* and then the actual **page number** then the **text** *of* followed by the actual **number of pages** in the report. This can be seen in Figure 7.9.

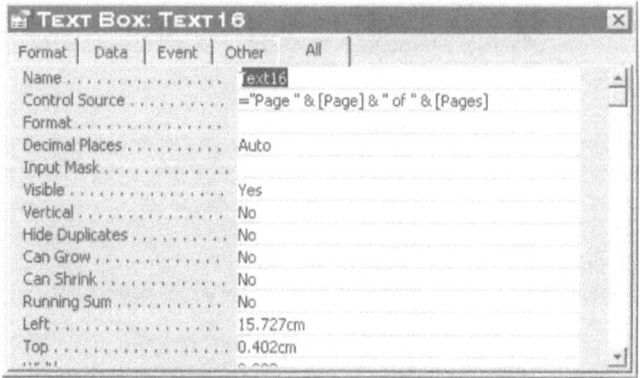

***Figure 7.9** An unbound text box displaying page numbers.*

The items within quotes are taken literally and displayed, while the items in brackets *[ ]* are **fields** or **functions** supplied by Access.

Using the expression builder in reports

You can build these **expressions** yourself by using the **expression builder**. Re-examine the previous example and view the **properties** of the **page number object** again.

- Select the control **source row** for the **page number object**, as shown in Figure 7.9.
- Select the **expression builder** button to display the **expression builder window**, as shown in Figure 7.10.

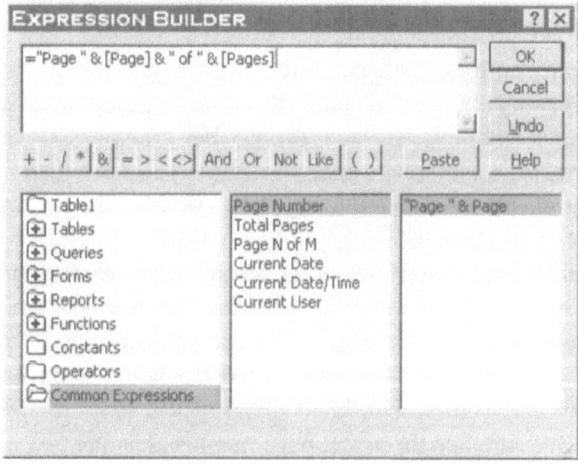

***Figure 7.10** The expression builder window.*

- Select **Common Expressions** from the **objects column** on the left; you can now see how this expression could have been built using the *Page N of M* option.

Adding calculated fields to a report

You can create calculated **fields** in a **report** in the same way that you created a calculated **field** within a **form**. Although our example has no **fields** that would require totalling, you could provide a **count** of the number of records and display this at the base of the **report**. To add a count to the bottom of the group:

- Open your report in a **design view.**
- Open the **toolbox;** use the icon on the toolbar to do this as shown in Figure 7.11.

Figure 7.11 The toolbox icon.

Make some room in a **group footer** area by extending the footer base line and start dragging from the top of the **group footer** row towards the bottom of the page. You only need enough space to place your **count** on the report; see Figure 7.12.

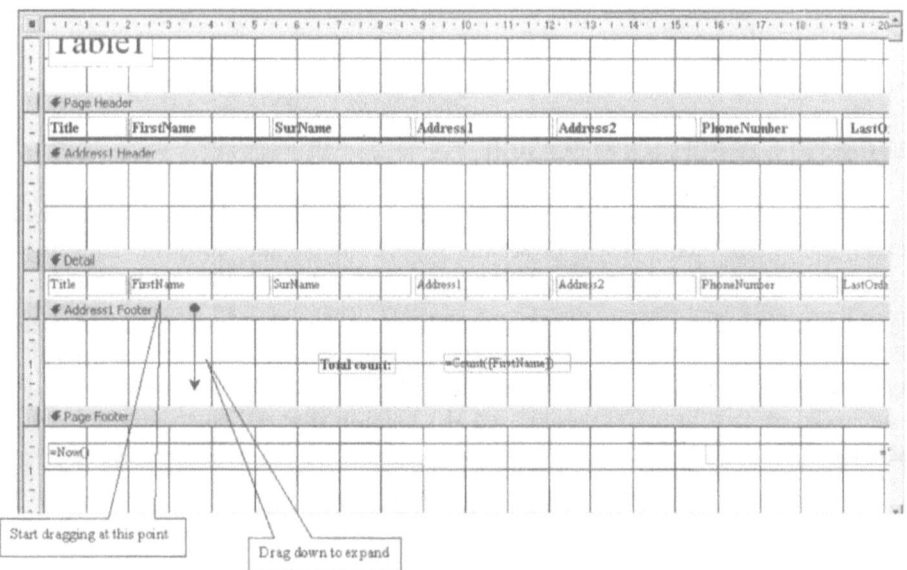

Figure 7.12 Using the mouse to expand an area.

- Now place an unbound text box onto the report.

- Change the label text to *Total count.*
- Set up the properties for the Control Source to =Count([SurName]) as shown in Figure 7.13.

In the example the *SurName* field is used to provide the **count** of the number of records.

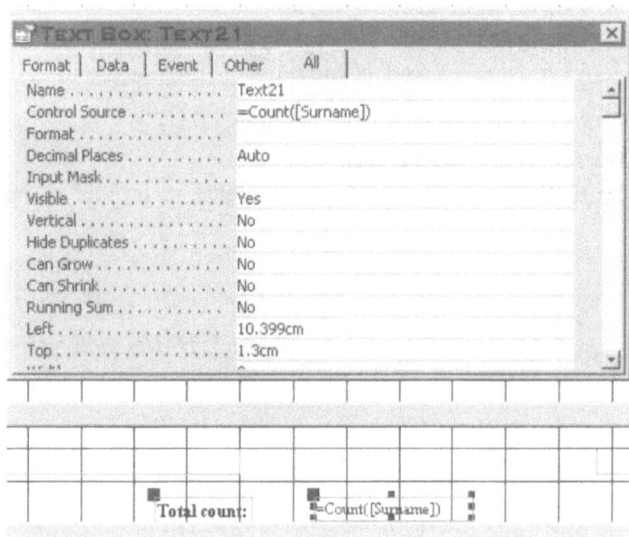

Figure 7.13 A count function used in an unbound text box.

Creating a report from scratch

In this section you will create a **report** that is similar in layout to the previous example but this time you will create the **report** without the aid of the **AutoReport wizard**. To create a **report** from scratch you need to know which **table** you want to base the **report** on - what is the **record source?** Then you will need to decide what type of **report** you want to create - is it to list all the records down the page with fields running from left to right? This is a **tabular report** style. Perhaps you want to show one record on each page? This is classed as a **column report**. To create a report from scratch:

- Select the Report object tab from the database window.
- Select **New report** and then **Design View** as shown in Figure 7.14.
- Select the **table** for the data source from the **pick list** as shown in Figure 7.15, *Table1.*

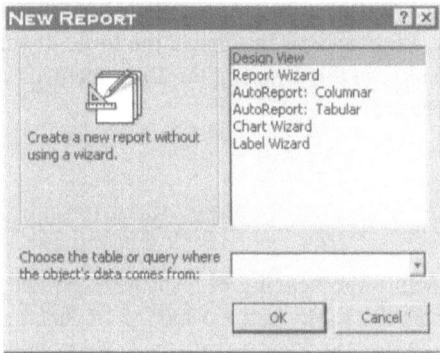

Figure 7.14 *Selecting Design View for a new report.*

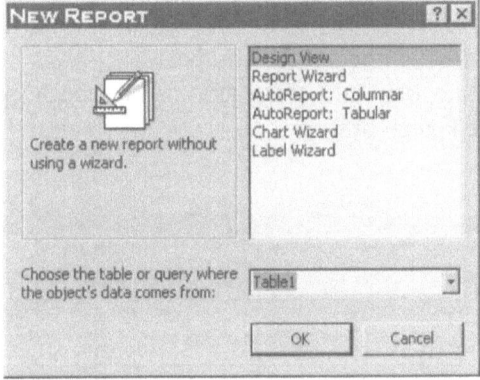

Figure 7.15 *Selecting a table for the reports record source.*

Figure 7.16 *Viewing the header and footer areas.*

Once the design window is open you can see there are three main areas on the **form**, this will depend on the **View** options in force at the time. If you cannot see the header or footer areas you can change this by using the View menu as shown in Figure 7.16.

The main report areas are:

- Page header
- Detail
- Page footer

These are used to define the heading of each page printed, the reports content or details to be printed from the **table,** and the footing of each page printed. Initially all three areas are blank as shown in Figure 7.17. You place the **fields** on the report one by one by using the **field list button** to display the **fields** and then by dragging the **fields** from the **field list** onto the reports **detail** area.

Once the field list box is open you can drag your first field onto the detail area of the report:

- Select the *Title* field from the field list box.
- Drag it onto the detail area of the form; leave enough space on the left for the text label; see Figure 7.18.

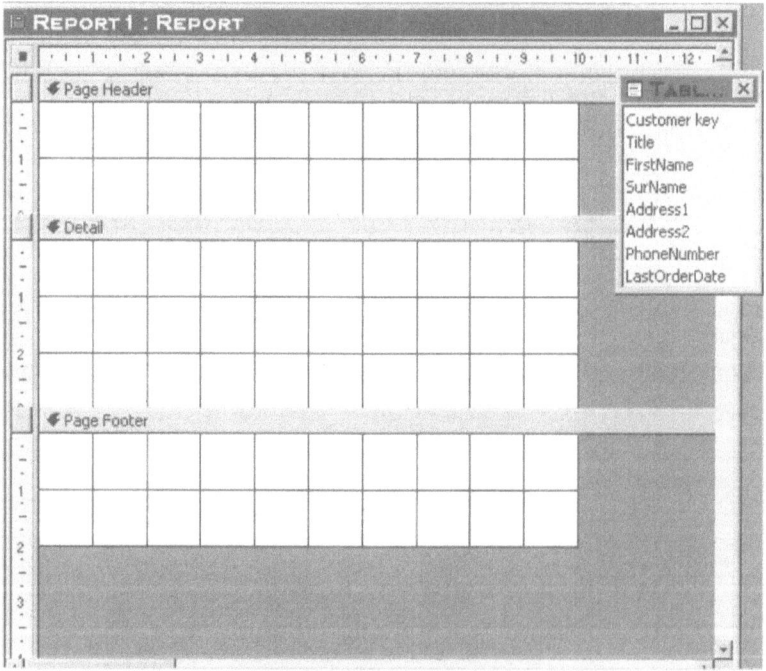

Figure 7.17 *Blank report design and field list window.*

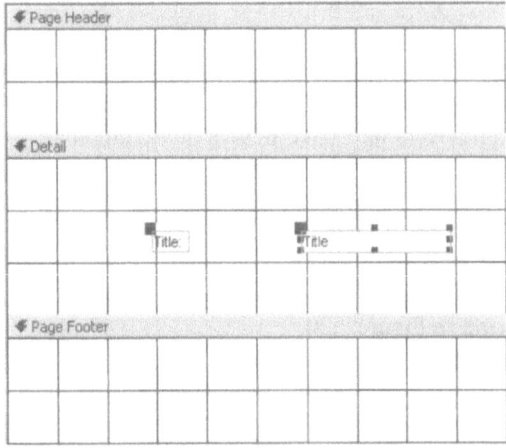

Figure 7.18 Result of dragging field onto report.

Now repeat the process until the layout looks similar to that shown in the example in Figure 7.19. Remember you can move **objects** around the **report** by selecting the outline frame with the mouse.

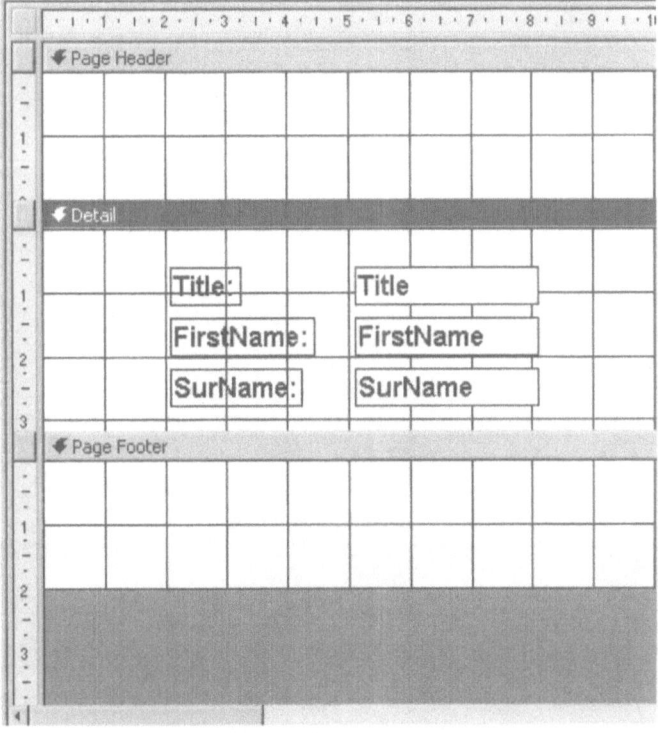

Figure 7.19 Final layout for the report.

If you **preview** the **report** it will look like the example shown in Figure 7.21. The reason for this can be seen in the **Detail block properties**; the **Force New Page property** may be set to **none**. This forces the **report** to print each **detail** entry on the same page until the page is full; only then will a new page be produced. You can set the **detail** block to produce a new page **before** the **detail** starts to print. To view the detail block properties:

- Select the **detail** row heading.
- Select **properties** or right-click the mouse on the **detail** row heading.
- Change the **Force New Page** option to produce a new page **before** the section prints, as shown in Figure 7.20.
- The view after the change can be seen in Figure 7.22.

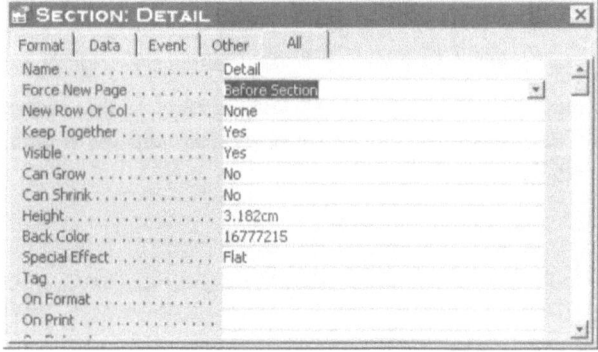

Figure 7.20 *Changing the Force New Page option.*

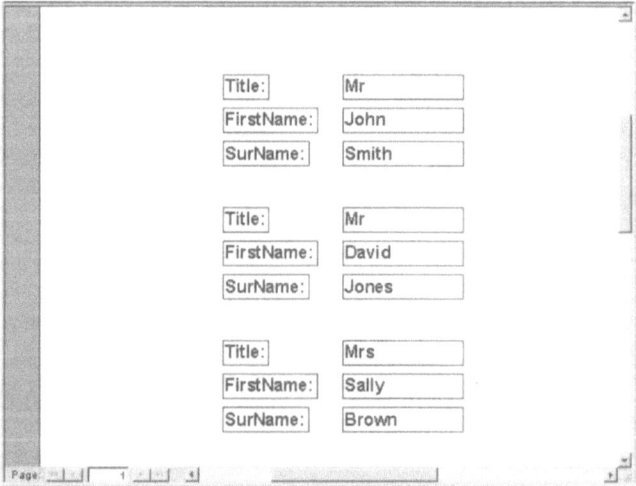

Figure 7.21 *Preview before changing the Force New Page property.*

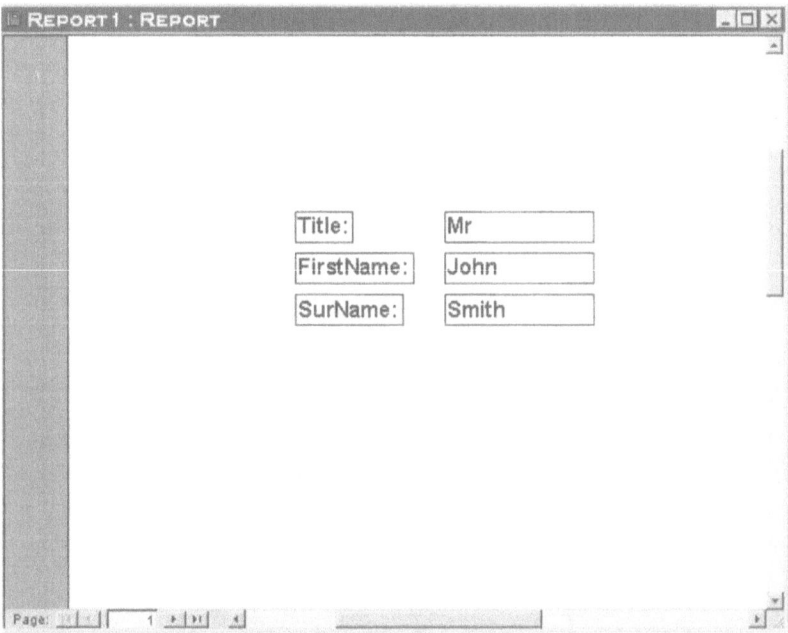

Figure 7.22 *Results of changing the detail Force New Page properties.*

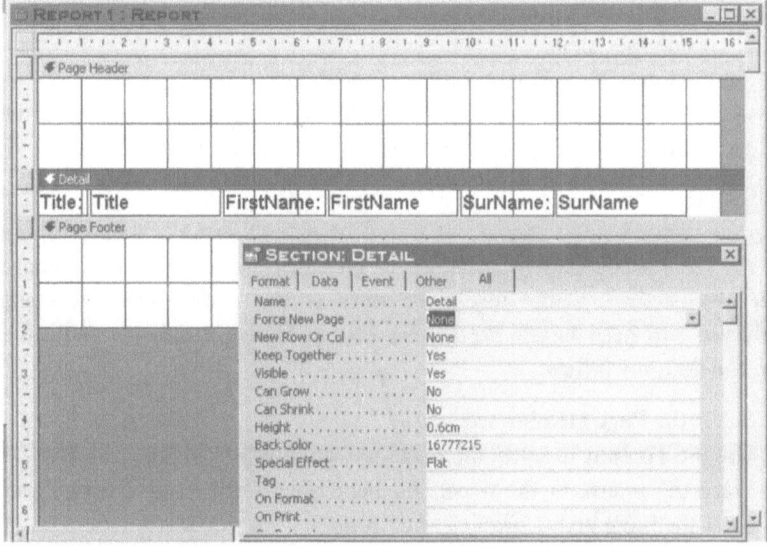

Figure 7.23 *A tabular layout without a Force New Page option.*

You can convert a **column report** to a **tabular** style by moving the fields around within the **detail** section and changing the **Force New Page properties** for the **detail** section again.

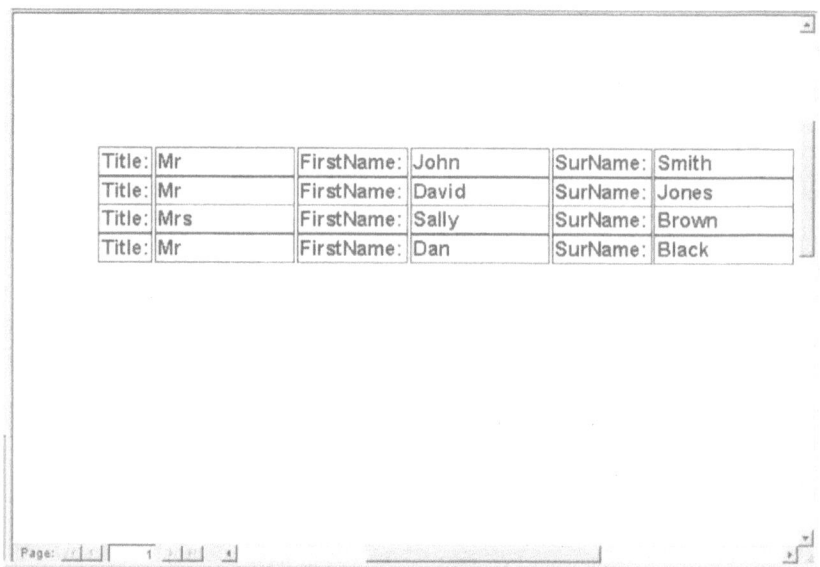

Figure 7.24 Restyled tabular report.

To re-create the example shown in Figure 7.24:

- Move the fields up against the top row of the **detail** section and place them alongside each other.
- Set the **Force New Page** property of the **detail** section to none.
- Decrease the size of the Page Footer by dragging it from the top of the details section to remove any blank or white space between the two sections.

To complete the **report** you need a **report title**, a **page number** and the total **number of pages** for the **report**. It would be nice to **sort** the records by *SurName*, **group** the records together by the town or city they are located in and **count** up the number of customers within any given town or city (*Address2*). To continue the example you will need to add the **report title** and **page numbers**. With the **report** open in the **design window**:

- Select the **Page Header** section.
- Use the **Toolbox** to select the Label tool as shown in Figure 7.25 and 7.26.
- Place the mouse in the upper left hand side of the **Page Header** section and enter the **label** text, *Customers by Location*.
- Select the **label** and increase the font size to 14 points.
- Enlarge the **label** to accommodate the larger size text by double-clicking onto one of the **size handle** boxes. The effects of this can be seen in Figure 7.27.

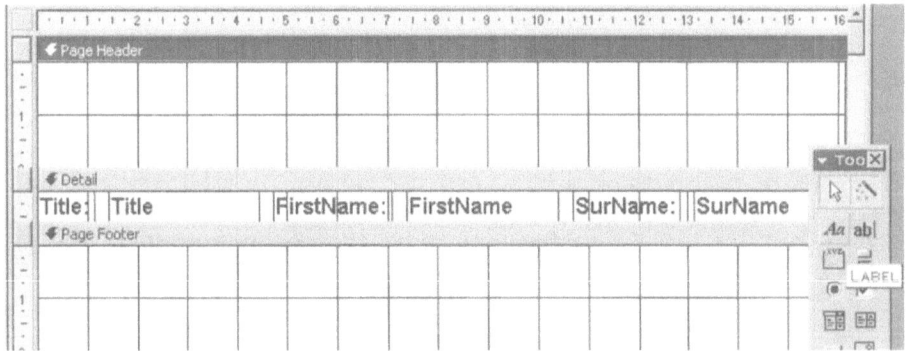

Figure 7.25 *Selecting the page header and the label icon from the toolbox.*

Aa

Figure 7.26 *The label tool.*

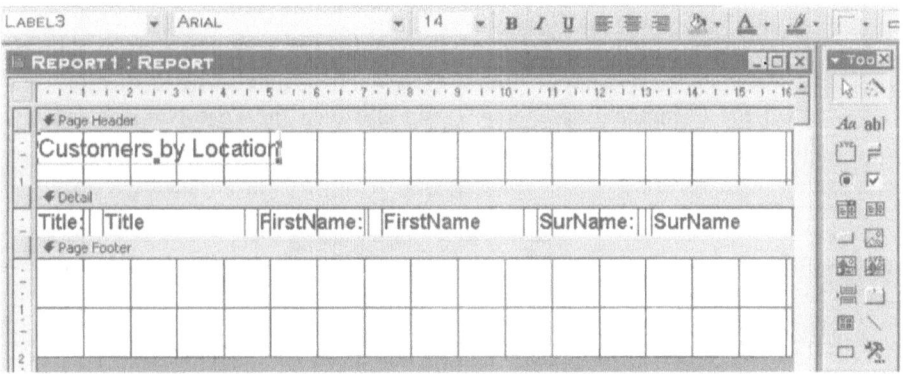

Figure 7.27 *Enlarged label in page header.*

Now you need to add the fields for the **page numbers** at the base of the page, within the **Page Footer** section:

- Select the **Page Footer** section.
- Add an **unbound text box** by using the text box icon from the toolbar as shown in Figure 7.28.
- Place it in the bottom left of the **Page Footer** section.
- When the **text box** has been placed onto the **Page Footer**, alter the **caption property** of the **label** part of the **text box**, as shown in the example in Figure 7.29.
- The **caption** has been changed from *Text4* to *Page* by using the **properties** of the **label**.

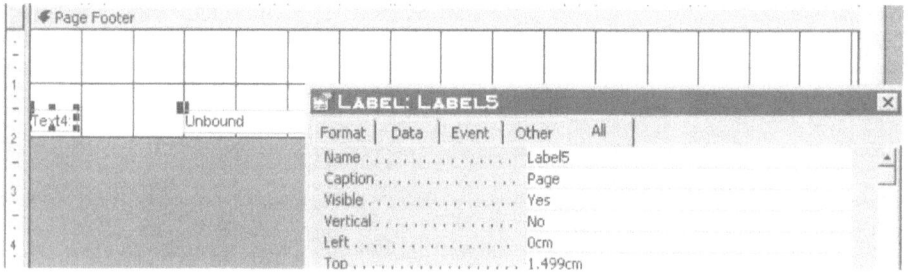

Figure 7.28 *The text box icon.*

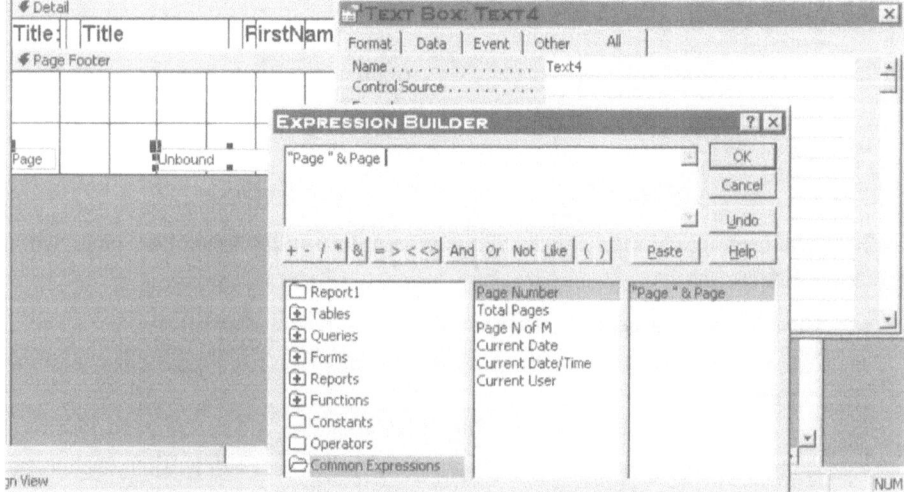

Figure 7.29 *The properties for the label part of the unbound text box.*

The **unbound text box** has no **data source** to display a value from; therefore you need to set a value to display within the **unbound text box**. To do this:

- Select the properties for the unbound text box.
- Set the Control Source property.
- Use the expression builder button to build the page numbering expression.
- Select the Common Expressions group and then the Page Number option as shown in Figure 7.30.

Figure 7.30 *Using the expression builder to produce a page number.*

The **Page Number** expression is available as a pre-built function and consists of the word *Page* and a function called **Page** in the form:

"Page" & Page

The first part of the **function** is not required as you already have the word *Page* displayed on the **report** as the **unbound text box** Label. This has been removed from the **expression builder window** as shown in Figure 7.31. The word *of* and the **function Pages** have been added to the **expression**; this will display the current **page number** followed by the text *of* and then the total **number of pages** for the **report**. This is a long-winded way of producing the **page numbers**, but it does show you how the pre-built **function, Page N of M** is constructed.

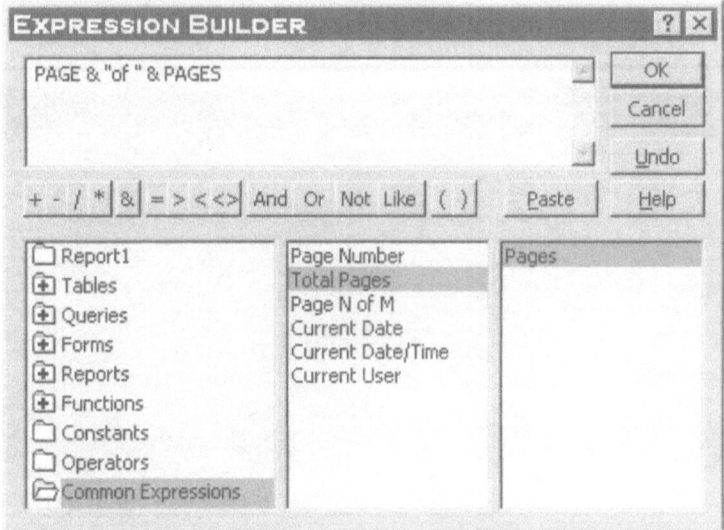

Figure 7.31 *Expression to produce the current and total number of pages.*

In the next example you will add the town or city part of the address from the **table**, then **sort** the records on the report into *SurName* order.

- Use the mouse to right-click on the report.
- Select **Sorting and Grouping** from the shortcut menu as shown in Figure 7.32.

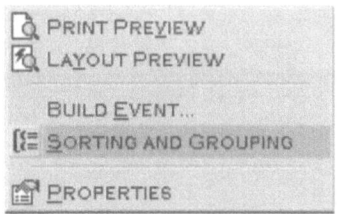

Figure 7.32 *Selecting Sorting and Grouping from the shortcut menu*

You need to **sort** the records by the *SurName* field but **group** them into order using the town or city field; in the example the field that contains the town or city is called *Address2*.

- From the **sorting and grouping** window select the first row and pick the *SurName* field from the pick list.
- Choose ascending for the sort order, as shown in Figure 7.33.

There are two rows in the **sorting and grouping properties window** relating to the **group header** and **footer**; in both cases these options have been set to **No**. This means that the **header** and **footer** will not be displayed on the **report**. The **header** and **footer** are not required if you are only **sorting** records.

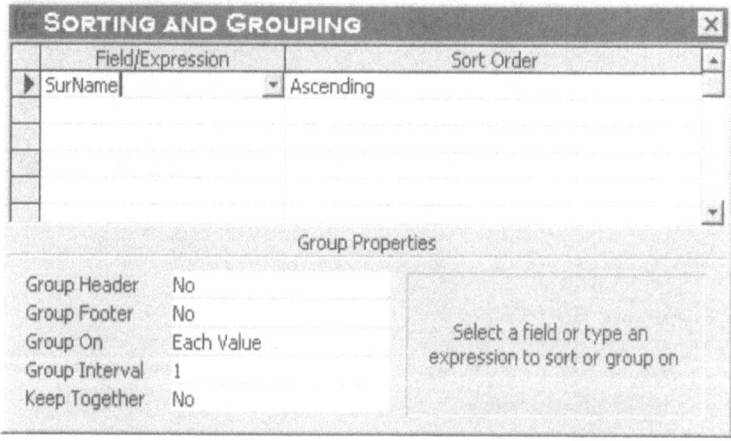

Figure 7.33 Setting a sort field without group headers and footers.

To set the **grouping** for the records:

- Select the second row in the **sorting and grouping** window
- Pick the *Address2* field from the pick list.
- Set the **group header** and **group footer** options to Yes.

The example in Figure 7.34 shows these options after setting the **group header** and **footer** on.

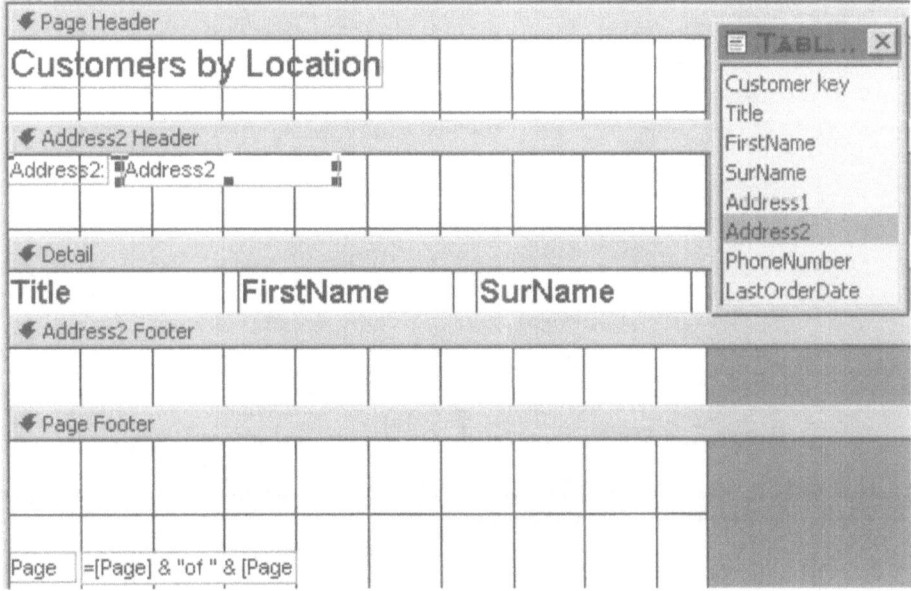

Figure 7.34 Setting the group header and footer properties.

Now you need to add the *Address2* **field** to the **report**; it needs to be placed into the **group header** section of the *Address* group. In addition the **labels** need to bee removed from all the **fields** within the **detail** section. To place the new field on the report:

- Open the field list.
- Drag the field into the group header as shown in Figure 7.35.

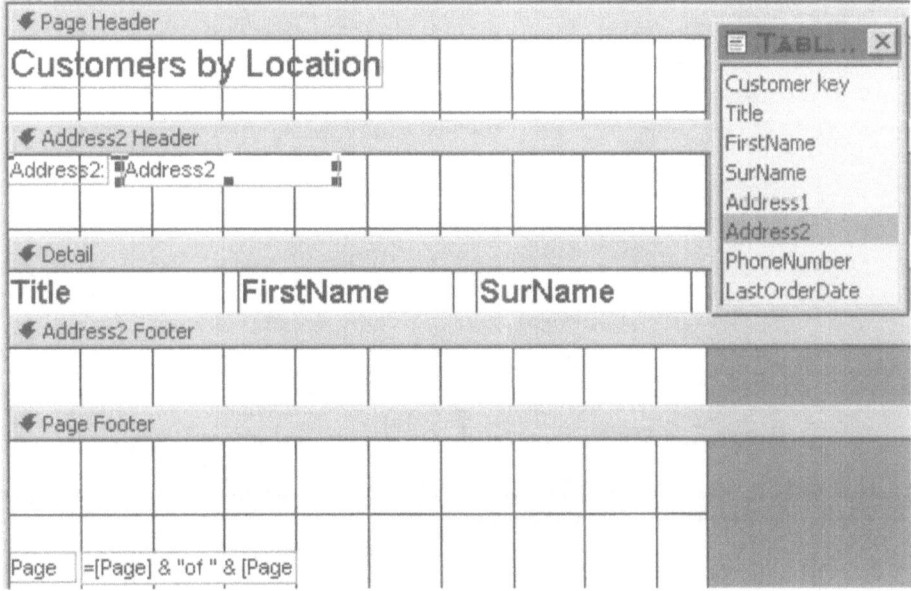

Figure 7.35 Adding the Address2 field using the field list box.

The final stage is to add the **count** for the number of customers in each town; this will be placed into the *Address2* **group footer** section.

- Add an **unbound text** box into the *Address2* **group footer**
- Open the **text box properties**.
- Set the **control source** to:

=Count ([SurName])

This will produce a **count** of all the *SurName* entries for each **group** of records. However, if you **preview** the **report** it may look strange as the **sorting** and **grouping** needs to be adjusted. The **report** may look a little like the one shown in Figure 7.36.

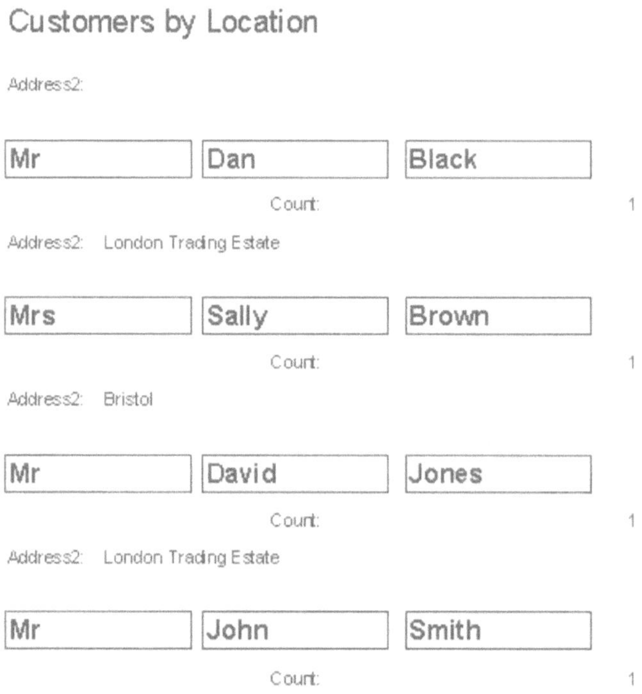

Customers by Location

Address2:

| Mr | Dan | Black |

Count: 1

Address2:   London Trading Estate

| Mrs | Sally | Brown |

Count: 1

Address2:   Bristol

| Mr | David | Jones |

Count: 1

Address2:   London Trading Estate

| Mr | John | Smith |

Count: 1

Figure 7.36 Sample report with incorrect sorting and grouping.

This can be corrected by adjusting the **Sorting** and **grouping properties** in the **report** design. To do this you will need to:

- Open the **sorting and grouping** window.
- Select the whole of the *Address2* row as shown in Figure 7.37.
- Drag the *Address2* row up onto the first row, using the mouse. The order will appear as shown in Figure 7.38.

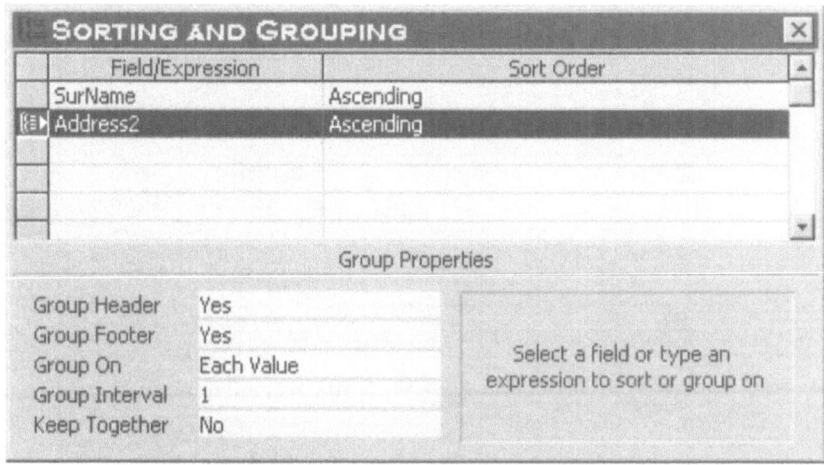

Figure 7.37 *Selecting a row within sorting and grouping window.*

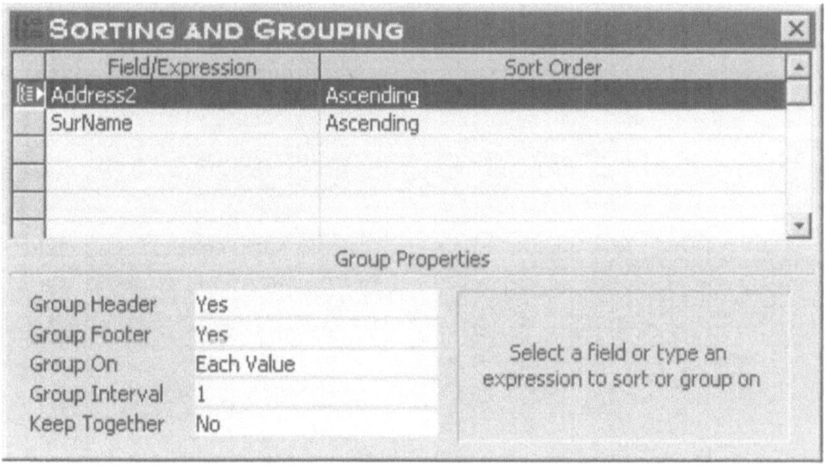

Figure 7.38 *Results after dragging Address2 field onto the first row.*

Having adjusted the **sorting** and **grouping** properties the **print preview** will look similar to the example shown in Figure 7.39.

Customers by Location

Address2:

Mr	Dan	Black

                     Count: 1

Address2:   Bristol

Mr	David	Jones

                     Count: 1

Address2:   London Trading Estate

Mrs	Sally	Brown
Mr	John	Smith

                     Count: 2

Figure 7.39 *Preview report with corrected sorting and grouping options.*

8
SQL

Introduction

Behind every **query** you create is an **SQL** statement. **SQL**, or Structured Query Language, is designed to help deal with **table** manipulation. Although it is designed to conform to a standard there are always deviations to any standard; however, most dialects will contain many familiar keywords.

Using SQL

If you re examine the **query** you created earlier - *(Query1)* in design mode, you can view the **SQL** statements that were created by Access when you saved the **query**. To do this use the **VIew I SQL VIEW** menu.

The **SQL** statement can be broken down into sections.

> **PARAMETERS** *title Text (255);*
> **SELECT** *Table1.Title, Table1.SurName*
> **FROM** *Table1*
> **ORDER BY** *Table1.LastOrderDate;*

The **Parameters** keyword defines the **parameter** value, its **name** and **type**. In this case the name is *Title*; it is of a *text* **data type** and has a maximum **size** of 255 characters. The **Select** statement is used to identify the **fields** to be selected while the **From** statement identifies the **table source**. Finally the **Order By** statement defines the **sort** order.

There are many who advocate the use of **SQL** and the real advantage is that it can be transported to a certain degree from product to product. Many database management systems now employ **SQL** statements.

As far as Access is concerned you can use an **SQL** statement as a **record source** for a **form**, **report** or **field**. This means you do not have to create and save a **query** each time within the database.

Key SQL statements

In this section you will examine some of the key **SQL** statements.

Select
The **Select** statement is used to **select fields** from a given **table**, for example:

> *SELECT SurName, FirstName, Address1*

This will **select** only the three named **fields;** *SurName, FirstName* and *Address1*. There is a variation on this, and that is to use a **SELECT DISTINCT** statement. The **Select** statement does what its name implies: it selects **fields**. It selects all the records for those **fields**, so if there are **duplicates** it will show them. However, if you use the **DISTINCT** keyword then **duplicate** records will be eliminated.

> *SELECT DISTINCT SurName, FirstName, Address1*

This example selects the same three **fields** but this time it eliminates **duplicates**.

From
Once you have selected your **fields** you need to define which **table** these come from. This is when you use the **FROM** keyword. So, to complete the previous example:

> *SELECT DISTINCT SurName, FirstName, Address1*
> *FROM Table1;*

Notice that the completed **SQL** statement ends with a semicolon.

Where
To select a specific **group** of records you specify the **criteria** in the **query** design. The **Where** keyword allows you to define the selection; for example, your **criteria** may select all the entries from the *Title* **field** that contain the text *Mr* within *Table1*. So your **SQL** statement may look something like this:

> *SELECT SurName, FirstName, Address1*
> *FROM Table1*
> *WHERE Title = "Mr";*

Order by

The **ORDER BY** keyword allows you to **sort** the results into **ascending** or **descending** order. If you follow on from the last example, then to **sort** the selected records into *Title* and then *SurName* **order**:

> **SELECT** *SurName, FirstName, Address1*
> **FROM** *Table1*
> **WHERE** *Title = "Mr"*
> **ORDER BY** *Title, SurName;*

The default **order** is to **sort** into **ascending order**; to define **ascending** or **descending** you need to use the **ASC** or **DESC** keywords. In the next example the *Title* **field** is **sorted** into **ascending order** and the *SurName* **field** into **descending order**.

> **SELECT** *SurName, FirstName, Address1*
> **FROM** *Table1*
> **WHERE** *Title = "Mr"*
> **ORDER BY** *Title ASC, SurName DESC;*

As

To rename a column in a **query** you used a **label** with a colon suffix in the form:

> *Label text: [FieldName].*

The **SQL** equivalent of this is to use the **AS** keyword. Say you want to rename the *SurName* field to *LastName*. If you reuse the previous example again it should look like this:

> **SELECT** *SurName AS LastName, FirstName, Address1*
> **FROM** *Table1*
> **WHERE** *Title = "Mr"*
> **ORDER** *BY Title ASC, SurName DESC;*

Built-in functions

There are a number of built-in **functions** you can use within a **query** or your **SQL** statement; you used some of these earlier.

- SUM   produce a total
- COUNT   count the number of occurrences
- AVG   average
- MIN   maximum
- MAX   minimum

To produce a **count** of the number of *SurName* entries on *Table1*, the **SQL** statement would look like this:

> **SELECT COUNT***(SurName)*

***FROM** Table1;*

Adding SQL to Access objects

You can use an **SQL** statement instead of a **table** or **query** as the **record source (data source)** for a **form** or **report**. To demonstrate this look at the **select query** created earlier, *Query1*.

Add the **fields** to the query so they match the data on the **form** called *Form 1*.

- Open the **query** in **design view** and add the **fields** as shown in Figure 8.1.
- While in **design view** use the **View | SQL View** menu to select the **SQL** option.
- Highlight the **SQL** statements and **Copy** them using the **Edit | Copy** menu; see Figure 8.2.

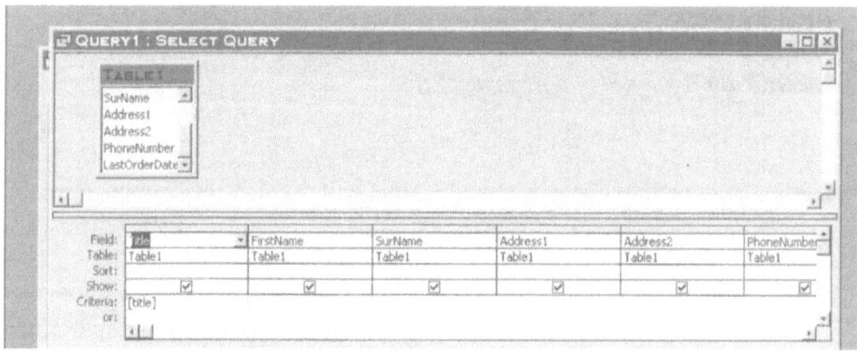

***Figure 8.1** Reworked Query1 example with new fields.*

```
QUERY1 : SELECT QUERY
PARAMETERS title Text ( 255 );
SELECT Table1.Title, Table1.FirstName, Table1.SurName, Table1.Address1, Table1.Address2, Table1.PhoneNumber, Table1.LastOrderDate
FROM Table1
WHERE (((Table1.Title)=[title]));
```

***Figure 8.2** Viewing the SQL statements of a query.*

Close the **query** and **save** the changes. Return to the **design** of *Form1*; you will use the **form properties** to change the **record source** from *Table1* to the **SQL** statement. To do this:

- **View** the **form's record source properties**.
- **Delete** the name of the table *Table1*.
- **Paste** in the **SQL** statement you copied earlier.

When you open the **form** the **parameter** box you set up to **filter** the selection by *Title* is displayed; see Figure 8.3. Fill in the *Title* you require, e.g. *Mr*, and the **form** will display only those records that match.

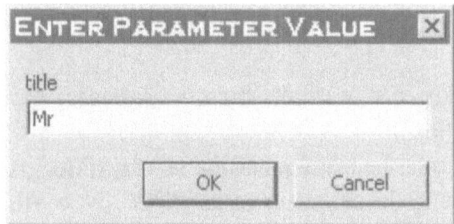

Figure 8.3 *Entering the required title.*

SQL specific queries

There are special types of **SQL queries** available within Access; these are known as **SQL SPECIFIC queries**. These are designed in a different way to those you have created so far by using the **query** by design tool. There are four forms of **SQL Specific queries** available and these are:

- Union query
- Pass-through query
- Data-definition query
- Subquery

Union queries

This **query** combines **fields** from one or more **tables** into one output **field**. For example, if you want to combine the address lines from the customer table *Table1* into one single output column, then you could create a union query to combine the two address **fields**.

Pass-through query

This type of query sends commands directly to **ODBC** databases, for example Microsoft FoxPro, using commands that are acceptable to the server. For example, you can use a **pass-through query** to retrieve or change records on the server. For the exact nature of the structure and syntax of a **pass-through query**, you need to refer to the documentation for the **SQL** database server to which you're sending the query. **ODBC,** or Open Database Connectivity, is a standard used for connecting and accessing data within an **SQL** server database; such as a Microsoft **SQL** server.

Data-definition query

This type of **query** can be used to create and modify **table structures**, or to create **indexes** in a database such as Microsoft Access or Microsoft FoxPro.

Subquery

This type of **query** consists of an **SQL SELECT** statement inside a **select** or **action query**. You can enter a **Select** statement in the **field row** of your **query** design to define a new **field**, or in the **Criteria row** to define your selection **criteria**. You can use **sub queries** to:

- Test for the existence of results from the **subquery** (use the **EXISTS** or **NOT EXISTS functions**).
- **Find** any values in the main **query** that are **equal to, greater than**, or **less than** values returned by the **subquery** (using **ANY, IN**, or **ALL functions**).
- Create subqueries within sub queries (nested subqueries).

Creating a table using a data-definition query

In the following example a **data-definition query** uses the **CREATE TABLE** statement to create a **table** named *People*. The **name** and **data type** for each **field** is defined along with the *PersonalID* **field:** an **index** that marks it as the **primary key**.

CREATE TABLE People
*([PersonalID] **integer**,*
*[LastName] **text**,*
*[FirstName] **text**,*
*[Birthdate] **date**,*
*[Phone] **text**,*
*[Notes] **memo**,*

*CONSTRAINT [Index1] **PRIMARY KEY** ([PersonalID]));*

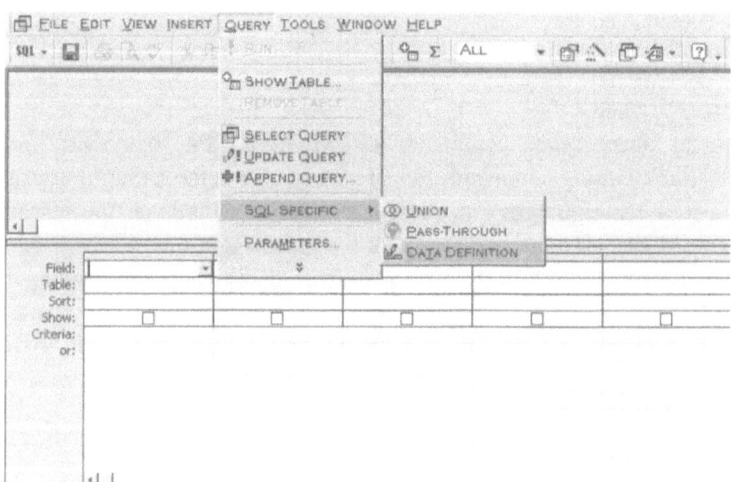

Figure 8.4 Creating an SQL specific data-definition query.

To re-create the example shown you will need to:

- Create a **new query** and then select **design view**.
- When the **add table window** appears, **close** it without adding any **tables**.
- Use the **Query** menu and select **SQL Specific.**
- Select Data Definition as shown in Figure 8.4.

When you have completed this step you will need to add the **SQL** statements as shown in example you have just used.

> **CREATE TABLE** *People*
> *([PersonalID]* **integer**,
> *[LastName]* **text**,
> *[FirstName]* **text**,
> *[Birthdate]* **date**,
> *[Phone]* **text**,
> *[Notes]* **memo**,
> **CONSTRAINT** *[Index1]* **PRIMARY KEY** *([PersonalID]));*

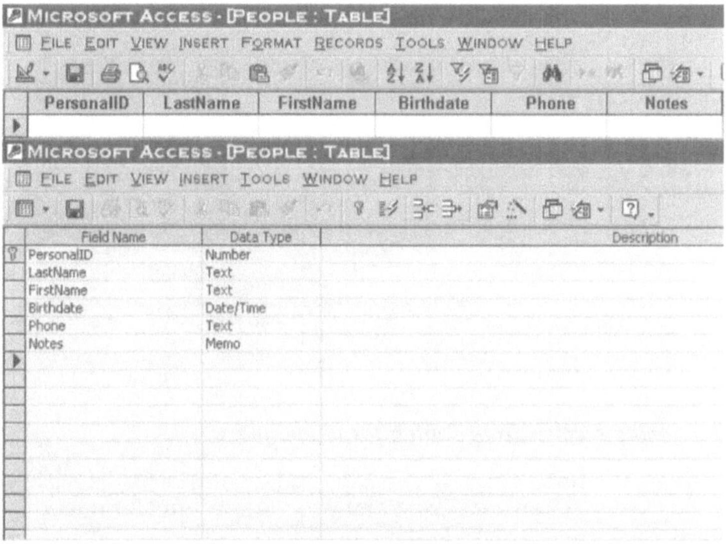

Figure 8.5 The data structure for the table created with a data-definition query.

When you run the **query** you will have created a new **table** called *People;* this will be added to the **table objects** within your database. The resulting **table** and its **structure** are shown in Figure 8.5.

Creating a union query

You can merge the results of two or more **queries, tables**, or **SELECT** statements, in any combination, in a single **UNION** operation. The following example merges the names and personnel numbers from two tables of personnel for two geographical regions. Using a UNION SELECT statement merges the *SurName, PersNum* fields from a table named TableA and the SurName, PersNum fields from TableB:

> **SELECT** *TableA .SurName, TableB.PersNum*
> **FROM** *TableA*
> **UNION SELECT** *TableB.SurName, TableB.PersNum*
> **FROM** *TableB*

By default, no **duplicate** records are returned when you use a **UNION** operation. All **queries** in a **UNION** operation must request the same number of **fields**, but the **fields** do not have to be of the same **size** or **data type**. However, you would not normally merge the results of two different field types when using a **UNION** query; for example, there would be little reason to combine a **Logical** field (Yes/No) with an Address field. The results of the **union query** used in the example are shown in Figure 8.6. The input tables *TableA* and *TableB* are shown in table 8.1 and 8.2.

Table 8.1 Example records from TableA for union query.

Title	FirstName	SurName	Address2	PersNum
Mr	John	Smith	South East	9876
Mr	David	Jones	South East	9843
Mrs	Sally	Brown	South East	9812
Mr	Dan	Black	South East	9823

Table 8.2 Example records from TableB for union query.

Title	FirstName	SurName	Address2	PersNum
Mr	Brian	Adams	North	1243
Mr	John	Smith	North	1223
Mrs	Ann	Jones	North	1267
Mr	David	Johnstone	North	1523

Figure 8.6 *The result of a union select query.*

Creating a subquery

In the next example an **SQL** statement is used to define the selection **criteria** for the *Total value* **field** within a **select query**, selecting records from the *Orderstable*. Only total order values that are greater than the **average** order value are selected. The **query** has been designed from the *Orderstable*; six **fields** have been added to the **design grid** and the *total value* **field** has been used to specify the selection **criteria**. The selection **criteria** is an **SQL** select statement that generates the **average** *total value* from the *Orderstable*. The whole of the **SQL** statement is enclosed within brackets, with the exception of the **>** (**greater than**) **operator**. This is used to specify that the **total value field** must be **greater than** the **average** value. The **query** design is shown in Figure 8.7 while the **SQL** statements used as the selection criteria (the **subquery**) are shown below. The resulting output is shown in Figure 8.8.

>*(SELECT AVG([Total value]) FROM [Orderstable])*

Order Number
date
qty
cost each
Total value
Field:
Table:
Sort:
Show:
Criteria:
or:
CustomerKey
OrdersTable
Order Number
OrdersTable
date
OrdersTable
qty
OrdersTable
cost each
OrdersTable
Total value
OrdersTable
>(SELECT AVG([Total value]) FROM [orderstable])

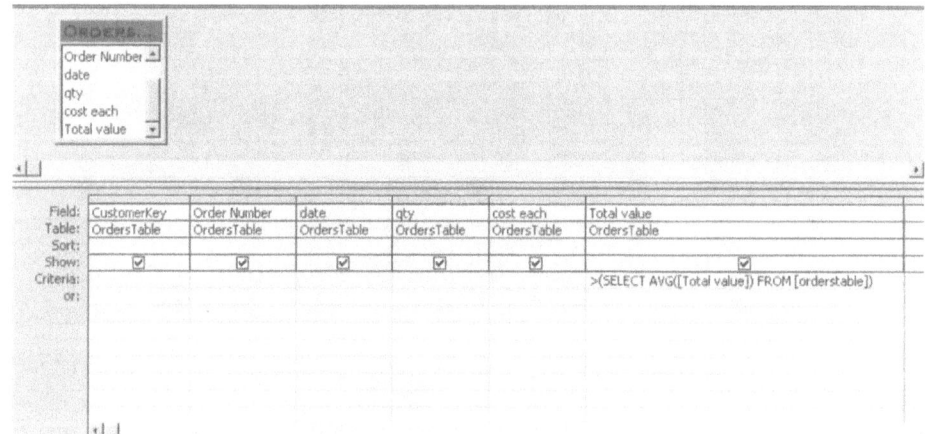

Figure 8.7 The subquery design.

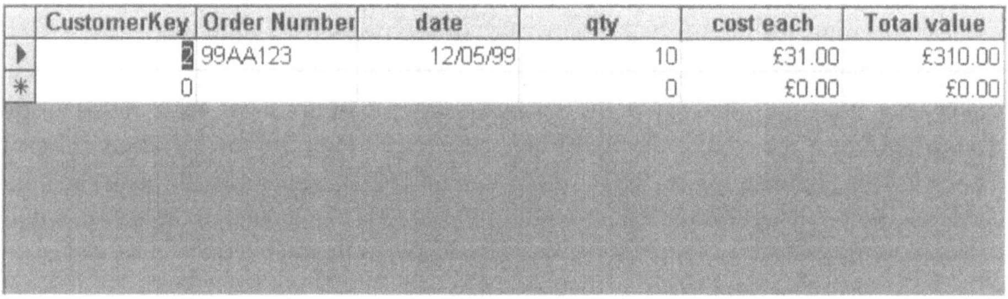

CustomerKey
Order Number
date
qty
cost each
Total value
2
99AA123
12/05/99
10
£31.00
£310.00
0
0
£0.00
£0.00

Figure 8.8 The output from a subquery.

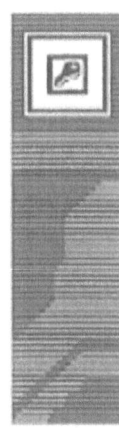

9
Using Multiple Tables

Introduction

You saw earlier, in the example shown in Tables 3.6 to 3.9 in Chapter 3, how you can use several tables to remove duplication within a database. In this chapter you will use a simplified form of these tables to examine how multiple tables can be used within your database. In the *Customer* **table** example, you can see that problems begin to occur when you add two or more **tables**. For example, if you wanted to identify which orders belonged to a specific customer, you might create a second **table** holding all the order details. The problem is how to identify which orders belong to a specific customer; you could try using the customer's company but there may well be several customers with similar if not the same company name. To overcome the problem you need to add a **key** or **unique field** to the *Customers* **table**, this could be used on the separate **table** containing the order details.

This is known as creating a relationship between tables; Access allows you to connect several sets of data to each other by using a key **field**. For example, the table examples in Chapter 3, Tables 3.6 to 3.9, were used to show how a simple customer ordering database could be designed to hold details relating to the customer's company, orders and goods descriptions. This information may be contained in several **tables**; for example, customer, orders, order details and product descriptions. There may be more than one **field** used to link the **tables** to each other. A customer number or code may link orders to customers. The orders may be linked to the order details and the order details may be linked to the product descriptions as shown in Figure 9.1. In the example there is a **one-to-many relationship** between the customer information and the customer orders; this means there may be many orders relating to a single customer. There is a **primary key field** on the *customer* **table** called *Cust ID*; this key will not allow any duplicate values to be entered in this field on the **table**. This is related to the *orders* table which contains a **foreign key** which is also called *Cust ID;* a **foreign key** will allow duplicate values in the **field** on the **table.**

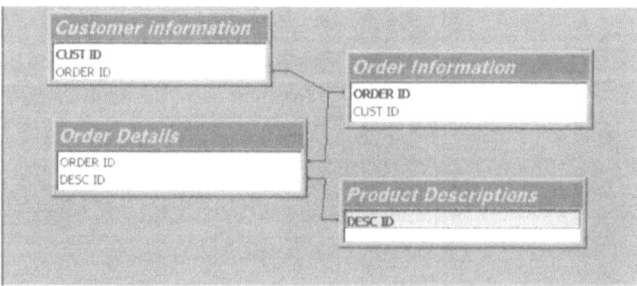

Figure 9.1 An example of how a customer table may link to other tables.

Creating relationships

The main advantage of creating a relationship between tables is that once created you can quickly collect sets of related data from separate tables and ensure that the data remains synchronized at all times; in other words, if you change something in one table it will reflect this change throughout the related tables.

To create a relationship between tables:

- Open the database window.
- Use the **Tools | Relationships** menu to open the relationships window, as shown in Figure 9.2.

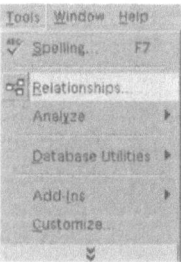

Figure 9.2 Showing tables using the relationships menu.

- Add the tables you want to link together to the view window as shown in Figure 9.3.

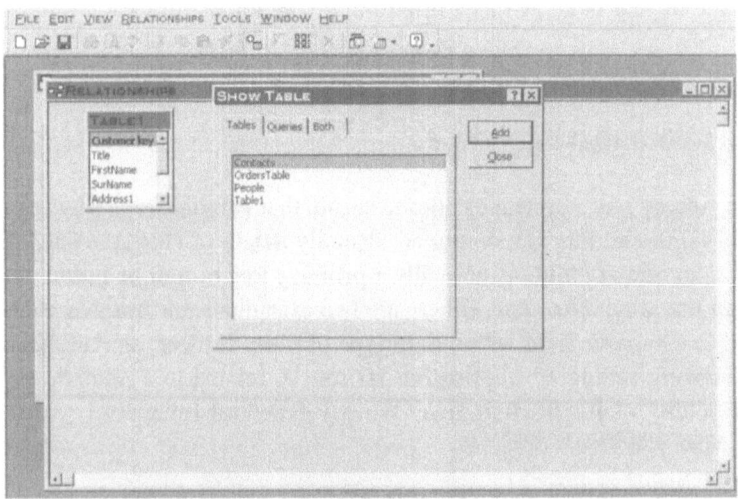

Figure 9.3 *Adding tables to the relationships window.*

- Drag the linking **field** from one **table** onto the matching **field** in the second **table**.
- In the example shown in Figure 9.4 the Customer key in *Table1* is linked with the CustomerKey in the *Orderstable*.

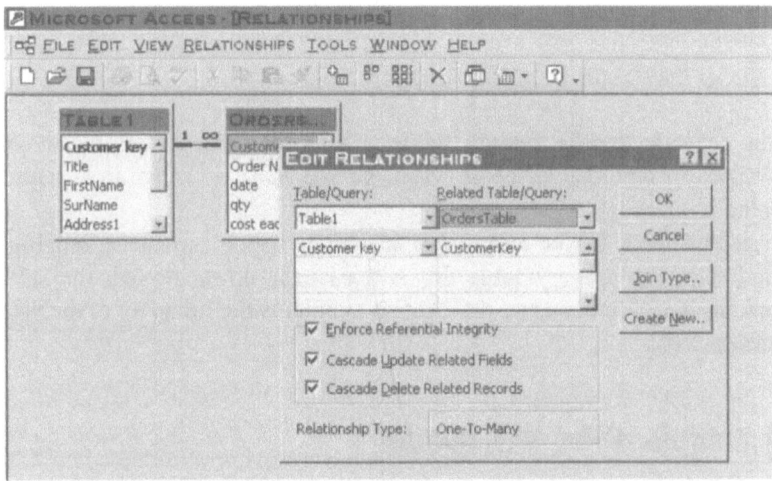

Figure 9.4 *Creating a relationship between two tables.*

- When the **edit relationships window** is displayed, which allows you to confirm how the **tables** are linked, select the **Enforce Referential Integrity check box** as shown in Figure 9.4.
- When complete select the **OK** button.

This type of join is known as a **one-to-many relationship** (one customer to many orders).

What is referential integrity?

Microsoft Access uses a system of rules to ensure that **relationships** between records in **tables** are valid, and that you do not accidentally **delete** or change related **data**. The **field** from the primary **table** is normally a **primary key** or **unique index**. The related **fields** have the same **data type.** (There are two exceptions: an **AutoNumber field** can be related to a numeric **field** with a **data type** of **Long Integer**, an **AutoNumber field** with a **property** setting of **Replication ID** can be related to a numeric **field** with a **property** setting of **Replication ID.**) When **referential integrity** is enforced, there are some rules you should observe:

- You cannot enter a value in a **key field** of a related **table** if it does not exist in the **primary key** field of the primary **table.**
- You cannot **delete** a record from a **primary table** if matching records exist in a related **table**.
- You cannot change a **primary key** value in the primary **table**, if that record has related records.

If **referential integrity** is enforced and you break a rule, Microsoft Access will display an error message and will not allow the change.

What does cascade related mean?

Using the **cascade update related fields** option will force Access to automatically **update** values in any related **tables** whenever you make a change to a **primary key** value in the primary **table**.

The same principle is true for the **cascade delete** option - whenever a **primary key** is **deleted** from the primary **table** this will **cascade** down through the sub **tables**. These options help you to ensure that Access maintains the **integrity** of the data where **relationships** exist.

Using multiple tables with queries

Before you can look further at the use of multiple **tables** it would be useful to create a second **table** to use with the customer contacts **table**:

- Select tables object tab from the database window.
- Choose the create table in design view option.
- Fill in the table design as shown in Figure 9.5. Note that the last two numeric fields are decimal with a currency format.

- **Save** the **table** giving it the name *OrdersTable*. When asked if you want to set up a **primary key** select the **No** option.

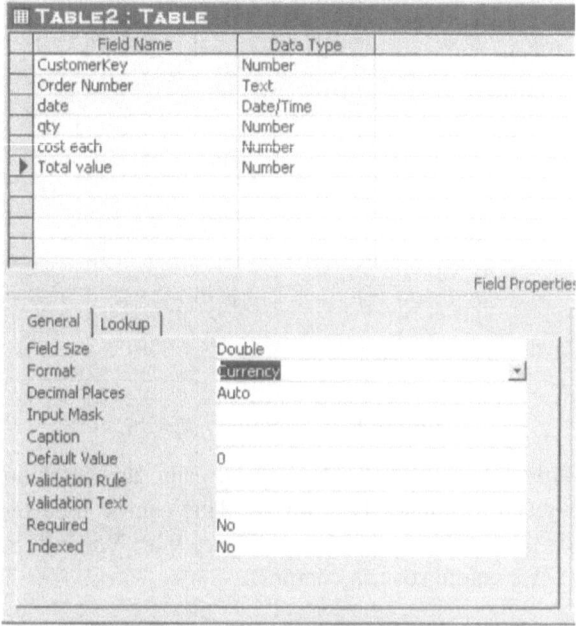

Figure 9.5 The design for OrdersTable.

You will need to modify the customer contacts table created earlier, *Table1*.

- Return to the **database window**.
- Select the **tables object tab**.
- Use the Design button to redesign this table.
- Using the **Insert | Rows** menu add a **new row** and fill in the details for the new **key field** as shown in Figure 9.7.
- This is to be the **key** or unique **field** so set its type to **AutoNumber;**, this way each entry will be assigned a unique number by Access.
- When you have created the new **field** set it as the **primary key** by selecting the **field row** and then using the **Primary Key** button on the **toolbar**, as shown in Figure 9.6.
- **Close** the table design saving it as *Table1*.

Figure 9.6 The Primary Key button.

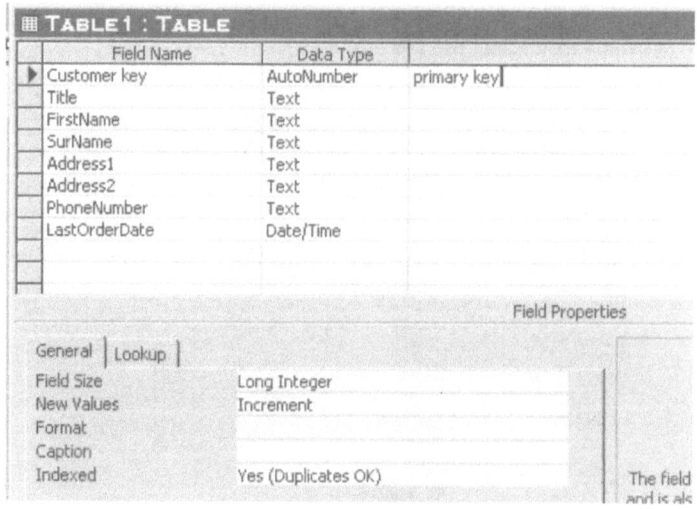

Figure 9.7 *Adding a new row.*

If you **open** *Table1* you can see the effect of using an **AutoNumber** field. Each record has been given a unique **ID** number. This can be used by Access to locate related records on other **tables** as shown in Figure 9.8. You will need to enter some data into *OrdersTable* before you can continue.

Customer key	Title	FirstName	SurName	Addre
1 Mr	John	Smith	Unit 24	
2 Mr	David	Jones	12 High S	
3 Mrs	Sally	Brown	Unit 1	
(AutoNumber)				

TABLE1 : TABLE

Figure 9.8 *Data with an AutoNumber field.*

Open *OrdersTable*. Enter the new records as shown in Figure 9.9. Notice that there are no entries for the last customer, customer **key** number 3.

ORDERSTABLE : TABLE

CustomerKey	Order Number	date	qty	cost each	Total value
1	12345GG	12/10/00	100	£1.00	£0.00
1	12333GK	01/10/99	100	£1.00	£0.00
2	99AA123	12/05/99	10	£31.00	£0.00
	0		0	£0.00	£0.00

Figure 9.9 *Entering new records for customer numbers 1 and 2.*

Now you have some data you can look at how this can be used with an Access **query**. To demonstrate this you will need to create a new **query** and join the orders in the *OrdersTable* to the customers in *Table1*. You can achieve this by creating a **join** within a **query** rather than setting up a **relationship**. This can be useful when you are trying to **join** several **tables** together to provide a quick listing. To create the multi-table query:

- Select the query object tab from the database window.
- Create a new **query** using the **design view** option.
- Add both *OrdersTable* and *Table1* to the **query** using the **Query | Show Table** menu as shown in Figures 9.10 and 9.11.

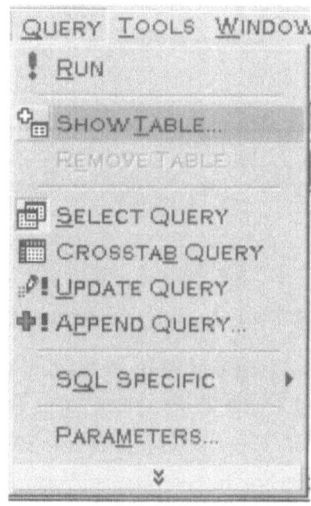

Figure 9.10 *Using the Show Table menu to add tables.*

Figure 9.11 *Both tables within the query design.*

To create the **join** between the two **tables** within the **query**:

- Highlight the *Customer key* **field** on *Table1*.

- Use the mouse to drag this onto the *CustomerKey* **field** on *OrdersTable*. When complete a **join** line will appear between the two **tables** as shown in Figure 9.12.

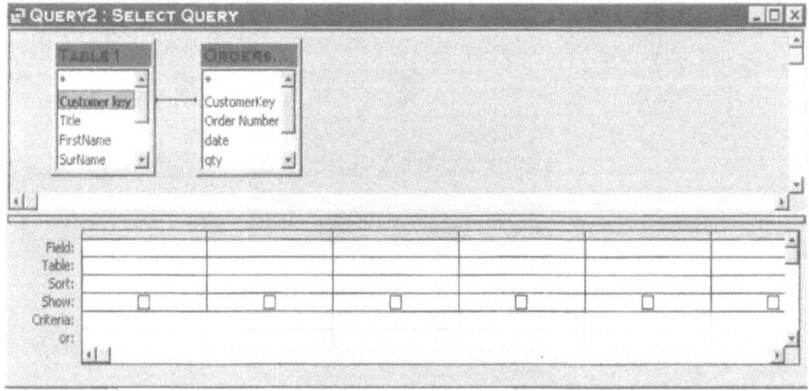

Figure 9.12 *A one-to-one join between two tables.*

To demonstrate how a basic **join** can help to display matching records from two or more **tables,** add the following **fields** to the query from *Table1*:

- *Customer key*
- *Title*
- *SurName*
- *Address1*

Now add the following **fields** from *OrdersTable*:

- *CustomerKey*
- *Order Number*

Having added the **fields** the **query** design will look like the one shown in Figure 9.13.

The resulting output will show only the records that match on both **tables,** in other words where the *Customer key* value in *Table1* is equal to the *CustomerKey* value in the *OrdersTable* table. This can be seen in Figure 9.14. You will notice that there is no entry for the customer with a *Customer key* value of 3 from *Table1*. The reason being there was no matching order on *OrdersTable* with a *Customerkey* value of 3.

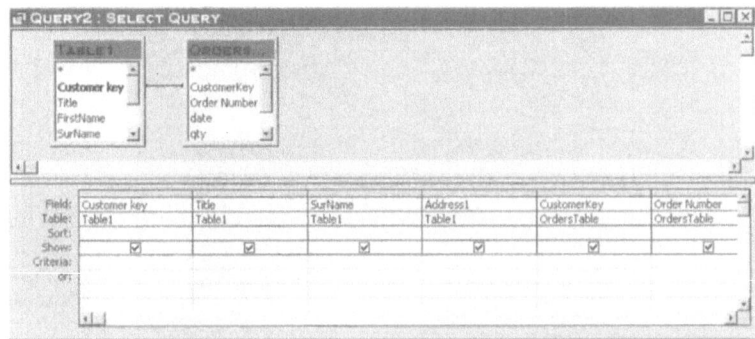

Figure 9.13 *Query design after adding fields from both tables.*

Customer key	Title	SurName	Address1	CustomerKey	Order Number
▶	1 Mr	Smith	Unit 24	1	12345GG
	1 Mr	Smith	Unit 24	1	12333GK
	2 Mr	Jones	12 High Street	2	99AA123
*	(AutoNumber)				

QUERY2 : SELECT QUERY

Figure 9.14 *The output from the joined table query.*

The default for a query **join** is to provide only the records where the **join fields** are equal in both **tables**; there are other ways of expressing the **joins** in a **query**. If you return to the design of the **query** you will be able to change the **join** type and then view the results again. To view or change the **join properties** do one of the following:

- Use the **View | Join Properties** menu.
- Right-click the mouse on the **join** line in the **query** design and select **Join Properties**.
- Double-click the mouse on the **join** line to view the **join properties**.

The **join properties** for the **query** used in the above example are shown in Figure 9.15. The name of each **table** used is shown along with the names of the **joined fields**. There are three options available-these allow you to select how the records are to be joined and displayed. In the example shown in Figure 9.15 the default is to show only the records that match on both tables. If you want to show all the customer details from *Table1* and any matching orders from the *OrdersTable*. The join would be changed to include ALL records from Table 1 and only those records from *OrdersTable* where the joined fields are equal.

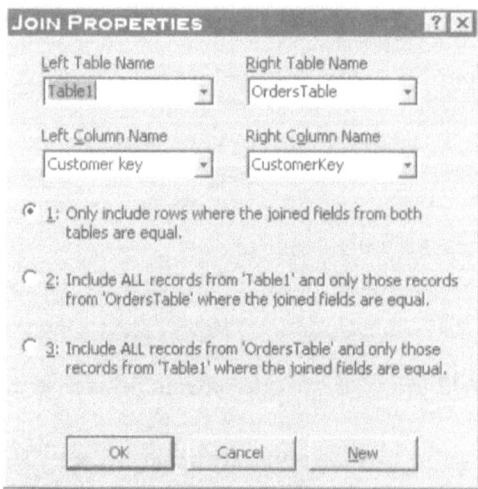

Figure 9.15 *Changing the join properties.*

Try changing the **join properties** in the last **query** to include all records from
Table1 and then **run** the **query** again and compare the results to those from the last
example. The new results are shown in Figure 9.16. This time the customer details
for *Customer key* value 3 are shown along with blank entries from *OrdersTable*, to
show that there are no order values on this **table**. When you have finished viewing the
results **save** the **query** and leave the name as *Query2*.

Customer key	Title	SurName	Address1	CustomerKey	Order Number
1 Mr	Smith	Unit 24	1	12345GG
1 Mr	Smith	Unit 24	1	12333GK
2 Mr	Jones	12 High Street	2	99AA123
3 Mrs	Brown	Unit 1		
(AutoNumber)				

QUERY2 : SELECT QUERY

Figure 9.16 *The results of changing the join properties.*

Using multiple tables with forms and subforms

There are times when you need to view the information from more than one **table** on a
single **form.** To do this either:

- Create a **query** to **join** the **tables** and then create a **form** based upon this **query**.
- Create two separate **forms** and embed one **form** into the other creating a
  master/child link between the two, having created a **relationship** for the two
  tables beforehand.

The later method is referred to as **main form/subform**. This is the method used in the next example. There are two steps to complete:

- Creating the **main form** from the first **table**
- Then creating the subform from the second table.

You will create the **main form** from *Table1* and the **subform** from the O*rdersTable*.

- Start by returning to the forms object tab in the database window.
- Create a new **form** using design view and base it on *Table1* layout as shown in Figure 9.17. Do not forget to add a button to **close** the **form**, as this is always a good idea.
- Now **minimize** the **form** as shown in Figure 9.18. Next create a new **form** based upon *OrdersTable*. Use the layout shown in Figure 9.19.

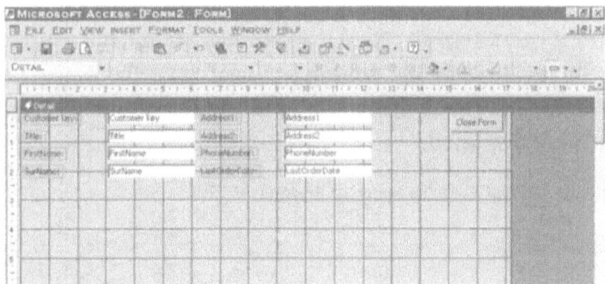

Figure 9.17 *The layout of the main form from Table1.*

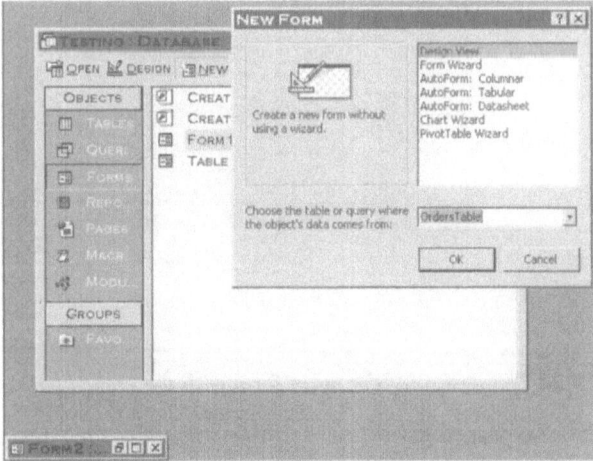

Figure 9.18 *The minimized main form and the new form window for the subform.*

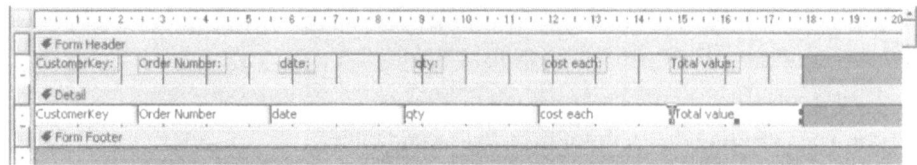

Figure 9.19 *The layout for a subform based on OrdersTable.*

You will notice that in the example the **labels** for the **fields** have been placed into the **form header**, if you cannot see the **form header;** use the **view** menu to display it.

When you have completed the design for your **subform, save** it using the default name of *Form3.* Having completed both forms, all that remains is to embed the **subform,** *Form3,* into the main form, *Form2,* and then set the **subform properties** for the **master/child links**.

- **Restore** the design of the **main form** *Form2* onto the screen but do not **maximize** it - you need to resize it so you can see the **database window** as well.
- Use the mouse to drag the **subform** *Form3* onto the **detail area** of the **main form,** *Form2*, and resize the **subform** within the design of the **main form** so all the details are displayed.

The final design layout can be seen in Figure 9.20.

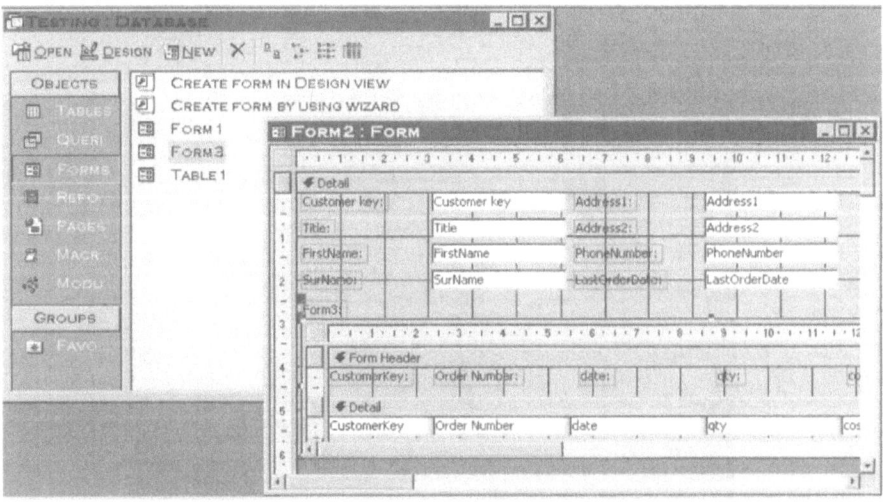

Figure 9.20 *The design of the main form with the embedded subform.*

Finally, display the properties for the subform and set the **master/child** link fields up so they match, then set the subform to show **continuous** records.

- Select the **data properties** for the embedded **subform** *Form3* and set the **master field** to *[Customer Key]*, this is the **key** or **unique field** on the **main form**.

- Now set the **Child field** to *[CustomerKey]*, this is the matching **key field** on the **subform**. See Figure 9.21.
- Now **close** and **save** the **form** as *Form2*.

If you **open** the **form** and view the results you will see two sets of **records selectors.** One set at the bottom of the **form** is used to select the main **table** record and one set within the **sub form** to select the sub **table** records. All the customer orders will match the main customer **key**.

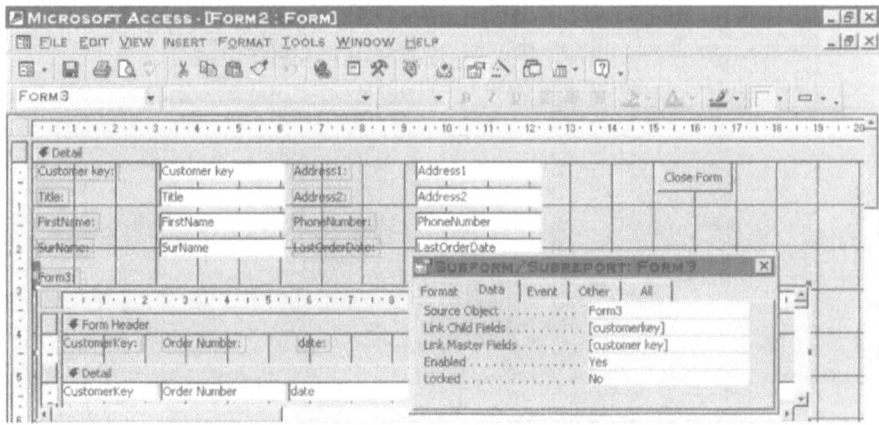

Figure 9.21 *Setting the master/child link fields on the main form properties.*

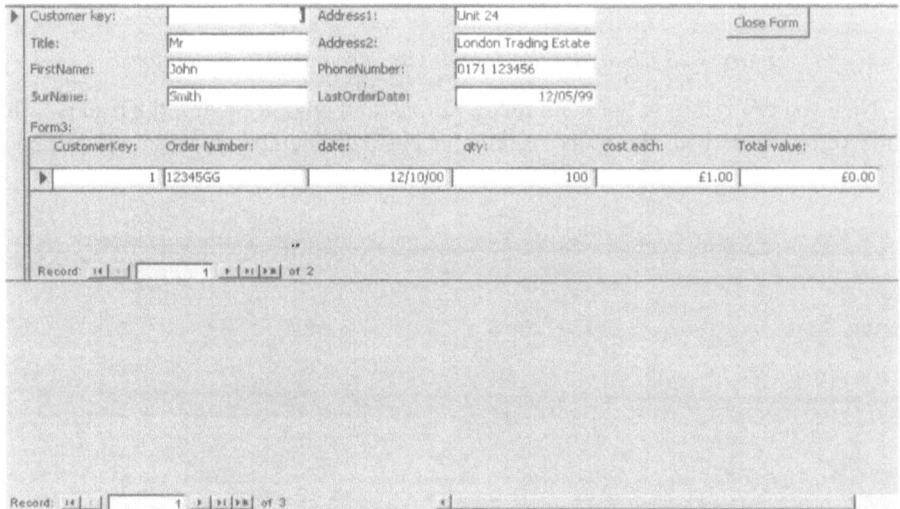

Figure 9.22 *Main form and subform displaying single records.*

In the example shown in Figure 9.22, there are three **main form** records, of which record number 1 is displayed. The **subform** is showing only the first of two matching records from the sub **table**. This is due to the **subforms default view property**.

The last step is to change the **properties** for the **subform** and get it to display multiple matching records:

- **Close** the main **form**, *Form2*.
- Return to the **design** of the **subform**, *Form3*.
- Open the **properties** window for the **form.**
- Change the **default view** for the **subform** to **Continuous Forms**; this will force the **form** to show multiple records, as shown in Figure 9.23.
- **Close** the **form** design and **save** the changes.

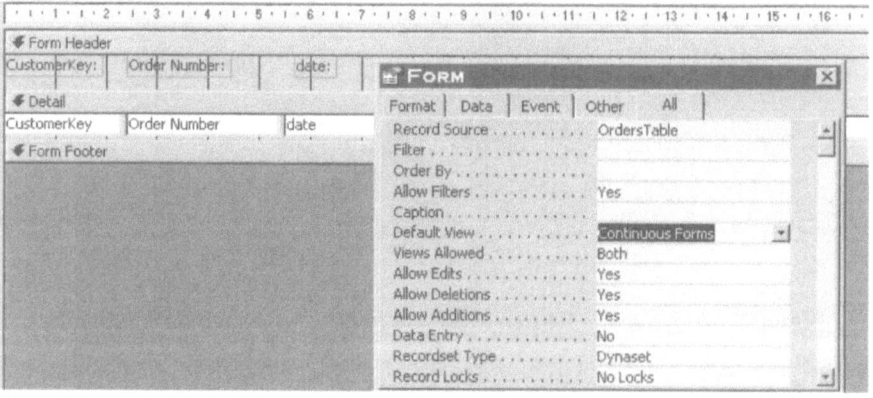

Figure 9.23 Changing the default view property for the subform.

Now you can return to the main **form**, *Form2,* and **open** it to view the results. This time you will see both the order records for customer number 1, as shown in Figure 9.24.

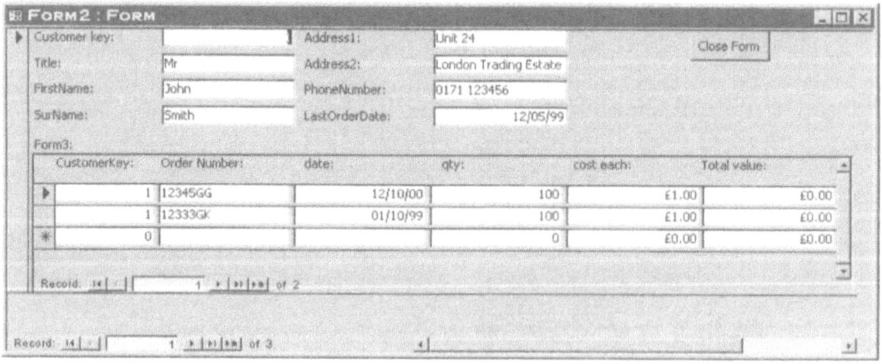

Figure 9.24 The result of changing the subform default view to Continuous Forms.

Using AutoNumber fields as primary keys

The previous example shows how main **forms** and **subforms** can be **linked** or joined together using a common **field.** You will need to bear the following points in mind when using this method, when there are no **relationships** built into the **database.**

In the previous example, **auto numbering** is set on the *Customer key* **field** of *Table1*, but the *CustomerKey* **field** in *OrdersTable* is set to a **numeric** so there can be more than one duplicated value. In other words you can have several orders for each customer. There is a problem when adding new records using the new **main/subform**; while **Auto Number** will provide the next **unique** number for the new customer, there is no control over the value you can type into the **subform's key field.** So in theory the next new customer would be number **4,** but you could fill in the orders key with a value of **6,** there would be no objection. However, this means these orders will never be **linked** to the new customer, as shown in Figure 9.25.

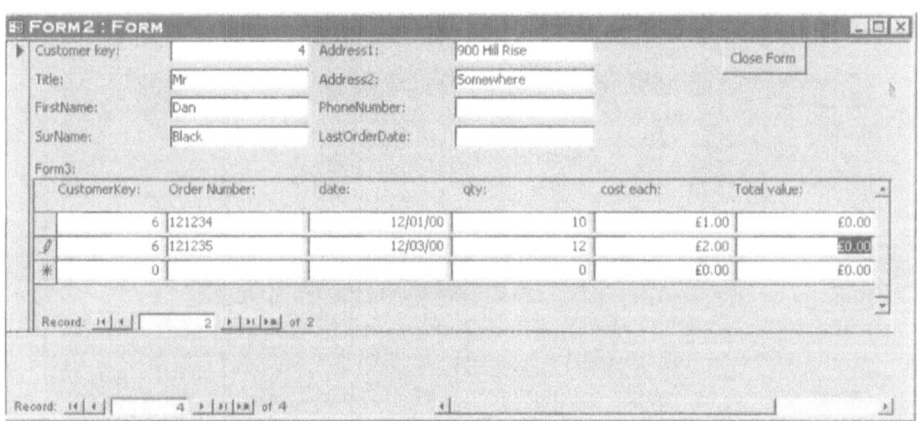

Figure 9.25 Adding an incorrect order key on the subform.

If you use the **Tools I Relationships** menu to view the **relationships** for the database, you could add both *Table1* and *OrdersTable* and **join** the two customer **key fields.** By setting the **referential integrity,** you can then force the integrity of the **key field** values, as shown in Figure 9.26.

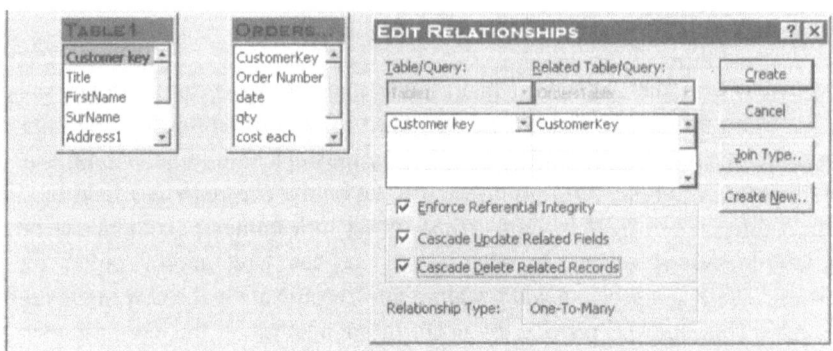

Figure 9.26 *Editing the relationship between two tables.*

If you use the main/**subform** again and try to add a new customer with an incorrect key value for the order. The **relationship** model for the **database** will stop this and produce a warning message as shown in Figure 9.27.

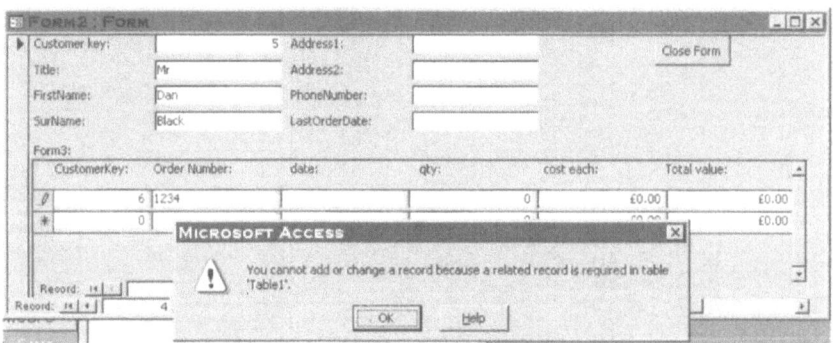

Figure 9.27 *Adding a customer key of 5 and an order key of 6 produces an error.*

If you correct the **key field** value for the new customer order to match the value entered on the main **form** the **relationship** will be satisfied and the new record will be accepted onto the underlying **tables** see Figure 9.28.

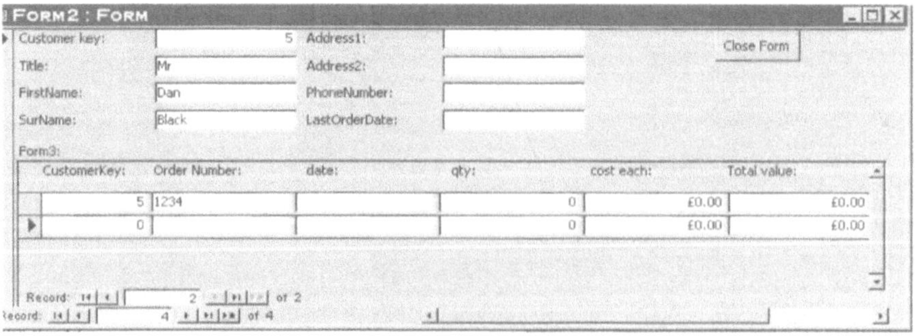

Figure 9.28 *Correct entry for customer key and order key.*

Designing reports for multiple tables

Having looked at some of the principles behind the use of multiple **tables**, the next thing you need to do is to create a **report** based on one or more **tables**. One way to do this is to create a **query** that selects the records you require from your **tables**, then design a **report** based on this **query**. This way you can check that the **joins** work in the **query** before you go on to create the **report**.

In the next example you will **join** customers with orders within a **query** and then use the results in a **report**. The first thing to do is create a **select query** to **join** the two **tables** together.

- Select the **query tab** from the **database window** and then select the **new** button to create the new **query**.
- Add the following two tables to the design grid: *Table1* and *OrdersTable*. The **join** between the two tables is maintained by the **relationships** you set up earlier.
- Add the *Customer key, Title, Firstname* and *Surname* **fields** from *Table1*.
- Now add the following **fields** from *OrdersTable: Order Number, date, qty, cost each, Total value*, as shown in Figure 9.29.
- Now **close** and **save** the **query** as *ReportQuery*.

Now you can start the design of the report:

- Return to the database window and select the reports object tab.
- Select the new report button from the toolbar.
- Select the Report Wizard option and use the *ReportQuery* query as the data source for the report as shown in Figure 9.30. Select the OK button and then pick all the fields from the next window as shown in Figure 9.31.

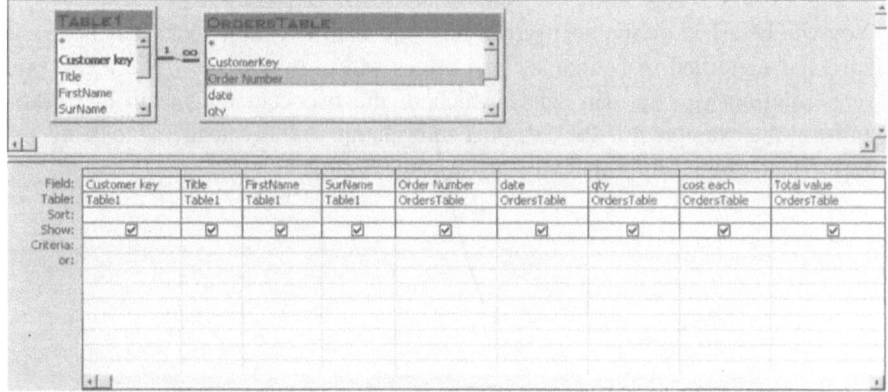

Figure 9.29 *Adding fields from both tables within a select query.*

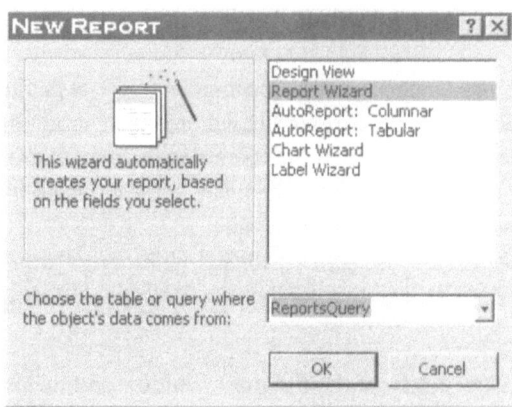

Figure 9.30 Creating a report based on the ReportsQuery query.

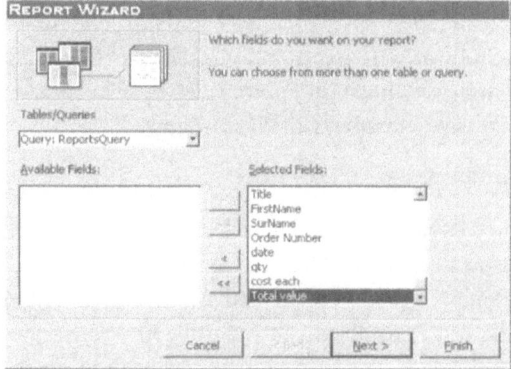

Figure 9.31 Adding all the fields to the report using the report wizard.

You will be asked on the next screen how you want to **group** your data. The **report wizard** has identified that there are two **tables** within the **query**. As the two **tables** have a **relationship** you can select which of the two contains the main **group** of records; in the example it is the customer information that is considered to be the main **group**. The customer information is held within *Table1*.

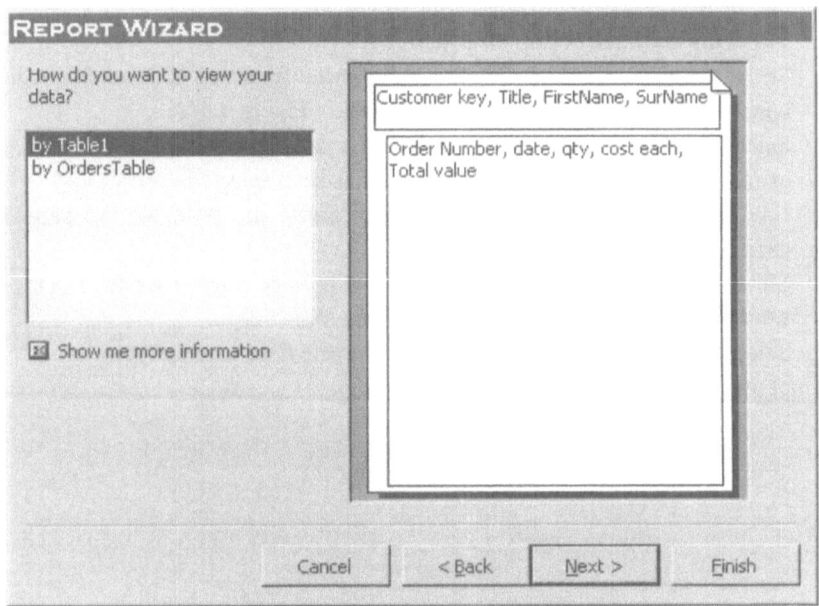

Figure 9.32 *Selecting the main group of records from Table1.*

- Select *Table1* as the main group as shown in Figure 9.32.
- Select the **Next** button to move on and choose any **grouping order** for the **report**. In this case choose *Customer key* as the main **group** for this **report** as shown in Figure 9.33.

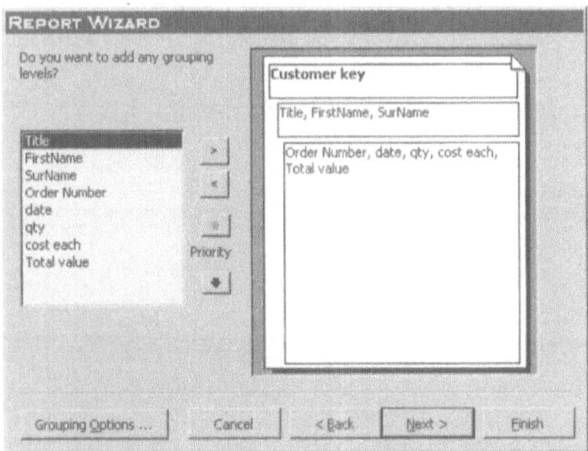

Figure 9.33 *Adding group levels to the report.*

- Select the **Next** button to move on to set the **sort order** and add any **summary options** for the **report**.

- Set the **sort order** to the *date* of the order.
- Select the **summary options** button.
- Select the **Sum** checkbox for the *Total value* **field** and then click on the **OK** button to confirm the **summary options;** see Figure 9.34.
- Select the **Next** button to move on and choose the layout for the **report.** In the example shown the **Align Left 1** layout has been selected.
- Use the **Next** button to move on and choose the style for the **report;** the example uses **Soft Grey** style.
- Move on again using the **Next** button and provide a name for the report, in the example the report is named as *Customers And Orders*.
- Select the Finish button to get Access to create the report for you.

The final **report** is shown in Figure 9.35 and 9.36.

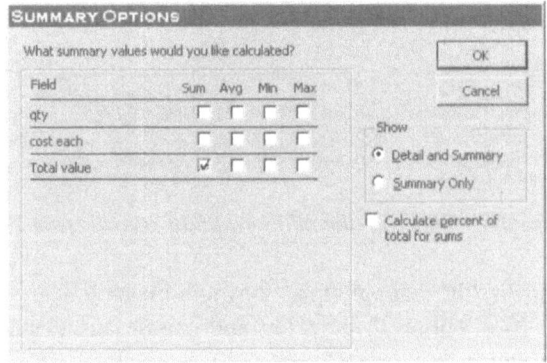

Figure 9.34 Summary options.

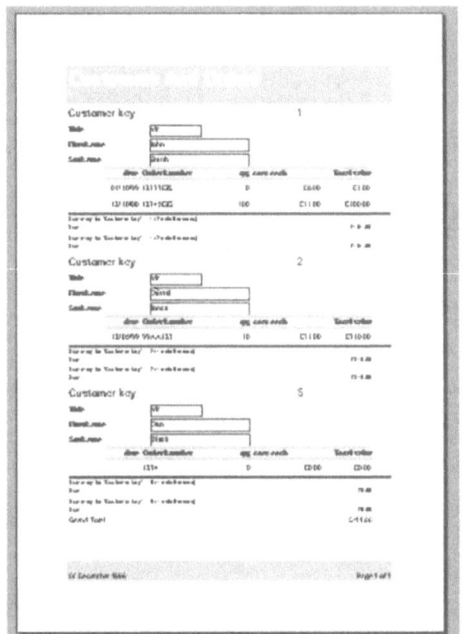

Figure 9.35 *Report layout example.*

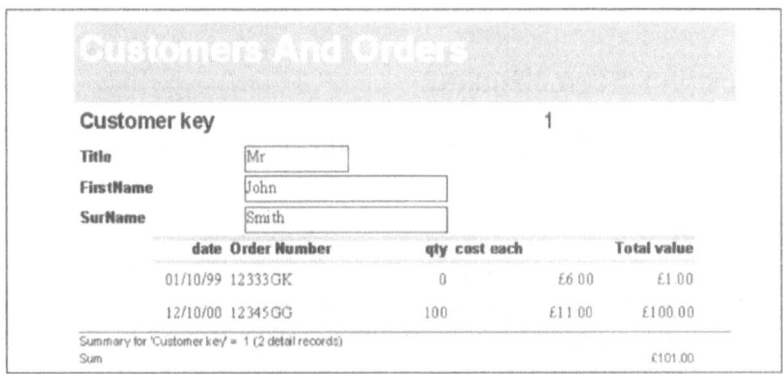

Figure 9.36 *Extract from report example.*

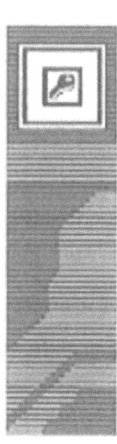

10

Using Macros

Introduction

A **macro** is a set of instructions or actions which perform a task, perhaps to open a **report** or perform a calculation. **Macros** enable you to automate repetitive tasks. A **macro** can be a sequence of **actions**, or it can be a group of macros. You can also add **conditions** to your **macro**. You may assign your **macro** to a **button** on a **form** if you wish. A **macro** will run each **action** row in turn, from the top down.

Macro design screen elements

There are two main columns within the **Macro design window: Action** and **Comment**.

Action column

This is used to select the **actions** you want performed from the **action list box** provided. Some **actions** will also require an additional set of **action arguments;** for example, if you use a **macro** to open a **report** you will need to supply the **report** name as an **action argument**.

Comment column

You can use this column to supply comments or text to describe what the **action** line is supposed to do; this is useful to others who may need to understand what the **macro** is doing.

Action arguments

These are the additional items of information that certain **actions** will require; it may just be the name of a **table** or **report**.

Creating a macro

For example, suppose you want to calculate the order value for the previous main/**subform**. The principle is to take the order quantity and multiply this by the unit value to produce the order value.

- Select the Macro object tab from the database window.
- Select the New button to create a new macro.

Enter your first **action** on the first row in the **action column**; enter any descriptive comments on the right of this in the comments column.

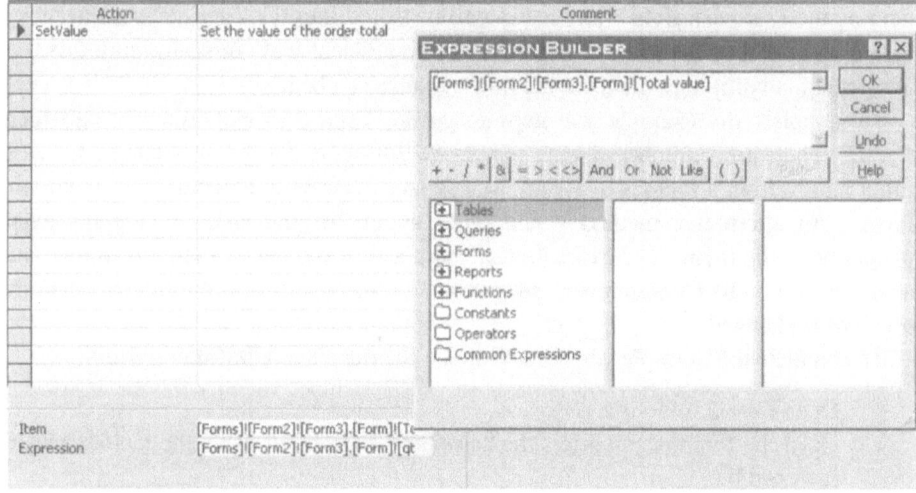

Figure 10.1 Using the expression builder to enter an action argument.

The **actions** may require **arguments** depending on the **action** type in use; if so then the **arguments** box will be shown in the lower part of the **macro** window. In the example the **action** being used is **SetValue**; this is used to set the value of an **object** by using a specific **expression**. There are two **arguments** for this **action;** the first is used to identify the **item** you are setting the value of, while the second **argument** is used to set the **value** of the object. If you look at the example in Figure 10.1 you can see that the **action argument** for the **object** has been built using the **expression builder**, in this case the **item** is referred to as

[Forms]![Form2]![Form3].[Form]![Total value]

This is the full **identifier** for the field called *Total value* which exists within the **subform** called *Form3* which again is contained within the main **form** called *Form2*. You will notice a **comment** line to the right of the **action row**; this is used to help remember what the **action** is for.

- Set the **Action** column to **SetValue** on the first row of the **macro**.
- Then either use the **expression builder** or type into the **Item argument** the name of the **object** you are setting the value of, in this case *[Forms]![Form2]![Form3].[Form]![Total value]*
- Having completed this, move to the **Expression Argument** and either use the **expression builder** or type in the following **expression** to set the value for the **item**
  [Forms]![Form2]![Form3].[Form]![qty]*[Forms]![Form2]![Form3].[Form]! [cost each]
- Close and save the macro as *Macro1*.

This **expression** will take the current record on the **subform** and multiply the *qty* field by the *cost each* **field**. The result will be stored into the *Total value* **field** by the **SetValue action** of the **macro**. There are more efficient ways of performing this type of calculation but it does demonstrate how a **macro** can be used.

To complete the example you need to get the **macro** to **run** from the **sub form** *Form2*. There are a number of ways to achieve this but by far the most common way to run a **macro** from a **form** is to assign the **macro** to a **command button** placed onto the **form**. An alternative method would be to assign the **macro** to an **objects event property** on the **form**. For example you could assign the macro to the *qty* **object** and attach it to the **On Change event property**, in other words **run** the **macro** when the *qty* **field** is changed.

To complete the example you need to attach the **macro** to a **button** on *Form2*:

- Open *Form2* in design view.
- Open the **toolbox** and select the **command button,** ensuring the toolbox wizard is turned on.
- Place the **command button** into the **header** of *Form3*.
- Select the **Miscellaneous** category and then select **Run Macro** action.
- Select the **Next** button and select the **macro** to **run**, in this case *Macro1* as shown in Figures 10.2 and 10.3.

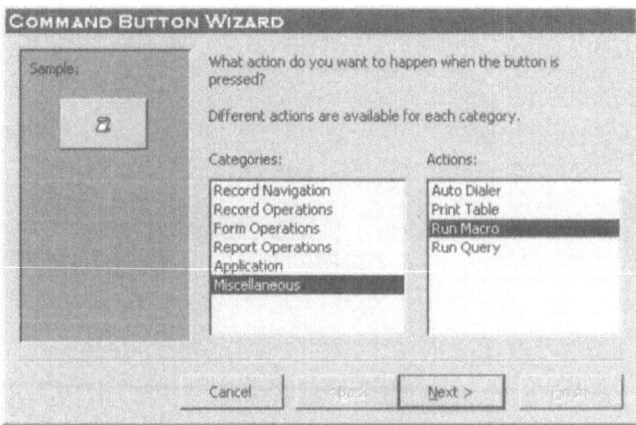

Figure 10.2 *Selecting the category and action for a command button.*

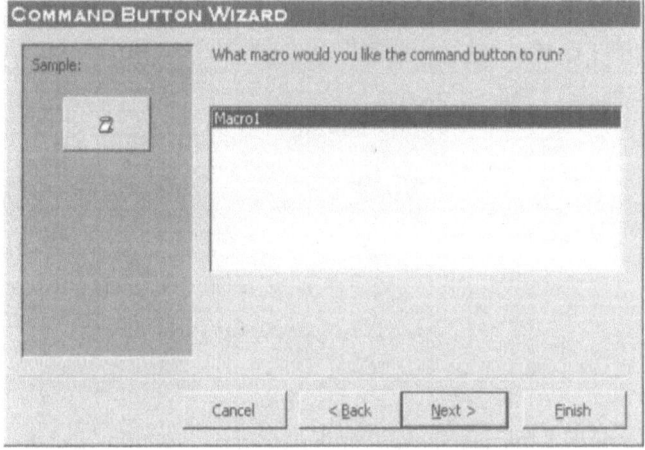

Figure 10.3 *Selecting the macro to run from the command button.*

- Select the **Next** button and then fill in the **text** to be displayed on the **command button**, i.e. *Calculate Total* as shown in Figure 10.4.
- Select the **Next** button again and enter a name for the **command button object**. Finally, select the **finish** button to place the **command button** onto the **form** as shown in Figure 10.5.
- **Close** and save the design changes on *Form3*.

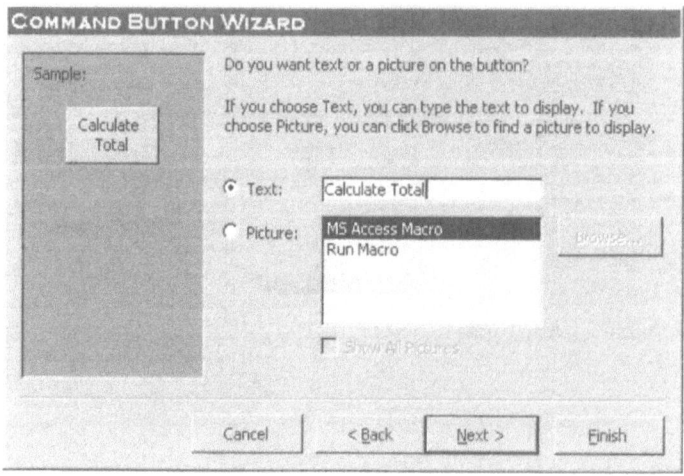

Figure 10.4 *Editing the text for a command button.*

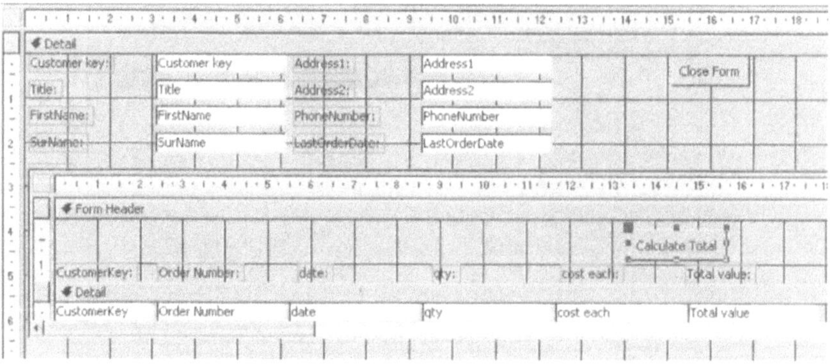

Figure 10.5 *The command button placed onto the sub form header.*

If you open *Form2* in data view and then select an order on the **subform** you can see the effects of running the **macro** by using the **command button** you placed on the **form**. In Figure 10.6 the first order row on the **sub form** has been selected and then the **command button** has been used to calculate the new order total. In this case, the *cost each* **field** containing the value **1** multiplies the *qty* **field** containing the value **100** producing the *Total value* **field**.

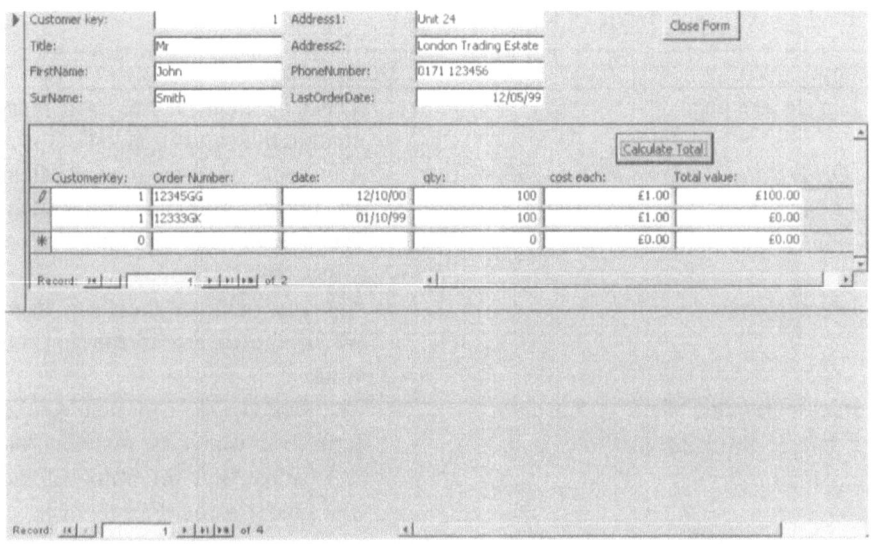

Figure 10.6 *The result of using the command button.*

Setting conditions within a macro

Having completed your first **macro** you can probably see how they can be used to calculate values on **forms**, but what happens if you do not want to calculate a value all the time? Sometimes you may only want to produce a value when all the necessary information is present. Before continuing, look at the macro condition examples, shown in table 10.1.

Table 10.1 *Macro condition examples.*

Example	Description
[*City*]="London"	The *City* field on the form must contain the word "London".
[*OrderDate*] Between #2-Feb-1999# And #2-Mar-1999#	The value of the *OrderDate* field on the form is no earlier than 2-Feb-1999 and no later than 2-Mar-1999.
IsNull([*Qty*])	The *qty* field on the form from which the macro is run has no value.
[*City*]="London" And Forms![Form3]![*qty*]>100	The value in the *City* field on the form from which the macro is run is London, and the value of the *qty* field on the Form3 form is greater than 100.

In the previous **macro** example there would be no point in calculating the total order value if the quantity was missing. In this case you may want to produce a **message** to tell you that the quantity is **zero** or blank. How you could display a message based on a condition set within a macro?

- Open the previous **macro,** *Macro1* in design mode.
- Turn the **conditions** column on; either use the **View|Conditions** menu or the **button** from the **toolbar;** see Figure 10.7 and 10.8.

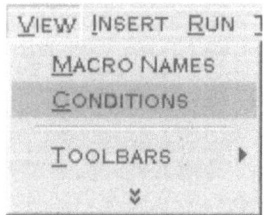

Figure 10.7 View | Conditions *menu.*

Figure 10.8 *Macro conditions button on the toolbar.*

There are two things you have to decide before you continue:

- What form is the **message** is to take?
- What is the condition expression?

The **message** is a warning to the user that the quantity value is missing, so it may take the form of a statement along the lines *There is no quantity value, please enter this and try again.* What about the condition itself? You are checking to see if there is a value other than **zero** within the quantity **field**; if there is then you want to perform the calculation. If there is no value then you do not want to produce the calculation but you will need to display your **message** instead. You need to have two **actions** within the **macro**, one to perform the calculation and one to display the warning **message**. Each **action** will need a **condition expression**. In longhand notation the **expressions** may look something like this:

- If the quantity is **not equal** to **zero** and the quantity is **not blank** then perform the calculation.
- If the quantity is **zero** or the *quantity* is **blank** then show the warning **message**.

The **condition** column does not require you to use the **IF** keyword so the calculation **condition** would look like this:

[Forms]![Form2]![Form3].[Form]![qty]>0 And
Not IsNull([Forms]![Form2]![Form3].[Form]![qty]).

This is the full **identifier** for the **object** on the **form**. Remember that *[qty]* is part of *[Form3]*, which is part of *[Form2]*, which in turn is part of the *[forms]* **object** group. The **condition** checks to see if the *qty* **field** contains a value greater than **zero** and that it is not null. The **null** keyword is an Access **function** to test for missing values. The **message condition** might look like this:

[Forms]![Form2]![Form3].[Form]![qty]=0 Or
IsNull([Forms]![Form2]![Form3].[Form]![qty]).

The **condition** checks to see if the *qty* **field** contains a **zero** value or a **null** value, **IsNull**. Now you have decided what **message** to display and the **condition expressions** to use you can go on and modify the **macro**.

- **Open** the macro in **design view**.
- Add the message box action to the second row; use a warning message as shown in Figure 10.9.
- Now add the condition to the SetValue action row:

[Forms]![Form2]![Form3].[Form]![qty]>0 And Not
IsNull([Forms]![Form2]![Form3].[Form]![qty]).

- Now add the condition for the message box action:

[Forms]![Form2]![Form3].[Form]![qty]=0 Or
IsNull([Forms]![Form2]![Form3].[Form]![qty]).

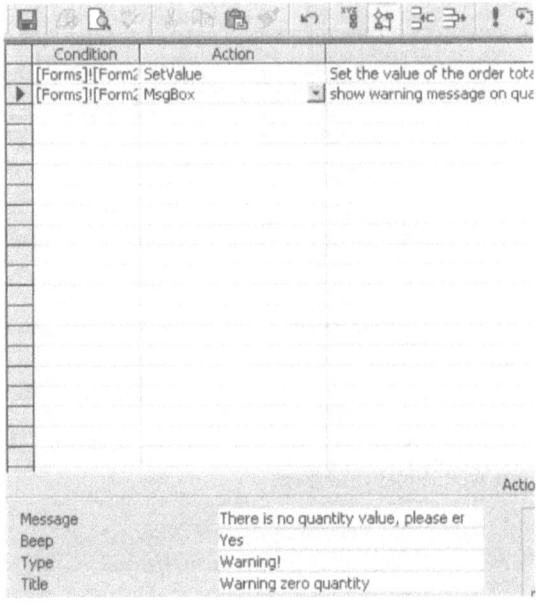

Figure 10.9 *The message condition and action arguments.*

- Close and save the macro.
- View the results by opening the **form** *Form2* and setting *qty* to **zero**.
- Then use your **command** button to try to calculate *Total value*; your **message** will be displayed as shown in Figure 10.10.

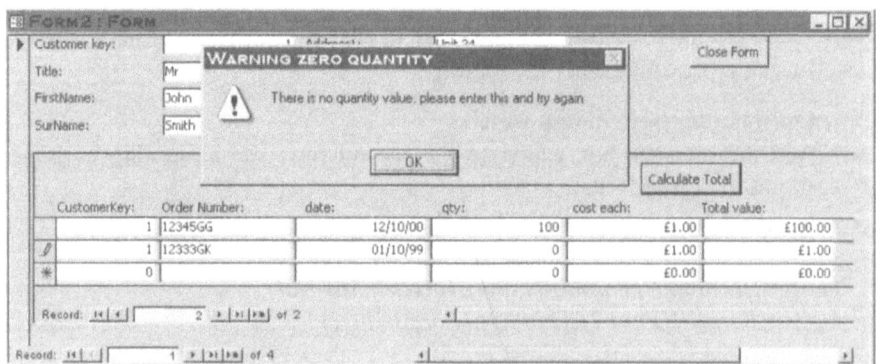

Figure 10.10 *The message from the conditional macro.*

Adding a macro to an existing button

So far the **command button Wizard** has been used to assign **macros.** You can assign the **macro** yourself by turning off the **toolbox wizard** and then placing a **command button** onto your **form.** If you examine the **properties** of the **command button** you can set the **On Click event** to **run** the **macro** of your choice by selecting it from the **list** of **macros** available.

Look at the design for the **form** you created earlier, *Form2*, and examine the **event properties** for the **command button**; see Figure 10.11.

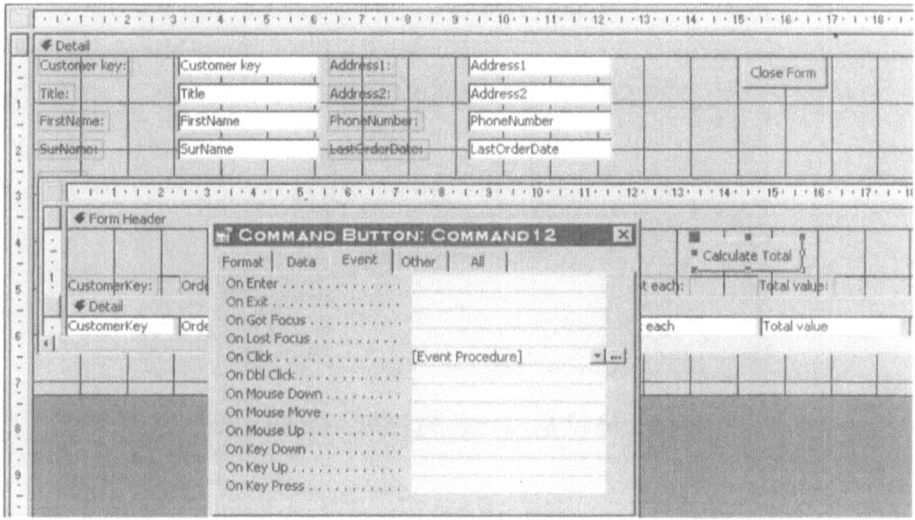

Figure 10.11 A command button's On Click event property.

The **button** has an **On Click event**; behind this is a **Visual Basic module** created to **run** the **macro**.

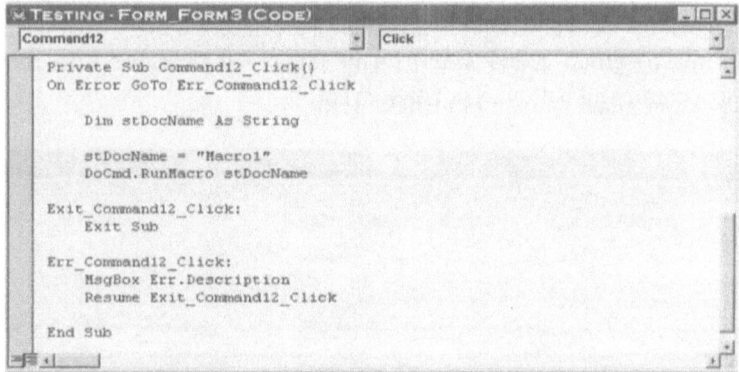

Figure 10.12 A command button's event code.

If you use the **expression builder** you can examine the **event procedure's Visual Basic** code created by the **wizard**. There are a number of lines required to enable the **macro** to **run,** as shown in Figure 10.12.

The alternative is to create the button, select the **On Click event**, then pick the **macro** from the list of available macros using the **list** button; see Figure 10.13.

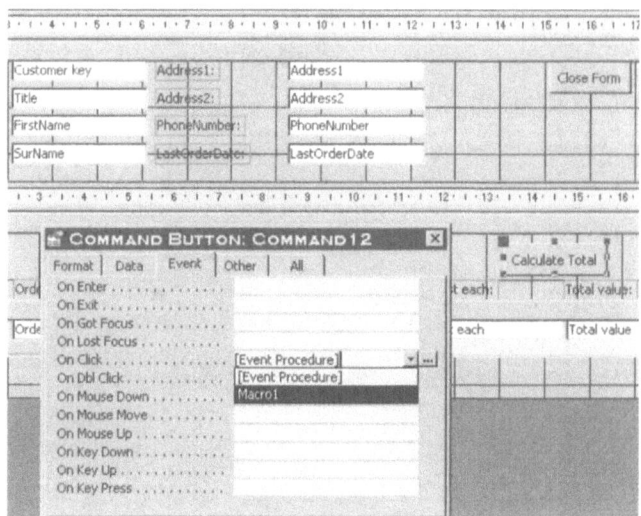

Figure 10.13 Replacing an event with a macro.

Using macro names with macro groups

Macros can be grouped together in one **macro** file known as a **macro group**. Each individual **macro** is given a unique name or **label** which helps to identify it. As macros run from the first row down it is common practice to leave a **blank** row at the end of each set of **macro** instructions. In the example shown there are two macros called *mac1* and *mac2* respectively. Figure 10.14 shows the **macro** design, each macro is held within the macro group called *Macro1* and Figure 10.15 shows how they can be assigned to a **command** button's **On Click event**.

Macro Name	Condition	Action	Comment
mac1	[Forms]![Form2]![Form3].[Form]![qty]>0 And Not IsNull	SetValue	Set the value of the order total
	[Forms]![Form2]![Form3].[Form]![qty]=0 Or IsNull([Form	MsgBox	show warning message on quantity va
mac2		Beep	
		MsgBox	

Figure 10.14 Two macros *mac1* and *mac2* within a macro group file, *Macro1*.

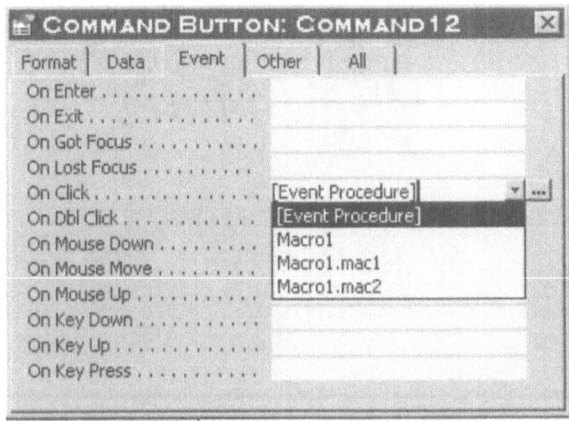

Figure 10.15 *Selecting a macro from a group.*

11

VB Modules

Introduction

Visual Basic is Microsoft's underlying development language for all Office components; with this language you can manipulate not only the product you are currently using but also any Office **object** or **ActiveX** component. While the language is reasonably easy to use, the **syntax** and **methods** require more time to fully understand.

While it is not possible to cover all the Visual Basic programming concepts in a book of this size, it does need to be included for the sake of completeness. This chapter covers some common **commands**, **functions** and **methods** for an Access data base.

Objects and events

Before you look at the examples included within this chapter, it is worth mentioning some concepts relating to the use of Visual Basic with Access. The code you create is commonly applied to an **Objects Event** by using the **event properties** for that **object**. For example a **button** on an Access **form** is considered to be an **object**, and this will have its own set of **events**. You use the mouse to **click** onto a **button** so the **button** **object** has an **On Click event**; you can also **tab** on and off a **field** using the **tab** key. This is known as getting the **focus** and losing the **focus** and so there are two related **events** called **On Got Focus** and **On Lost Focus**. If you look at the **form** you designed earlier, *Form3*, you can examine the **properties** for the **button** that produces the calculation and view the **events**; see Figure 11.1.

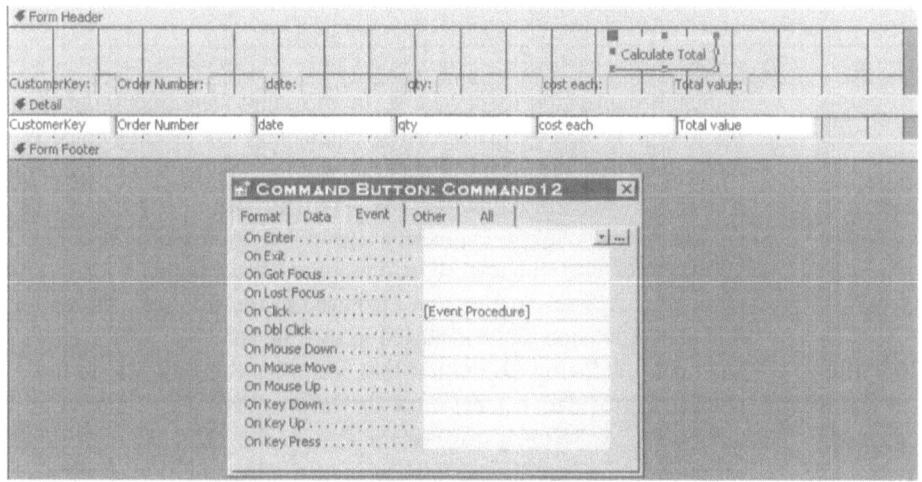

Figure 11.1 *A command button On Click event.*

So you can think of any item on a **form** or **report** as an **object** and each **object** contains a set of characteristic **properties**. Within these **properties** you will find in most cases a set of **events** that you can use to attach a set of instructions from a **macro** or a **Visual Basic procedure**. You can obtain more information about **events** and **event procedures** by using the online **help** guide, look under the subject heading of *Events and Event Properties Reference*.

Displaying a message

There are times when it would be useful to communicate with the user; there are a number of Visual Basic **functions** that can be used to help you achieve this. One such **function** is known as the **Message box function**. This allows you to display a **message** on the screen, in a similar way to the **macro** example you created earlier; however, you would be using **Visual Basic code** instead of a **macro**. You can use the **MsgBox** to display a **message** containing a warning or information. For example, you can use the **MsgBox** function with **validation macros**. When a **control** or **field** fails a **validation condition**, a **message** box can display an **error message** and provide instructions about the kind of data that should be entered. Every **command** or **function** in Visual Basic has a specific structure; this is known as the **command syntax**. The syntax of the **MsgBox** function is :

MsgBox(prompt[, buttons] [, title] [, helpfile, context])

The component parts of the **Msgbox function** are described in Table 11.1.

Table 11.1 Message box components

Item	Description
prompt	A String expression displayed as the message. The maximum length of prompt is approximately 1024 characters. If prompt consists of more than one line, you can separate the lines using a carriage return character (Chr(13)), a linefeed character (Chr(10)).
buttons	Optional. A Numeric expression specifying the number and type of buttons to display, the icon style to use, the default button.
title	Optional. A String expression displayed in the title bar. If you omit this the application name is placed in the title bar.
helpfile	Optional. A String expression that identifies the Help file to use. If helpfile is provided, context must also be provided.
context	Optional. A Numeric expression that is the Help context number assigned to the appropriate Help topic by the Help author. If context is provided, helpfile must also be provided.

Note that, to make use of **help files** and **help context** options, you need to have access to the **Help file compiler**; this is normally supplied with the developer's edition of Access.

Many of the Visual Basic **functions** contain component parts that are optional and therefore not required to get them to work. The following example is used to display a simple warning **message** using only the **prompt** component, which is the minimum requirement.

MsgBox("Please enter a value that is greater than 0").

This would result in the **message** *Please enter a value that is greater than 0* being displayed on the screen. This is not quite complete but gives you an idea of how the **function** is used; to enable the **function** to work and continue the example you need to add it to the **form** you used in the main/**sub form** example, in this case *Form3*. To demonstrate how you could use this you will add a **message** to the *cost each* **field** on the **form** and add this as an **event** on the **field**. The **event** you will use in this case is the **On Got Focus event**.

- Open *Form3* in design view.
- Select the *cost each* field and view its **properties**.
- Select the **On Got Focus event property**.
- Use the **expression builder** button and then choose the **Code builder** option from the next window; see Figures 11.2 and 11.3.

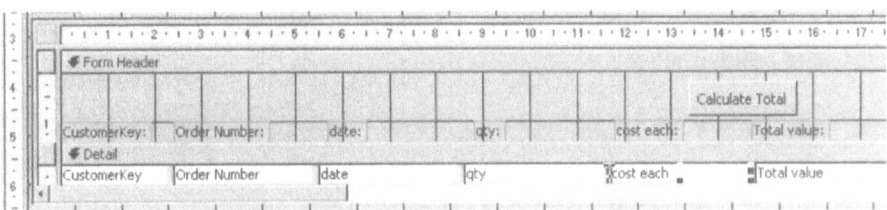

Figure 11.2 *Selecting the cost each object.*

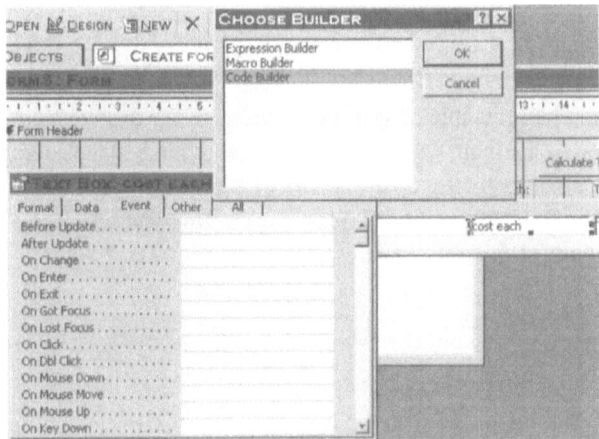

Figure 11.3 *Selecting the On Got Focus event and using the Code builder.*

The **Visual Basic editor window** will display with a pre-built **procedure** for the **On Got Focus event**. The *cost each* **field** gets the **focus** when the cursor moves onto the **field** this will run the **On Got Focus event**. A **procedure** is identified by the key words **Sub** and **End Sub;** in the example the **procedure** is called *cost_each_GotFocus*. So the start of the **procedure** is identified by the line:-

Private Sub cost_each_GotFocus

The end of the **procedure** is identified by the line:

End Sub

The lines in between these two **statements** are the program **code** lines; in this case you want the **message** *Please enter a value greater than 0* to be displayed.

- Type in the Msgbox() function line as shown below and in Figure 11.4:
  Msgbox("Please enter a value greater than 0")
- Close the Visual Basic window and return to the form design.

You will see that the **On Got Focus event** line within the **field properties** now contains the statement *[Event Procedure];* this is used to indicate that this **event** now has an underlying **procedure**. To re-edit these **procedures** at any time use the **expression builder** button.

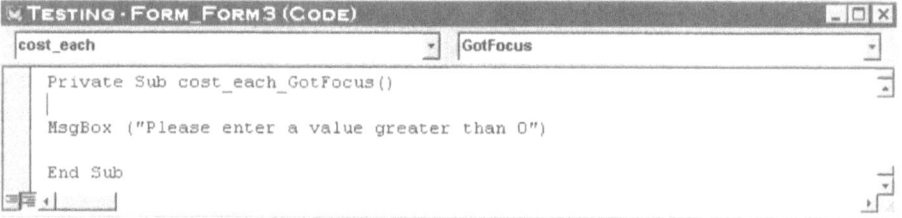

Figure 11.4 A message box used with an On Got Focus event.

- When you have completed this, **close** and **save** the changes to *Form3*.
- Now **open** the main **form**, *Form2*, and then move to the subform, *Form3*.
- **Tab** or **click** onto the *cost each* **field**. The **message** you created using the **MsgBox function** will be displayed each time you **tab** onto a *cost each* **field**; see Figure 11.5.

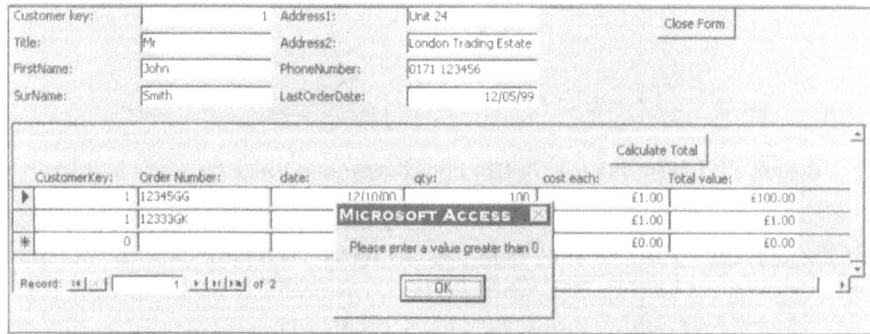

Figure 11.5 The message box produced by the On Got Focus event.

Asking for a value

You have looked at a Visual Basic **function** that allows you to display a **message** onto the screen, the next logical progression from that would be to ask for a value. You do not have to store the value onto the **form** or within the **form's** underlying **data source**, it could be used just for calculation purposes. Continuing with the same theme as before, suppose that when you enter the *cost each* value on the **form** you want to know what the cost would be if it were converted into dollars.

You would need to work out what the current exchange rate was and then display the result of your calculation. In a long hand format this might look something like:

dollars = cost each multiplied by the exchange rate.

If the *exchange rate* was something like **2.5** dollars and the *cost each* was **1.00** then the calculation might become:

*1.0 * 2.5 or Dollars = 1.0*2.5.*

As the result will be a varying value dependent on the *cost each* value, it is a **variable** and as such you will need to set this up in Visual Basic, so that the result of the calculation will be stored into a **variable** that can be reused later. So the aim is to wait for the *cost each* value to **change**, ask for an *exchange rate* and then display the result on the screen. The **function** that allows you to ask for a value is known as the **InputBox function**; its **syntax** is shown below and the elements are explained in Table 11.2.

InputBox(prompt[, title] [, default] [, xpos] [, ypos] [, helpfile, context])

Table 11.2 *InputBox components table.*

Item	Description
prompt	Required. String displayed as the message. The maximum prompt is approximately 1024 characters.
title	Optional. String displayed in the title bar of the dialog box.
default	Optional. String displayed in the text box as the default response.
xpos	Optional. Numeric expression that specifies the horizontal distance of the left edge of the dialog box from the left edge of the screen.
ypos	Optional. Numeric expression that specifies the vertical distance of the upper edge of the dialog box from the top of the screen
helpfile	Optional. String that identifies the Help file to provide context-sensitive Help for the dialog box.
context	Optional. Numeric that is the Help context number assigned to the appropriate Help topic

So, to ask for a value for an *exchange rate* the **InputBox function** might look something like this:

InputBox("Please enter Exchange rate")

This again uses the minimum requirements for the **function**. Now you need to apply this to the previous **form** example; this time you will attach the Visual Basic code to the **Change Event** of the *cost each* field. This means the **function** will run each time you **change** a value within this **field**.

- Open *Form3* in design view and select the **On Change event** from the *cost each* **field** *properties.*
- Use the **expression builder** to build the code for this **event** by choosing **Code Builder.**

The first thing to do is set up the **variable** to hold the *exchange rate;* in this case you will call this *Dollars.* To set up a **variable** to hold a value in Visual Basic you need to use the **Dim** statement. In the example shown the **Dim** statement has been used to set up a **variable** called *Dollars* and defined **As** a **variant,** a value that is defined as a **number** or **text** or **date** by the value stored within it when it is first used. You could have set it up as a **numeric, date** or **text** value but **variant** is suitable in this case. The statement is:

Dim *Dollars As* **Variant**

This defines the **variable** name and the **type** of value it will be used to hold. The next line is used to ask for some **input** on the screen, by using the **InputBox function.** The **message** to be displayed by the **function** is contained within quotes and is known as the **prompt.** When the user responds to this by typing in a value it is stored into the **variable** called *Dollars.* This can be seen in Figure 11.6.

The next stage is to perform the calculation using the **variable** value and the value from the *cost each* **field** on the **form,** Remember that this **field** is part of the *Form3* **object** which in turn is part of *Form2,* so the full **identifier** for the **field** would be:

[Forms]![Form2]![Form3].[Form]![cost each].

The **InputBox function** part of the calculation is shown in Figure 11.7, the **Msgbox function** is used to display the results on the screen, when you have completed the code

- Construct the *cost each* **change event** as shown below.
- **Close** the Visual Basic window and then **close** and **save** the form.

```
Private Sub cost_each_Change( )
Dim Dollars As Variant
Dollars = InputBox("Please enter Exchange rate ")
MsgBox ("The cost in dollars " & [Forms]![Form2]![Form3].[Form]![cost each]
* Dollars)
End Sub
```

When you reopen the **form** and **change** or overtype a *cost each* value you will be asked for an *exchange rate* value. Once the value has been entered into the **InputBox** and you have selected the **OK** button then you will see the resulting **MsgBox function** display the result of the calculation as shown in Figure 11.8.

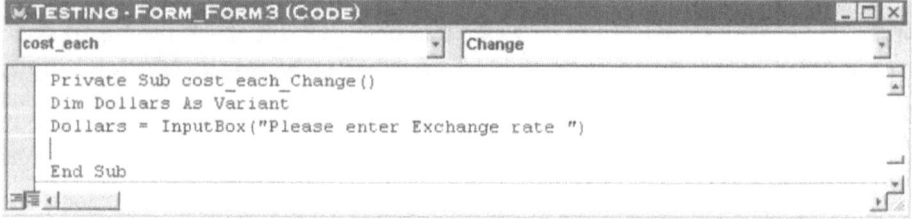

Figure 11.6 Setting a variable and using the InputBox function.

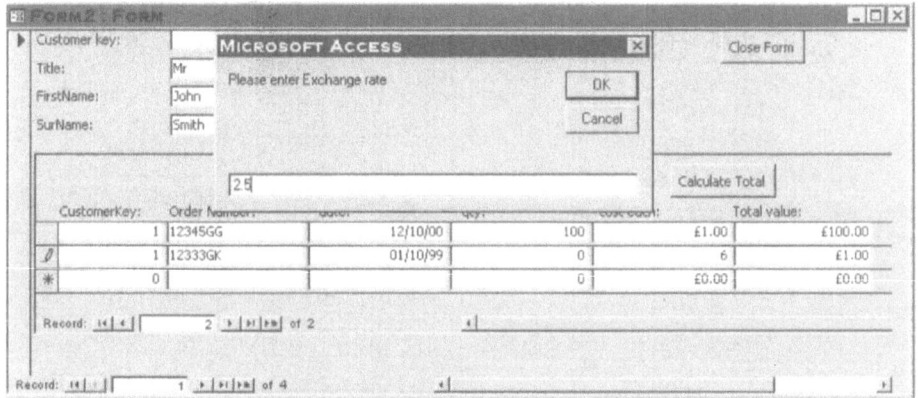

Figure 11.7 An InputBox function in action.

Figure 11.8 The MsgBox function in action.

Setting values on a form using Visual Basic code

Having looked at two Visual Basic **functions,** one to display **messages**, and one to prompt for values while using a **variable** to store the value. You will find that there are occasions when you want to apply these kinds of functions to store the results of calculations on a form. You could use a Visual Basic function rather than a **macro** that uses a **SetValue action** to perform the calculation. Say you need to store the resulting *exchange rate* onto your main form, *Form2*, after you have performed the *exchange rate* calculation. To do this you will need to place an **unbound text object** onto the form as shown in Figure 11.9 and then modify the Visual Basic code that runs from the **On Change event** of the *cost each* **field**.

- Open your main form, *Form2*, in design view.
- Use the **toolbox** to add an **unbound text box** onto the top of the **form** as shown in Figure 11.9.
- Open the **properties** for the new **unbound text box** and change its **name** to *ExchangeRate*.
- **Close** the form and **save** the changes.

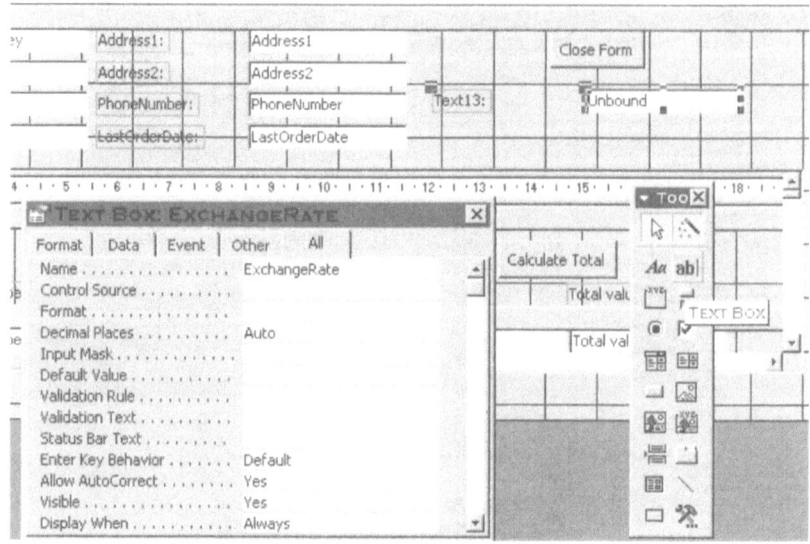

Figure 11.9 Adding an unbound text box and changing its name.

- Open the **subform**, *Form3* in design view.
- View the **event properties** for the **On Change event** of the *cost each* **field**.
- Use the **expression builder** button to redisplay the existing Visual Basic code.
- Modify the code by adding the final line to set the value of the *ExchangeRate* **field object**, as shown in the program listing below.

```
Private Sub cost_each_Change()
Dim Dollars As Variant
Dollars = InputBox("Please enter Exchange rate ")
MsgBox ("The cost in dollars " & [Forms]![Form2]![Form3].[Form]![Cost
each] * Dollars)
[Forms]![Form2]![ExchangeRate] = [Forms]![Form2]![Form3].[Form]![Cost
each] * Dollars
End Sub
```

Close and **save** the changes to the Visual Basic code, then open *Form2* and try changing one of the *cost each* values, you will see the resulting calculation displayed within the **text box** at the top of *Form2*.

Using a logical statement within a procedure

Sometimes there are occasions when you need to decide how to handle a value within a **field** or passed to a Visual Basic **procedure** by a user. These are often the times when you need to use a **conditional** or **logical** statement; this executes a group of statements, depending on the result of a **conditional expression.** Its **syntax** is shown below and the elements are explained in Table 11.3.

If condition *Then* *[*statements*]* *[Else* elsestatements*]*

Or, you can use the block form syntax:

If condition *Then*
*[*statements*]*
Else
*[*elsestatements*]*
End If

Table 11.3 *If components table.*

Part	Description
Condition	One or more of the following two types of expressions:
	A numeric or string expression that evaluates to True or False.
	If Null, treated as False.
Statements	One or more statements; executed if *condition* is True.
Elsestateme nts	One or more statements; executed if *condition* is False.

So how can you use this? Look at the example you used earlier to calculate an exchange rate in the **form** called *Form2.* You set up a Visual Basic **procedure** to calculate an exchange value; you can review this if you **open** the form in **design view** and examine the **On Change event property** of the *cost each* **field**. See Figure 11.10 and the Visual Basic code listing below.

```
Private Sub cost_each_Change( )
Dim Dollars As Variant
Dollars = InputBox("Please enter Exchange rate ")
MsgBox ("The cost in dollars " & [Forms]![Form2]![Form3].[Form]![cost each]
* Dollars)
[Forms]![Form2]![ExchangeRate] = [Forms]![Form2]![Form3].[Form]![cost
each] * Dollars
End Sub
```

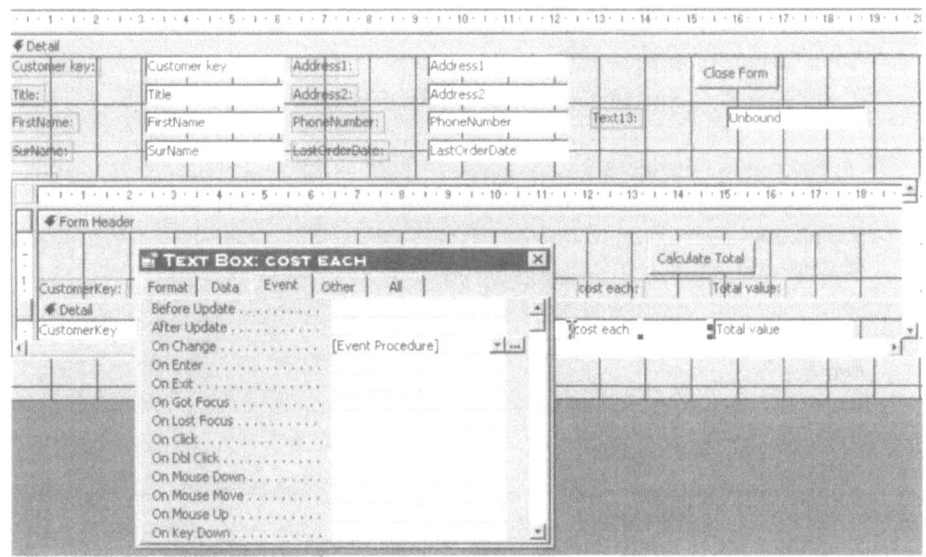

Figure 11.10 *Using If statements.*

What is missing is a check to see if the user places a **zero** value in the **field**. To do this you could use a **validation** check in the **field properties** or use a **conditional If** statement in the **procedure**. If you modified the existing Visual Basic code for the **On Change event** of the *cost each* **field** to include an **If** statement, it might look something like the listing shown below.

Private Sub cost_each_Change( )
Dim Dollars As Variant
Dollars = InputBox("Please enter Exchange rate ")
If Dollars = 0 Then
    MsgBox ("Cannot calculate exchange value as exchange rate was zero")
Else
    MsgBox ("The cost in dollars " & [Forms]![Form2]![Form3].[Form]![cost
each] * Dollars)
    [Forms]![Form2]![ExchangeRate] =
[Forms]![Form2]![Form3].[Form]![cost each] * Dollars
End If
End Sub

In the example, an **If** statement has been added to check if the value typed in response to the **InputBox** statement was **equal** to the value **zero**, if so then the lines of code are executed following the **If** statement until an **Else** or **End If** statement is encountered. In this case the message *Cannot calculate exchange value as exchange rate was zero* is displayed on the screen in a message box. The next line of code to be executed will be the **End if** statement, so the *ExchangeRate* **field** would not be calculated. However, if the value typed in by the user is **not zero** then the lines of code after the **Else** statement are executed and the *ExchangeRate* **field** on the **form** is calculated. In other words, **IF** the value typed in and stored in the *Dollars* **variable** is **equal** to **zero** **THEN** show the ***message*** *Cannot calculate exchange value as exchange rate was zero* on the screen and stop, **ELSE** the value typed into the **variable** *Dollars* was **not equal** to **zero** so calculate the *ExchangeRate* **field** and finish.

Final notes

I hope that you have had the chance to use some of the techniques shown within this book and it has given you an insight into how the Access 2000 product can be used. I have tried to keep the examples as simple as possible as it would be impossible to cover all the features and **functions** that are available within this volume. There are, as ever, several different ways to achieve the same result, and there is so much you can achieve by using the **SQL** language and by clever use of the Visual Basic **procedures** when attached to the **events** of an **object**. There are other areas that I could have covered given a few hundred more pages. I hope that I have given you enough information to allow you to experiment and explore the product with more confidence, there are several examples contained within the Access online help and there are several other publications in the *Essential* range that are worth exploring as further reading.

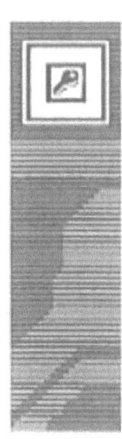

12
Further Reading

Other titles

There are a number of other titles available that enable you to examine Relational Database design in more detail as well as furthering your skills in the use of Visual Basic. I have listed some useful titles below:

- A Guided Tour of Relational Databases and Beyond, Mark Levere and George Loizou, 640 pages in soft back format, ISBN 1-85233-008-2, Published by Springer-Verlag.
- Inside Relational Databases, (including examples in Access), Mark Whitehorn and Bill Marklyn, 264 pages in soft back format, ISBN 3-540-76092-X, Published by Springer-Verlag.
- Essential Visual Basic fast, John Cowell, 232 pages in soft back format, ISBN 1-85233-207-7, Published by Springer-Verlag.

Useful Web sites

There are also several Web sites that may prove useful for further information again I have listed these below:

- http://www.Microsoft.com/Office
- http://www.Microsoft.com/Office/Enterprise/Entsupport.htm
- http://www.Springer.co.uk

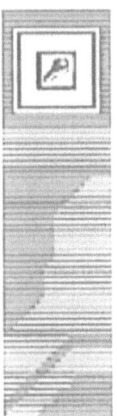

Index